Eton College Lists, 1678-1790

Richard Arthur Austen-Leigh, Eton College

ETON COLLEGE LISTS

1678—1790

ETON COLLEGE LISTS

1678—1790

EDITED BY

R. A. AUSTEN LEIGH

(Author of " Bygone Eton," " The Eton Guide," etc.)

ETON COLLEGE:

SPOTTISWOODE AND CO., LTD.

1907

HAS TABVLAS

QVAS VETERRIMAS, ALIAS ALIVNDE, COLLIGERE POTVIT

NE QVA ETONENSIVM QVAMVIS ANTIQVORVM NOMINA

ITA POSTERORVM INCVRIA DELEANTVR

VT SVB IISDEM NVTRITORVM PENETRALIBVS

MEMORIA PENITVS EXCIDANT

EDMONDO WARRE

PER ANNOS XXI INFORMATORI CLARISSIMO

GRATO ANIMO

ETONENSIS

CONTENTS.

PREFACE.

My object in publishing the present volume is to supplement as far as possible the records of the School previous to 1791, when the School Lists first began to be printed. Before that date, in the absence of any printed record, it has been hitherto almost impossible to say whether any particular boy was at Eton or not, and it is my hope that the lists here printed with the accompanying index may to some extent remove this difficulty.

The present volume contains lists for the following years, viz.: 1678, 1698 (printed in Appendix I.*), 1706, 1707, 1718, 1725, 1728, 1732, 1742, 1745, 1747, 1753, 1754 and 1756—1790. I should not have presumed to print so incomplete a collection, had I any expectation that by a longer delay I might be able to discover an appreciable number of the missing lists. But taking into consideration the fact that Etonians have been collecting these MS. lists for some seventy years, and moreover that during the last four years I have done all in my power, both by circulars to Old Etonians and by public advertisements, to discover further lists, I think it better to publish at once those in existence than to defer publication indefinitely. For it is, I fear, hardly probable that a complete set of lists even for the first half of the 18th century will ever be brought together, though I am not without hope that this volume, by exciting interest in the subject, may lead to further discoveries.

To many these lists, containing little but bare surnames, may appear uninteresting enough, but as a necessary foundation on which some future commentator may build a real register of 18th century Etonians, I hope they will have their value. Such a register, though not impossible, must be a work of great labour, for the names themselves give little clue to identification. But there are certain sources of information that it may be well to indicate for the benefit of future workers in this field. In the first place the Christian names and parentage of all Collegers are

This list only came to light after the others had already been printed.

easily accessible from the baptismal certificates which they had to produce to prove their age, and which have been kept among the College archives. These go back continuously as far as 1714, and are to be found for a few odd years previous to this date. In the next place it should not be difficult to trace any boys with titles, whether peers, sons of peers, or baronets. With regard to the great bulk of boys who were neither Collegers nor noblemen Dr. Barnard's entrance-book (preserved in the College Library), giving the Christian names, is of the greatest assistance for identifying the 1100 boys who entered the School between 1754 and 1765. It is possible too that other entrance-books may yet be discovered. Other sources are the Admission Books to Colleges at the Universities, which (at least in several cases at Cambridge), besides giving the Christian name and parentage of each undergraduate, specify the school from which he came, its head master's name, and the number of years the boy spent there. Some of these registers have been already published, notably those for St. John's College and Gonville and Caius College at Cambridge : the names of Etonians found at these and at other colleges are being gradually published in the periodical *Etoniana*. Further, a considerable number of Etonians may be gleaned from such books as the *Dictionary of National Biography*, Nichols' *Literary Anecdotes of the* 18th *Century* and his *Illustrations of the Literary History*, and Jesse's *Memoirs*, while another source not to be neglected is the list of subscribers to the edition of *Musae Etonenses*, published in 1755, most of whom were in all probability Etonians.

While this collection may claim to be fairly complete from 1752 onwards, there are many gaps in the first half of the 18th century. It is mortifying, or it would be mortifying were any other school in question, to reflect that Winchester, thanks to the untiring efforts of the late Mr. C. W. Holgate, can shew a complete set of rolls from 1723 onwards, besides no less than forty-four previous to that date beginning with the year 1653. But apart from Winchester, I know of no school, with the exception of Merchant Taylors' and possibly our ancient rival, Westminster, that can shew so many early lists as Eton.

It remains for me to express my most grateful thanks to all those who have been kind enough to entrust me with their lists, to the late Duke of Rutland, the late Earl of Romney, the Right Hon. L. V. Harcourt, M.P., Sir L. E. Jones, Bt., Sir J. W. Buchanan-Riddell, Bt., Sir W. W. Portal, Bt., Mr. C. W. Campbell,

Miss B. Chetwynd-Stapylton, Mrs. Chute, Mr. A. Clark-Kennedy, Mr. Lionel Cust, Rev. G. R. Dupuis, Mr. J. E. Eastwood, Miss Ellison, Rev. N. T. Garry, Mr. T. C. Garth, Mr. S. H. le Fleming, Mr. G. E. Lloyd-Baker, Miss M. Mason, Mr. R. Orlebar, Rev. J. H. Snowden, Mr. V. F. Tufnell, and Mr. A. Wyatt-Edgell. Also to the Provost and Vice-Provost of Eton for granting me access to many documents; to Sir H. C. Maxwell Lyte for help and encouragement; to Mr. G. E. Cokayne for assisting me to identify many of the noblemen's names; to Mr. Wasey Sterry for generously placing at my disposal his collection of notes dealing with Eton; to Mr. Herbert Chitty, Mr. B. P. Lascelles, Rev. H. A. James, D.D., and Mr. G. F. Russell-Barker for information with regard to the numbers at Winchester, Harrow, Rugby and Westminster; to Mr. F. L. Clarke of the Bursary, King's College, for enabling me to date many of the lists by reference to the register of admissions to King's, and to all others who have helped me with advice and encouragement.

Further, I should like to express in particular how much I owe to the labours of the late Mr. H. E. Chetwynd-Stapylton. Mr. Stapylton, while engaged on his annotated School Lists from 1791 to 1892, found time to collect and make transcripts of many lists of the 18th century, and at one time even thought of publishing his collection. But abandoning that idea he gave his transcripts to the Eton College Library. Although I have in every case made my own transcript from the original, Mr. Stapylton's discoveries and his notes as to where the originals were to be found have naturally been of the greatest assistance.

I should like also to mention how much I owe to the example of the late Mr. C. W. Holgate in the admirable work he did with regard to the Long Rolls at Winchester, work that I can only hope to imitate *longo intervallo*.

In conclusion I need scarcely say how glad I should be if any one possessing lists for years not represented in this volume would let me know of them.

                                    R. A. AUSTEN LEIGH.

March 1907.

INTRODUCTION.

THE EXTENT OF THE SERIES, 1678–1790.

THE present volume contains a complete series of lists from 1756–1790 and the following lists previous to 1756, viz. 1678, 1698 (see Appendix I.), 1706, 1707, 1718, 1725, 1728, 1732, 1742, 1745, 1747, 1753 and 1754. When Mr. Stapylton presented his collection of transcripts to the Eton College Library in 1895 it contained lists for the following years, viz. 1678, 1718, 1725, 1732, 1742, 1745, 1752, 1754, 1757, 1762–1771, 1773, 1775, 1778–1783, 1785, 1788, and 1789. It will be seen that Mr. Stapylton's collection appears to include a list for 1752, but on closer investigation this proved to be a list not for 1752 but for 1753. The year 1753 being the first year for which I have seen more than one list, I have printed two, viz. for January and December, as they are practically a year apart. With the exception of the lists for the years 1698, 1732 and 1745, I have in every case been able to consult the original MS.

THE GAPS IN THE SERIES.

It will be seen that there are many gaps in the series previous to the year 1756, and it may be asked what chance there is of any further lists being discovered. From the very considerable number of lists that have been brought to light in the last few years, I feel no doubt that there are many more scattered about the country which will gradually emerge, as family papers come to be calendared. Meanwhile there is some proof that certain lists once extant have, temporarily at any rate, disappeared. Thus in the table of "Comparative Numbers of the School at different periods," which is given on the last page of the *Eton Calendar* and which was presumably taken from actual lists, it will be noticed that numbers are given for the years 1708, 1720, 1739 and 1755, for none of which have I been able to discover lists. This table first appears, as far as I know, in the original *Eton Calendar* that was edited in 1842 by G. J. Dupuis, who makes the following remark in his prefatory notice:

The Lists of Eton School were first printed and published in the year 1791, and have continued to appear, very nearly in their original form, annually at each successive Election. Before that period, Manuscript Lists were prepared once in each School-time by the Head Master, and presented by him to the Provost: this custom still continues. In still earlier times, "Bills" of the School (as they were called), written on long narrow rolls of paper or parchment, are the only memorials to be met with. They are of course extremely rare.

When I wrote to the Rev. G. R. Dupuis, asking if he possessed any lists that had belonged to his father, G. J. Dupuis, he kindly sent me certain papers, among which was the transcript of the list of 1698 evidently in G. J. Dupuis' handwriting. The papers, however, contained no trace of the lists for 1708, 1720, 1739 or 1755. They did, however, include an elaborately drawn up table of numbers at Eton School for the following years: 1693, 1697, 1698, 1705, 1707, 1708, 1713–28, 1732, 1735, 1737, 1739, 1741, 1743–50, 1752–62, 1764–70, 1772–80, 1786, 1791, 1793–6, 1798, 1800–1 (see Appendix II.). As the numbers of Upper and Lower School are given separately in nearly every case, it looks almost certain that whoever compiled this table had seen lists for all the above-mentioned years. I imagine the table to have been compiled by Dr. Goodall, from the fact that among Mr. Dupuis' papers is a slip containing the words "Old Eton Lists and Papers which were once Dr. Goodall's," and if so it certainly seems as if all these lists were in existence about a hundred years ago.

Possibly such of these lists as belong to the seventeenth and early eighteenth centuries may have been those referred to in Nichols' "Literary Anecdotes": *

I possess Rolls of Eton College and School, of the close of the 17th Century with the early parts of the 18th, preserved by Stephen Apthorp, many years Assistant, and finally Fellow of it. E. Jones.

Mr. Sterry made a search for these lists in 1889, and finally traced the matter down to a Mr. Charles Sturges Jones, of West Street, Chichester, who remembered his father possessing

* Vol. IX., p. 699 (additions to eighth volume, p. 428).

" several long parchment rolls about three or four inches broad, and containing a long list of names of Old Etonians." Mr. Jones remembered too that his father had gone to dine with the Provost of Eton some forty or fifty years before (i.e. before 1889) and "that he then took the said Rolls with him and presented them to the Provost or Head Master of that date." It is therefore quite possible that this series may yet be brought to light.

One other piece of evidence for the existence of other lists may be quoted from a letter to Mr. Chetwynd-Stapylton, written in 1861 by Lord Monson, in which the following sentence occurs:

I have had a letter from Mr. Lambert Larking, the antiquary of Kent, and he tells me of Mr. Clayton having the largest and oldest collection of Eton Lists he ever saw......Mr. Clayton's collection contains a Montem List about 1743.

I have not been able to discover anything about this collection, and it is possible that *printed* Eton Lists are referred to.

THE RECOVERY OF THE LISTS.

Incomplete as the present collection of lists is, it has only been brought together after a very considerable number of years, and I now propose to give as far as is possible the dates at which the various lists have been brought to light.

1832. In the January number of the *Gentleman's Magazine*, a list for 1781 (headed wrongly "1779–1780").

1834. Mr. Angelo lent a list for 1767 to Rev. R. B. Byam.

1843. Dr. Hawtrey caused a list for 1745 to be printed by E. P. Williams.

1851. The list for 1732 was printed in Eliot Warburton's "Memoirs of Horace Walpole and his Contemporaries," Vol. I., pp. 78–81.

1855. The Rev. J. Ayre presented lists for 1766, 1767, 1768 and 1769 to the College Library.

1862. Dr. Okes, Provost of King's, presented the roll for 1718 to the College Library.

1865. The list for 1678 was printed at the end of *Etoniana* (by the Rev. W. L. Collins).

In the course of this year Lord Abingdon wrote to Lord Romney begging the loan of certain lists (which

b

must have been those for 1752, 1762, 1768, 1771 and 1789) on behalf of Mr. Chetwynd-Stapylton. The last-named also had seen by this time Mr. Hatch's list for 1764 and the Mason roll for 1775.

Lord Abingdon seems also to have borrowed Mr. Riddell's roll for 1762 for Mr. Stapylton.

Mr. A. Wyatt-Edgell lent a list for 1766 to Mr. Stapylton.

Colonel Tighe of Rossana sent Mr. Stapylton a printed list for 1780.

Mr. R. N. Cust lent Mr. Stapylton a list for 1754.

Mr. Ingalton Drake bought the five Frankland lists for 1776–1780 at a sale in London.

Mr. Wasey Sterry discovered the list for 1742 in a copy of " Alumni Etonenses " in the Bodleian Library.

On June 21 appeared an article in the *Eton College Chronicle* by Mr. Stapylton, stating the extent of his collection at that date. From this article it appears that he had seen besides the lists previously mentioned, a collection made by Mr. Williams' assistant (George Davis) for the following years : 1754, 1757, 1768, 1778, 1779, 1781 and 1783 (Lower School only). Further Mr. Stapylton had seen a list for 1764, lent by Mr. Jesse, a roll for 1766, belonging to Sir W. S. Trelawny, a list for 1788 (of which the origin is not mentioned), and one for 1789 lent by Archdeacon Holbech.

Mr. R. M. Harvey presented a list for 1764 to the College Library. In the second edition of the "History of Eton College," published this year, Sir H. C. Maxwell Lyte mentions a list for 1766 existing at Belvoir Castle.

In the Report of the Historical MSS. Commission, published this year, Mr. Le Fleming's list for 1761 is mentioned.

At the Eton Loan Exhibition the following lists made their appearance (among others already mentioned):

No. 412. MS. volume of Eton Lists 1763–69, lent Mr. G. E. Lloyd Baker.

No. 413. Absence Roll, lent by the Earl Brownlow. (No date is given, and I can learn nothing of this item.)

No. 414. Absence Roll, lent by Mr. Wyndham S. Portal. (This is for 1769.)

No. 415. Absence Roll 1771, lent by Mr. C. Chute.

No. 416. Absence Roll 1772, lent by the Earl of Darnley.

1895. When Mr. Stapylton presented during this year his collection of MS. transcripts to the College Library, it contained in addition to those previously mentioned, transcripts of two lists in the College Library both dated 1773 (one of which however is really for 1774), of lists for 1782, 1783, 1785 also in the College Library, and of a list for 1782, lent by Rev. J. W. Hawtrey.

1899. Mr. C. W. Holgate, in his book "Winchester Long Rolls 1653–1721," p. 184, mentions that the item described in the third Report of the Historical MSS. Commission, p. 276, as "1707 Narrow paper roll, 8 or 10 feet long. Names of persons in Winchester School," is really an Eton list.

1901. I came across a MS. list for 1762 bound up at the beginning of a volume of printed School Lists, 1791–1810, in the possession of Messrs. Spottiswoode & Co.

1903. Mr. A. B. Ramsay and others presented a roll for 1769, purchased from Mr. W. G. Griffith, to the School Library.

Mr. R. S. de Havilland bought from a Reading bookseller lists for 1753 and 1754.

1904. I was lent by Mr. R. Orlebar lists for 1747, 1753 (2), 1754; by Sir L. Jones, lists for 1756, 1757 (2), 1758, 1759, 1760, 1761 (2); by Miss Ellison, two lists for 1761; by Mr. V. F. Tufnell, a roll for 1766; by Rev. J. H. Snowden, a roll for 1773. In addition I discovered a list for 1706 in the British Museum (Harl. MSS. 7025, f. 135), and was allowed to see at the Record Office a list (of which one quarter was missing) belonging to the Duke of Rutland, for 1762. Mr. Lionel Cust also kindly sent me a transcript of a list for 1781 belonging to Lord Darnley, and of a fragment of a list for 1758 belonging to Lord Brownlow.

1905. I was lent a roll (part of which is missing) for 1766 by Mr. L. V. Harcourt; by Mr. J. E. Eastwood a roll for 1728; Sir R. Payne-Gallwey also informed me that he possessed a list for 1766.

1906. Rev. G. R. Dupuis sent me a transcript of a list for 1698 in his father's (G. J. Dupuis') handwriting.

THE OWNERS OF ETON LISTS.

I will now give in detail the institutions and persons who have lists in their possession :

The British Museum possesses a list for 1706 (Harl. MSS. 7025 f. 135).

The Bodleian Library has lists for 1678 (Rawlinson MSS., B. 266, 146) and 1742 (Gough, Bucks, 6).

The Eton College Library has rolls for 1718 and 1766, and lists for 1753, 1754, 1764, 1766 (2), 1767, 1768, 1769, 1773 (2), 1775-90 (bound in two volumes).

The Eton School Library has a roll for 1769 (or possibly 1768).

The Earl of Romney has a roll for 1771, and probably one for 1752, and lists for 1768, 1789, 1790 (2).

Sir Lawrence Jones, Bt., of Cranmer Hall, Fakenham, lists for 1756, 1757 (2), 1758, 1759, 1760, 1761 (2).

Mr. G. E. Lloyd Baker, of Hardwicke Court, Gloucester, lists for 1762, 1763 (3), 1764 (3), 1765 (2), 1766 (3), 1767 (2), 1768 (2), 1769.

Mr. R. Orlebar, of Hinwick House, Beds, a roll for 1707, and lists for 1747, 1753 (2), 1754.

The Duke of Rutland for 1762 (quarter of one sheet missing) and 1766.

Miss Ellison, Kingsbury Lodge, St. Albans, 1761 (2).

Mr. T. C. Garth, of Haines Hill, Twyford, for 1725.

Mr. V. F. Tufnell, of Norwood House, Leamington, a roll for 1765.

Mr. J. E. Eastwood, of Enton, Witley, a roll for 1728.

Sir R. Payne-Gallwey, Bt., a list for 1766.

Mr. L. V. Harcourt, of 14 Berkeley Square, a roll for 1766 (incomplete).

Sir William Portal, Bt., of Malshanger, Basingstoke, a roll for 1769.

Mrs. Chute, of The Vyne, Basingstoke, a roll for 1771.

Rev. J. H. Snowden, S. Vedast, 25 Carlton Road, Putney Hill, S.W., a roll for 1773.

Miss M. Mason, of Aldenham Cottage, Yateley, a roll for 1775.

Sir J. W. Buchanan Riddell, Bt., a roll for 1762.

Mr. A. Wyatt-Edgell of Cowley House, Exeter, a list for 1766.

Mr. Holbech, Farnborough, Warwickshire, for 1789.

Messrs. Spottiswoode & Co. have a MS. list for 1762 bound up at the beginning of a volume of School Lists for 1791–1810.

My own collection comprises lists for 1754, 1757, 1766, 1767, 1768 (2), 1769, 1770, 1778, 1779, 1783 (Lower School only) and 1788.

In addition to the foregoing the Rev. G. R. Dupuis has a transcript of a list for 1698.

Mr. A. Clark-Kennedy transcripts of lists for 1764 and 1767.

Mr. C. W. Campbell, of Ivy House, Hampton Court, for 1773.

Rev. N. T. Garry, of the Rectory, Taplow, for 1773.

Miss B. Chetwynd-Stapylton for 1764.

Early printed lists, of which the originals have disappeared, are :

For 1732 in Eliot Warburton's "Memoirs of Horace Walpole and his Contemporaries," Vol. I., pp. 78–81 (ed. 1851).

For 1745, printed by E. P. Williams, Eton, 1843.

For 1780, a broadside printed by Colonel Tighe of Rossana.

For 1781 in the *Gentleman's Magazine* for January 1832.

Lastly the following lists, believed to have existed at one time or another, have temporarily at any rate disappeared :

For 1752, belonging to Lord Romney.

For 1754, belonging to Mr. R. N. Cust.

For 1772, belonging to Lord Darnley.

For 1782, belonging to the late Rev. J. W. Hawtrey.

HEADINGS ON THE LISTS.

The most common heading is "Bill of Eton College," or "Bill of Eton School," though the word "List" not unfrequently occurs. The lists for 1745 and 1756 are styled "A Bill of Eton College and School." It may be remarked here that in the small School List published at the end of each Half, which is the lineal descendant of the first printed list of 1791, the list is styled "A List of Eton College," but the list of boys on p. 11 is headed "Eton School."

Though the term "Bill" occurs in the last list printed in this volume, viz. for 1790, the expression was discarded in favour of "List" when the names were printed for the first time in 1791, and has never reappeared, though "Bill" is found in the MS.

volume as late as Election 1797. The expression "Bill," however, still survives in the Eton vocabulary, e.g. "A 'Bill' off
Absence," and in the less pleasant sense of being "in the Bill."

At Harrow the earliest lists of the school that survive are
styled "Bills," and to this day at Harrow "Bill" is as well
known as "Absence" at Eton. Though some of the Eton Lists
are in the form of rolls, I do not think the expression "Roll of
the School" is ever to be met with.

METHOD OF PRODUCTION.

It is difficult to say exactly how the School Bills were made
out, but the extant MS. lists may be roughly divided into three
classes, those written (1) by boys, (2) by writing masters
(probably), (3) by headmasters. With regard to the first class,
in days when there were sometimes 500 boys in the School,
it must have been impossible for any one to have known
the order of the boys by heart. Some light is thrown on the
method of compilation by a letter dated July 7, 1698, from
Thomas Rawlinson to his father, in which he says, "As for the
Bill of the boys' names which I promised to send you in my first,
the great alteration in the school by the new boys coming which
are very numerous and the old ones going away hath put me to a
stop till I got the bills of every form singly ; as soon as ever I
have got them I will send them." (Rawlinson MSS. 862, 101 in
the Bodleian.)

Having borrowed copies of the bills for each form, a boy
would then proceed to copy them out in order usually on a sheet
of foolscap. Such a *modus operandi* will account for various
errors found, e.g. *Toote* for *Foote*, *Paylor* for *Reylor*. But in
other cases the spelling appears to be phonetic, and it would
seem that the names must have been written down as they were
called out, perhaps at Absence time.

The second class of list gives evident trace of having been
written by persons who practised calligraphy as a fine art. The
flourishes and twirligigs to be found in lists of about 1760–1770
could scarcely have been written by anyone but a writing-master.
Nor is there anything improbable in this supposition : the late
Mr. Holgate was confident that the long rolls at Winchester
were written by the writing-master, while at Harrow, where the
lists were not printed till 1845, nearly all those preserved in the
Vaughan Library for the early part of the nineteenth century are

said to be in the handwriting of Mr. J. F. Marillier, Writing and Mathematical Master from 1819-1869.   And there is the further evidence that the first printed list at Eton (for 1791) was "Published (by Permission) By W. Hexter," who was writing-master until 1842.   No doubt Eton writing-masters were able in this way to add somewhat to their incomes, and probably continued to do so till long after the lists had come to be printed, for I have met with lists written out in a formal hand till as late as 1820.

With the third class of lists we do not become acquainted until 1775 (the date of the first of those in the bound volumes in the College Library), but it is likely enough that it was the custom at a much earlier date for the Head Master to prepare a list for the Provost.   From 1775 to 1790, although many of the Lists of the Lower School, in the instances where separate lists for it have survived, are undoubtedly in the handwriting of the Lower Master (Dr. Langford), the complete lists for the School do not seem to be in the Head Master's hand, and I suspect that he employed a boy to write them out and contented himself with supervising the result and perhaps adding the date.   This would account for the occasional insertion of names, and for the fact that the date is so frequently added in another hand.   Later on in the days of Goodall's and Keate's rule, the lists are nearly always in the handwriting of the Head Master.

With regard to the lists in roll form, I am not able to throw any light on their origin or use.   It is possible that in early times the official school list, which it is but reasonable to suppose existed in some shape or other, took this form.   The form indeed may have been borrowed from Winchester, where it existed at least as early as 1653.   Or it is possible that rolls were specially prepared for the purpose of calling "Absence."   In this connexion it may be remarked that Items Nos. 413–416 in the Eton Loan Exhibition of 1891 are described in the Catalogue as "Absence Rolls," but I do not know that there is any actual proof that they were used for such purpose, for which they cannot have been particularly convenient.

DATES OF THE LISTS.

The most common date at which lists were made out was without doubt Election time, but as some of the lists included in this volume are obviously written out by boys, they might be made at any time which might suit a boy's whim, or his father's request. Where the lists are dated by the original scribe no difficulty arises, but the case is not so simple where the list contains no date, or where the date has been added at a subsequent period; for it often happens that the wrong date has been affixed. The only way, and it is often a rough way, of dating such lists is by placing them between the time when the boy at the top of College got King's and the time when his predecessor did. The date of admission to King's can be obtained from the archives of King's College, and the dismissal from Eton usually took place about ten days previously. Between 1688 and 1713 the list can also be dated by the admission of the Collegers, for which the date is given in the College Register.

FORMS.

In the earliest known account of Eton, namely that apparently furnished for the benefit of the grammar school at Saffron Walden in c. 1530 by Richard Cox, as well as in the *Consuetudinarium* by William Malim written in 1560, there were seven forms beginning with the seventh and ending with the first, and it is reasonable to suppose that this was the original number of forms in existence at Eton, as it would be the simple and obvious way of grouping the seventy scholars. The same number seems to have existed at Winchester, whence Eton borrowed so many of her customs (see the account, also furnished for the school at Saffron Walden, by John Twychener, c. 1530). It may be remarked here that, supposing seven to have been the conventional number of forms in old times, few of the older schools now go beyond a sixth. Westminster, however, is an exception, still having a seventh, while St. Paul's has even an eighth.

After the lapse of nearly four centuries since Cox's time, we find that there now exist at Eton a Sixth, Fifth, Remove, Fourth and Third Form (neglecting all sub-divisions for the moment). Thus it will be seen that in the course of some 350 years the Forms have suffered a diminution at either end, besides an interpolation in the middle. In 1678, the date of the earliest extant list, we find a 6th, 5th, 4th, 3rd, 2nd, and Bible Seat, which must be taken as synonymous with First Form, whenever it does not form a separate subdivision. The Seventh has already gone; it is less usual for the higher forms to disappear than for the lower, and one can only imagine it to happen owing to a very unusual number of boys leaving at the top of the School. Exactly when the Seventh disappeared at Eton is impossible to say, but a likely time would perhaps be during the Civil Wars, when a great many of the bigger boys may have gone off to fight. The Seventh Form had similarly disappeared at Winchester c. 1650, for the Sixth is the highest form mentioned in the poem long attributed to Christopher Johnson, Head Master 1561-1571, but now known to have been written during the Headmastership of John Pottinger (or Potenger), who was Head Master 1643-1653.

It is a common occurrence to find that the lower forms at a school have disappeared, and this has doubtless been due in part to the rise of preparatory schools, which have led to boys going at a much later age to public schools. But even before the days of preparatory schools, we find a similar process in operation at Winchester, where as early as 1653 the only forms remaining are the 6th, 5th and 4th (and since then the 4th has disappeared). At Eton, however, the 2nd and 1st forms remained until 1869-1870.

Simultaneously with the disappearance of the top and bottom forms, a practice has sprung up of interpolating one or more forms. At Eton this form was called " Remove," at Westminster " Shell," and other schools have not been slow to adopt the practice. Thus at Harrow and Shrewsbury we find both a Shell and a Remove, at Rugby a Shell, at St. Paul's a Remove, at Merchant Taylors' and St. Paul's a Transitus Form.

It is difficult to explain the necessity for the introduction of these forms, except either on the theory that an extra form was needed, or that such a form as the Remove indicated originally a probationary or intermediate stage. This expression in its latter-day sense is first found in the list for 1718, though there seem to be traces of the existence of such a form both in the 1706 and 1707 lists. But in the sense of promotion the word is found at least as early as 1609, for we read in a letter of that date,* "[Phil Litton] hath stept a forme higher at this Christmas remove, and is now under the Schoolemaster's tuition." Also the " Lag Remove" as part of Third Form occurs in the list for 1698.

SUB-DIVISIONS OF FORMS.

The list for 1698 is the first to give us any definite names for sub-divisions of forms. In it we find Third Form divided

* Calendar of State Papers, Domestic Series, James I., Vol. LII. No. 9.

into six portions: the first merely bears the general title of Lower School, and then follow "Lower Greek," "Nonsense," "Scan and Prove," "Prosodia" and "Lag Remove." Of these, "Scan and Prove" and "Prosodia" appear in no other lists that I have ever seen, but in his MS. account of Eton Discipline written in 1766 Thomas James mentions the lessons studied by both these divisions. Thus he tells us both "Scan and Prove" and "Prosodia" did the same lessons as "Sense," with the exception that the former, instead of making sense verses, scanned and proved ten lines in Ovid's *Electa*, while the latter said instead a page in *Prosodia*, which they learnt at the end of the week. In the list for 1718 we find Second Form divided into two divisions, the first bearing the general title of Second Form and the second being called "Lower Remove." In the list for Jan. 30, 1753, Fourth Form is divided into a 1st, 2nd and 3rd Remove; Third Form into six removes, and Second Form into two. This was for the future the usual system. The six removes of Third Form had the following names assigned to them: Upper Greek, Lower Greek, Sense, Nonsense, Lag (or Lower) Remove and Unplaced. These names are by no means always given in the lists, but the first time they all appear is in the list of 1781.

Similarly Second Form was divided into an Upper and Lower Remove.

From the MS. book of Thomas James, afterwards Head Master of Rugby, we know what lessons these various forms did: that boys began Greek Grammar in Lower Greek; that Sense acquired its name because "some sense was given and rendered into Latin verse," whereas Nonsense did the same as Sense, except that "on Monday, Wednesday and Friday at 5 they made 6 nonsense verses out of a page of Terence, and Saturday at 11 they also made some nonsense verses."

The Last Remove in Third Form as well as Second Form devoted their energies to Latin Grammar and Translation, while First Form learnt nothing but Latin Grammar: the latter seem, according to James, to have been divided into two portions, the upper of which learnt "Syntax et as in praesenti" and did simple exercises, rendering three sentences at the beginning of *Exempla Minora* into Latin, while the lower portion said "Propria quae maribus" and the Accidence, and did no exercise.

These curious names were no doubt a source of bewilderment

to a good many parents; for instance we find the Countess of Courtown writing to her uncle, the Earl of Ailesbury :*

July 1, 1785: Courtown.

In about a fortnight I shall be expecting Richard, whom I shall think a great addition to our party. He writes me an excellent letter saying he has been sent up three times for good for making nonsense verses and that now he is put into sense. I believe one must be an Etonian to understand this language.

These names did not disappear from the printed lists until Election 1860.

The practice of calling forms by the lessons they learned obtained at other schools, and thus we find in the eighteenth century at Harrow a "Scan and Prove," "The Ovid Class," "Phaedrus," "Upper Selectae," "Under Selectae," "The Nomenclature," "The Grammar Class," "The Accidence," "Selectae e Profanis," "Ovid," "Selectae e veteri," "Nomenclator," "Terence," etc. Cf. too "Grecians" and "Great and Little Erasmus" at Christ's Hospital.

UPPER SCHOOL AND LOWER SCHOOL.

In Malim's time, as it was impossible to divide seven forms between the two schools, the middle or fourth form seems to have been a kind of sandwich form, for the Usher took it with the three lower forms at early school, and then handed it over to the Master who took it with the three higher forms. The disappearance of the seventh form probably resulted in the fourth being definitely made part of the Upper School, as it appears in the list for 1698, the first which marks off the Lower School.

The two schools were almost distinct organisations in the eighteenth century. The Lower Master chose and paid his own Assistants (who scarcely ever became Upper Assistants), held his own "chambers," and took an annual fee of four guineas from all boys in the Lower School, who paid nothing to the Head Master, except an entrance fee. Twice a year, once at the beginning of March, and again towards the end of September, boys could get their remove into the Upper School, and Dr. Barnard's entrance book gives the list, usually containing about thirty names, of those boys who "came into the Upper School" on each occasion. Certain initiatory rites on the part of the boys attended the promotion from Upper Greek to Fourth Form. Thus among the customs mentioned in the *Nugae Etonenses* of 1766 is that of "pelting the Upper Greek on their going into the Upper

* 15th Report of the Hist. MSS. Commission, App. Pt. VII. p. 241.

School." This practice developed into what was known as "booking" in Keate's time, or the practice of hitting over the head with the book each boy who made his way for the first time up the staircase into the Upper School.*

The numbers of the Lower School, which in the early part of the eighteenth century frequently exceeded those of the Upper School, began to decline about the year 1785, and it was finally abolished as a separate organisation under the new statutes in 1869, but names fortunately often survive actualities, and the office of Lower Master still survives. From 1870 till 1905 he held a limited jurisdiction over the Fourth and Third Forms, himself teaching the first division of the Fourth Form, and since Michaelmas 1905, keeping his former jurisdiction, he teaches the Second Division of the School. The separate chambers of the Lower Master were given up under Dr. Okes' lower-mastership, and W. A. Carter was the last who chose his own assistants.

THE ARRANGEMENT OF THE NAMES.

The usual arrangement of the most complete lists is as follows :

(1) The Staff (i.e. Provost, Fellows, and Masters).
(2) The Collegers.
(3) The Oppidans.

But in many lists no Staff is given : in one list alone, that for 1742, which is certainly written by a boy, the Staff are put at the end of the list. Similarly the Collegers are once found after the Oppidans (in a list for 1757), and of course they are frequently found intermingled with the Oppidans, sometimes distinguished by the initial "C." and at other times not at all.

THE STAFF.

The list of officials, where it is given, varies but little in the offices mentioned. The order is almost invariably, (1) Provost, (2) Vice-Provost, (3) Fellows, (4) Upper Master, (5) Lower Master, (6) Assistants, sometimes divided into Upper and Lower. Sometimes, however, the latter part runs, (4) Upper Master, (5) Upper Assistants, (6) Lower Master, (7) Lower Assistants.

The only occasions where other dignitaries are mentioned are :

(a) The list for 1745, which gives the Visitor at the top of the list, viz. Dr. Thomas, Bishop of Lincoln, and the Conducts, viz. Mr. Bostock and Mr. Hudgate (i.e. Huggett), after the Lower Assistants.

* Lyte's "History of Eton College," p. 599.

(*b*) The list for 1781 printed in the *Gentleman's Magazine* for January 1832, which gives the Provost of King's (Dr. Cooke) after the Provost of Eton.

(*c*) A list for 1788 (origin unknown), which gives, after the Fellows, " Busers " (i.e. Bursars) Rev. Dr. Norbury and Rev. Mr. Tew, who were two of the Fellows.

In addition this list gives the names of the Private Tutors, Dames and Extra Masters; while the list printed in the *Gentleman's Magazine* likewise gives the list of Private Tutors.

THE PROVOST.

The following is the list of Provosts for the period covered by the lists :

> 1665–1681, Richard Allestree.
> 1681–95, Zachary Cradock.
> 1695–1732, Henry Godolphin.
> 1732–46, Henry Bland.
> 1746–65, Stephen Sleech.
> 1765–81, Edward Barnard.
> 1781–91, William Hayward Roberts.

During the period under review, the Provostship ceased to be looked on as a mere piece of political patronage, and after Godolphin's time began to be regarded as the natural promotion either for a Fellow or for the Head Master.

VICE-PROVOST AND FELLOWS.

During the eighteenth century, the Fellowship gradually became confined almost entirely to Eton and King's men. There were however a few notable exceptions, among whom may be mentioned *William Berriman*, 1727–50, who was educated at Merchant Taylors' School and Oriel College, Oxford, and was the founder of the Berriman Exhibition : *John Burton*, 1733–1771, who was at Corpus Christi College, Oxford, the well-known divine: *William Hetherington*, 1749–78, at Eton but not at King's, who built the Chapel of Ease at Eton: and *Thomas Barnard*, 1772–8, whose only claim seems to have been that he was brother of Dr. Barnard, for he himself was neither at Eton nor King's and had spent many years in the Barbadoes.

THE UPPER MASTER.

Originally the "Master" *par excellence* described in the Statutes, as "Informator" by Malim, he came to be known as Upper Master, and finally as Head Master. In the list for 1698 he and the Lower Master are both described as "Masters."

In a list of Provost, Fellows and Masters given by Rawlinson* (*c.* 1710) Newborough is called "Chief Master." In 1742 we find "Head Master," and this is interesting as the list is written by a boy. The title does not reappear, except in the list for 1788 of which the origin is unknown, until the lists were first printed at Election 1791, since which date "Head Master" has always obtained.

During this period, all the Head Masters with the exception of Rosewell and Barnard were King's men. A good many of them too had been Assistants before they became Head Masters, though Rosewell, Snape, Bland and Barnard seem to have been exceptions.

HEAD MASTERS FOR PERIOD OF LISTS.

John Rosewell	1672–1682
Charles Roderick ..	1682–1689
John Newborough ..	1689–1711
Andrew Snape	1711–1720
Henry Bland	1720–1728
William George	1728–1743
William Cooke	1743–1745
John Sumner	1745–1754
Edward Barnard ..	1754–1765
John Foster	1765–1773
Jonathan Davies ..	1773–1792

HEAD MASTER'S EMOLUMENTS.

For the income and fees of an Eton Head Master in the eighteenth century we have two sources of information. In the first place there exists a paper in Warden Bigg's handwriting, written *c.* 1732.† From this we learn that he had two allowances, one of £50 and the other of £12, commons and lodgings reckoned as £30 for the year, spare chambers let to boys, which usually brought in £8 per annum. In fees he received one guinea entrance of all boys both in the upper and lower school, and an annual gratuity,

* Rawlinson MSS. B. 267 (Bodleian).
† Quoted by Mr. Kirby in his "Annals of Winchester College," p. 401.

usually of 4 guineas, from boys in the upper school. This fee however was never demanded, and it was reckoned that about a third of the boys paid nothing.

In the second place, Dr. Barnard's account book has survived, and from it we learn that in 1754 the charges for schooling were unchanged, being £4 4s. a year, £2 2s. a half year and £1 1s. a quarter, noblemen being charged double. Entrance fees varied from £1 to £10 10s., but the ordinary fee was £2 2s. The Head Master's official stipend was still the same, viz. £62, and in addition he received the following fees from each boy, which were known as " Gatherings":

	£	s.	d.
Michaelmas Sweeping	0	0	4
Christmas Firing and Candles and Sweeping	0	3	4
Lower School Candles and Sweeping ..	0	1	10
Lady Day Firing and Sweeping	0	1	10
Midsummer Sweeping	0	0	4

From these fees he received in a year from October 10, 1754, to September 29, 1755, the following sums:

			£	s.	d.
1754.	Oct. 10.	For Schoool Sweeping	5	14	0
		Given to Captain	0	5	0
	Dec. 7.	For Fire and Candles	41	0	0
1755.	Mar. 21.	Collection for Fire and Sweeping	17	3	6
	July	Collection for Sweeping ..	5	10	0

During the same period, the Head Master received £10 10s. for various Chambers and Studies, which were no doubt his original apartments at the west end of Long Chamber which he still let out. The studies seem to have been always let to Collegers.

What the Head Master made out of his " Gatherings " cannot be known, for it is to be presumed that he had to supply in return fires and candles in the winter months, and to provide for the sweeping out of the school.

Besides the above, the Head Master had one more source of income in the leaving presents, which seem to have ranged from £2 2s. upwards, though they often consisted of books. Writing in 1793 to Samuel Butler, Dr. James, the ex-Head Master of Rugby, says, "you know we have here no farewell presents; whereas the Master of Eton, you will find, by the custom of the place, receives a present of three, four, ten, twenty, etc., guineas (according to circumstances) from every boy that leaves his school in the upper part and not being on the Foundation."[*]

There is an instance of one boy, Baker, paying as much as £50, and the amount of income derived from this source reached the sum of £411 in 1763.

In addition to this present, or possibly in lieu of it, was the custom, which seems to date from Dr. Barnard's time, of boys of good birth giving their portraits to the Head Master.

This custom was not apparently peculiar to Eton, for it had prevailed at Winchester about the years 1729–1733, when the School became so fashionable under Dr. Burton. The portraits hang at Winchester in the Second Master's dining-room.

The custom when initiated at Eton happened to coincide with the most glorious period of English portrait painting, and the result is that, owing to the various Head Masters bequeathing these portraits to the College, the Provost's Lodge contains a splendid collection of portraits by Reynolds, Romney, Gainsborough, Lawrence, Hoppner, Beechey, etc. The average price paid for a head and shoulders portrait by Reynolds is said to have been only £35.

Cole[†] states that Barnard's income was every year above £1500, but out of that he presumably had to pay five assistants £44 2s. apiece.

In addition, the Head Master no doubt lived rent-free, and the official residence during the greater part of the eighteenth century was the house in Weston's Yard next to that known now as Savile House. Thus George, Cooke, Barnard, Foster and Davies all lived here. Sumner on the other hand, who as Lower Master was occupying the southern half of Savile House, then divided into two, seems to have remained on as Head Master in the same house.

THE LOWER MASTER.

The Lower Master was originally known as the Usher (the *Ostiarius* of the Statutes), and Rawlinson in his list, mentioned above, still employs that title, but in the list for 1698 the title is " master." In 1718 however we find the modern title of Lower Master. This title however was changed to Sub-Master in the first printed list for 1791, and to Under-Master from 1792–1809, but in 1810 became once for all Lower Master.

---

[*] " Life and Letters of Samuel Butler," Vol. I. p. 14.
[†] Brit. Mus. Add. MSS. 5835, p. 38.

LOWER MASTERS FOR PERIOD OF LISTS.

Charles Roderick	..	1676–1682
John Newborough	..	1682–1689
Stephen Weston	..	1689–1707
Thomas Carter ..	..	1707–1716
Francis Goode ..	..	1716–1734
John Sumner ..	..	1734–1745
Thomas Dampier	..	1745–1767
Henry Sleech ..	..	1767–1775
William Langford	..	1775–1802

The same document that gives the emoluments of the Master in 1732 also gives those of the Usher. We learn therefrom that he had only an allowance of £19 a year, that he had no right to any commons at all, but was nearly always invited to the Fellows' table, and paid nothing. That he had lodgings for himself, and let out studies besides to boys for about £6 a year, and that he received annual gratuities of four guineas from the Lower School, besides a guinea entrance from those under him.

In days when the numbers of the Lower School frequently exceeded those of the Upper, the post of Lower Master must have been reckoned distinctly good. He moreover chose his own assistants and even made a profit out of the transaction, if we may trust the following advertisement from the *London Evening Post* of November 9, 1731 :

Whereas Mr. Franc. Goode, under-master of Eaton, does hereby signify that there will be at Christmas next, or soon after, two vacancies in his school, viz. as assistants to him and tutors to the young gents ; if any two gentlemen of either University (who have commenced the degree of B.A. at least) shall think themselves duly qualified, and are desirous of such an employment, let them enquire of John Potts, pickleman in Gracious Street, or at Mr. G.'s own house in Eaton College, where they may purchase the same at a reasonable rate, and on conditions fully to their own satisfaction.

FR. GOODE.

N.B.—It was very erroneously reported that the last place was disposed of under 40s.

The Lower Master continued to choose his own assistants and hold his own chambers until Dr. Okes' time.

The old Lower School gradually shrank in proportion as preparatory schools became more common, and boys came to Eton at a more advanced age. It was finally abolished by the new statutes of 1869.

The Lower Master had evacuated his original chambers, which were at the east end of the range and underneath Long

Chamber, as early as 1718, for we find Mr. Carter, the Lower Master of that date, living in part of Savile House. As part of his chambers (or perhaps the whole) was used by College and known as Carter's Chamber, we may presume he was the first to evacuate these rooms. The Lower Master received rent for this room for a very long time.

THE ASSISTANTS.

Though only a Master and Usher were originally provided for the instruction of the Eton youth, as the numbers grew an increase in the teaching staff must have been needed. The first list of the staff that has survived is the list for 1698, where they are styled "Ushers." The next is that given by Rawlinson (B. 267, Bodleian), consisting of

Mr. Good	Mr. Simmonds
Mr. Wood	Mr. Curtiss
Mr. Beasley	Mr. Torrent
Mr. Antrobus	

From internal evidence the date of this list must be between 1708 and 1711. Hereafter we find lists given in 1718, 1728, 1742, 1745, 1747, 1753–1754, 1756–7, 1759–1774, 1778–1782, 1788, and 1791 onwards.

Harwood too in his "Alumni Etonenses" mentions others who became Assistants, and it is therefore possible to compile the following list of Assistants for the eighteenth century. Those names placed within square brackets occur only in Harwood; the rest are to be found in the extant School Lists: where the dates of their coming and leaving are not certain, they are enclosed in round brackets. The initials following certain dates denote that they then became Head Master, Lower Master, or Fellow.

LIST OF ASSISTANTS FOR PERIOD OF LISTS.

Thomas Johnson	..got King's	1683	(1698)
Gregory Parry	.. .. ,,	1685	(1698)
[Eldred Gaell	.. .. ,,	1687	
Thomas Carter	.. .. ,,	1690]–1707, L.M.	
John Lawley	.. ,,	1691	(1698)
William Willymott	.. ,,	1692	(1698)
James Upton	.. .. ,,	1693	(1698)
Richard Sleech	.. .. ,,	1693	(1698)

Richard Chair	..	..		(1698)
[William Wilson ..	..got King's 1694]			
Francis Goode	..	.. ,,	1695	c. 1710–1717, L.M.
Thomas Wood	..	.. ,,	1695	,,
William Beasley ..	..	,,	1696	,,
Robert Antrobus	..			(c. 1710, 1718)
[Richard Blythman	..	,,	1696	
Nicholas Mann ..	..	,,	1699]	
Samuel Symonds..	..	,,	1699	c. 1710
Francis Curtis	..	.. ,,	1700	,,
Samuel Torrent ..	..	,,	1702	,,
Samuel Gilman ..	..	,,	1704	(1718)
Charles Snape	..	.. ,,	1708	(1718)
William Antrobus	..	,,	1709	,,
Adam Elliot	..	.. ,,	1709	(1718, 1728)
Thomas Thackeray	..	,,	1711	(1718)–1728
John Burchett	..	..		(1718, 1728)
Charles Willats ..	..	,,	1712	,,
[Benjamin Archer	..	,,	1715	
William George ..	..	,,	1715]–1728, H.M.	
[Edward Littleton	..	,,	1716]–1726, Fellow	
Bartholomew Young	..	,,	1716	(1728)
John Ewer	..	.. ,,	1723	(1728)
John Sumner	..	.. ,,	1723	(1728)–1734, L.M.
Stephen Sleech ..	..	,,	1723	(1728)–1729, Fellow
[Ralph Thicknesse	..	,,	1726	(for 10 years)
John Goddard ..	..	,,	1726]	(1728)
Richard Dongworth				(1728)
[John Whaley	..	.. ,,	1727]	
Stephen Apthorp	..	,,	1728	(1742)–1758, Fellow
[John Sleech	..	.. ,,	1729]	
Peter Laynge	..	.. ,,	1730	(1742)
William Cooke	..	.. ,,	1730	(1742)–1743, H.M.
Joshua Barnes	..	.. ,,	1731	(1742–1747)
Thomas Dampier ..	..	,,	1731	–1745, L.M.
[Richard Lyne	..	.. ,,	1733]	
Septimius Plumptre	..	,,	1736	(1742–7)
John Reade	..	.. ,,	1738	(1742–5)
Robert Purt	..	.. ,,	1738	(1745–7)
John Reepe	..	.. ,,	1740	(1747)–1751, d. July
Henry Sleech	..	.. ,,	1741	(1747)–1767, L.M.
John Norbury	..	.. ,,	1742	1753–1783, Fellow

[Edward Young ..	..	„	1742]	
John Prior ..	.. got King's	1745	1760–1789
George Graham ..	..	„	1746	(1753)–1766
Robert Carey Sumner ..	„	1747	(1753)–1759
John Foster ..	..	„	1748	1754–1765, H.M.
John Ekins ..	..	„	1754	(1754)–1765
Richard Edwards..	..	„	1752	(1759)–1771
William Hayward Roberts	„	1752	1760–1771, Fellow
Graham Jepson ..	..	„	1753	1767–1770
Jonathan Davies ..	..	„	1755	1760–1773
Benjamin Heath ..	..	„	1758	1763–1771
Edward Hawtrey..	..	„	1760	1766–(1782)
William Langford	..	„	1762	1766–1775, L.M.
Humphrey Sumner	..	„	1762	1767–(1788)
George Heath ..	..	„	1763	(1778)–1792, H.M.
William Cooke ..	..	„	1765	1771–(1774)
William Foster ..	..	„	1767	(1773)–1790
George Savage ..	..	„	1769	1780–1799
William Cole ..	..	„	1772	(1778)–1779
Joseph Goodall ..	..	„	1778	1783–1801
Peter R. V. Hinde	..	„	1779	(1788)–1801
George Stevenson	..	„	1780	(1788)–1796
John Roberts ..	..	„	1780	(1791)–1800
Thomas Boggust ..	..	„	1783	(1791)–1792

Most of the Assistants were drawn from King's College, but one gathers from Mr. Goode's advertisement that this qualification was unnecessary for the Lower School. At any rate, I find only two instances of Upper Assistants not being King's men, viz. Robert Antrobus in 1718, who had been at Peterhouse, and Dongworth, who had been at Magdalene College, Cambridge, in 1728. Of Lower School Assistants there is Burchett (1718), who had been at Peterhouse. Chair, who from his position in the list of "Ushers" in the list of 1698 was probably a Lower School Assistant, graduated in 1697 from King's, but seems to have been only a "poor scholar" there.

Lower Assistants were not usually promoted to the Upper School, but Edwards seems to have been an exception.

In their tutorial capacity Lower Assistants had pupils who were in the Upper School and vice versa.

As far as salary went, the post of an Assistant at Eton must have been a good one, at any rate while the School was under

Barnard. The fee for tuition at this period was £8 8s. a year, see William Pitt's bill in 1719[*] and Edward Southcote's bill in 1764.[†] The private account book of W. H. Roberts, afterwards Provost, has been preserved, and is now in the College Library. In it he records that at " Christmas 1759 Dr. Barnard sent for me as Assistant to the School," and by the year 1764 he was receiving the following fees :

				£	s.	d.
Dr. Barnard	..	..	..	44	2	0
Mr. Sargent	..	..	..	130	0	0
Mr. Villiers	..	..	..	100	0	0
Mr. Cecil	..	..	..	50	0	0
Pupils	..	..	..	512	0	0
			£836	2	0

Sargent, Villiers and Cecil were no doubt private boarders that Mr. Roberts was allowed to take.

In 1767 Mr. Roberts did even better :

				£	s.	d.
Mr. Foster	..	..	..	50	0	0
Mr. Watsons	..	..	..	150	0	0
Mr. Sargent	..	..	..	50	0	0
Ld. Villiers	..	..	..	50	0	0
Mr. Cecil	..	..	..	100	0	0
Mr. Chauvet	..	..	..	100	0	0
Pupils	..	..	..	563	2	0
			£1063	2	0

It will be observed that Dr. Foster, the new Head Master, had apparently raised the small sum he allowed the Assistants. As the numbers declined under Foster, the post of Assistant became necessarily less profitable, so that in 1770 Roberts was drawing only £359 6s. from pupils, and in the following year he was probably not sorry to become a Fellow.

The Assistants must have lived in some of the small tenements that abounded in Eton in earlier times, and for a glimpse into the amount of their accommodation we may turn to a letter from John Hawtrey to his brother Edward, just appointed an Assistant :[‡]

[*] Lyte, 3rd ed. p. 294.
[†] *Eton under Barnard*, p. 30.
[‡] *History of the Hawtrey Family*, by F. M. Hawtrey, Vol. I. p. 197.

Eton, June 29, 1766.

Your chambers consist of two rooms without any furniture. The furniture for your Pupil Room may be bought here—any rubbish will serve, but the chairs and tables for your sitting-room you had better buy in London. Mr. Norbury used to sleep in his Pupil Room in a press-bed that shut up, made of wainscoat. I think you had better do the same. Take care to purchase a new one.

The *Countess of Atkins* sends her duty to you, and desires she may have the honour of waiting upon you; as her Ladyship is far advanced, I do not imagine you will fall in love with her, and therefore I would advise you to accept her service. Mr. Cole, the College barber, desires also that he may have the favor of dressing your wig, and my washerwoman to wash your linen. If you are not pre-engaged they will all do very well. Get an *Assistant's* wig and Bachelor's gown; but be sure bring no *Pease Blossom* coat. Mrs. Mary Young is very glad to hear of your arrival, and desired I would send her compliments to you.

Let me hear how soon you can possibly come to Eton. For my own part I do not conceive that Dr. Dampier will let you have the care of the third Form, but you may assure yourself I will go as far as I can upon that point, etc.

COLLEGERS.

Collegers are found in three different positions in these Lists.

   (1) Coming altogether at the beginning.

   (2) In groups at the head of each form.

   (3) Scattered about among the Oppidans.

And it is worth mentioning that Collegers to this day may be found in each of these positions, e.g.

   (1) All together at the beginning in the Absence Lists.

   (2) Placed in groups above the Oppidans in Sixth Form and Liberty.

   (3) Throughout the rest of the School scattered among the Oppidans.

Of the three systems, in the lists here printed, No. 1 is far the commonest, No. 2 only occurs in the lists of 1678, 1706 (mainly), and 1707. No. 3 is more frequent than No. 2, but not nearly so common as No. 1.

Before the lists came to be printed in 1791, I have seen no list in which the latter-day initials "K.S." are written, though the initials have apparently been interpolated in the printed lists for 1732 and 1745. Until the year 1788 I have come across no list containing the full term " King's Scholar." In the lists for 1788-90 the expression will be found. Before that, Collegers are either all written down under the heading of " Collegers," or if they occur among the Oppidans they are distinguished by the initial C. affixed to their names. The only exceptions are the lists of 1706, 1718, 1725, 1732, where Collegers are in no way distinguished from the rest of the School.

It is possible that the term King's Scholar, which was certainly familiar as early as 1661,[*] had fallen into desuetude and that it was revived out of respect to George III.'s interest in the School. Since 1791 "K.S." has always been the official designation of a foundation scholar, but colloquially the expression is still "Colleger," except when it degenerates into "Tug." College began to decline in numbers about 1760, and it is a slight blot on Barnard's reputation that when the School numbered over 500 under his vigorous rule, College should never have been full. There is indeed some ground for suspecting him of a dislike for College, for the mother of George Monk Berkeley says that when her son got into College Provost Barnard, who had been civil to him as an Oppidan, ceased to take any notice of him.

It will be found that boys who stood for College were generally already in the School as Oppidans : often they put off going into College till as late as possible, in fact till they were already high up in the School.

Instances may be met with where boys, after getting into College, reverted to the status of Oppidans (*e.g.* Portal, an Oppidan in 1769, a Colleger 1770–2, and an Oppidan again in 1773), and of course there are many instances where boys "gave by," *i.e.* gave up their nominations. Of these the most famous instance in the eighteenth century was George Canning, and his reasons for so doing will bear quoting :

Eton, Sept. 27, 1786.

I am now, my dear Sir, at the top of Eton School. I am the first of the Oppidants (Commoners you call them). I was to have been put on the foundation, but I did so much dislike the idea, and so evidently saw the great difference of behaviour and respect paid to the one situation in preference to the other that I prevailed on my uncle (being aided by the advice of Mr. Fox and Mr. Sheridan, who gave their opinions in my favour) to give up the idea. Hear some of my reasons and judge. A Colleger stays at Eton till Nineteen, then, if a vacancy falls out at King's College, Cambridge, while he is first in the School, he is translated thither, and enjoys an advantage of upon an average from first to last of about £50 p^r annum till he dies or marries : when a man goes into the Church the advantage is greater as he may chance by very good luck to get a living. These are the advantages. The contrary is—A Colleger rises much slower in the School and is consequently much later at the top ; he stays till nineteen, an Oppidant till seventeen—two years or a year even to a man whose

---

[*] Lyte, p. 263.

line is the bar, is surely an object: a Colleger may after all not go to King's if a vacancy does not fall: where *then* is the advantage? A Colleger among the boys even is not looked upon in near so respectable a light as an Oppidant: this was one of my principal reasons for my dislike. I gained my point, and have been some time in the 6th (the head) form.*

The election of Scholars, both for Eton and King's, took place by Statute between the Feast of St. Thomas of Canterbury (July 7) and that of the Assumption (August 15), and in practice usually fell in the last week of July or the first week of August. The panel consisted of the Provost, Vice-Provost and Head Master of Eton, together with the Provost of King's and two Posers from King's. Twenty-four boys were put on the Eton indentures, twelve on those for King's. The examination of candidates was purely formal, consisting of elementary questions which had to be answered in Latin. Election by merit was not introduced till 1844. Previously success was merely a matter of nomination, and according to Huggett (Sloane MSS. 4841, fol. 1) the electors nominated to the Eton indentures in the following order: the Provost of Eton chose the 1st, 3rd, 5th and 7th; the Provost of King's the 2nd, 4th, 6th and 8th; the Vice-Provost of Eton the 9th, 15th and 21st; the Senior Poser the 10th, 16th and 22nd; the Head Master the 11th, 17th and 23rd; and the Junior Poser the 12th, 18th and 24th. But Huggett does not say who nominated to the 13th, 14th, 19th and 20th places.

Royal influence was frequently exerted in Stuart times to get a boy nominated for College, but the electors seem to have been left alone in the eighteenth century.

OPPIDANS.

Little need be said of this branch of the School, except to note the various spellings of the word, viz. Oppidanes, Oppidants, Oppidents, Oppidans, etc. The expression is at least as old as 1561, for it occurs in Malim's "Consuetudinarium" and Sir Henry Maxwell Lyte notes having met with it in the Audit-book as early as 1557-1558.

In the eighteenth century, it is likely that a good many more boys came from Eton and Windsor than is the case nowadays, for in Barnard's account book there is a list containing names entitled "Windsor and Eton boys." Of one branch of the Oppidans it is necessary to say a little more, viz. *Noblemen.*

* Letter to Rev. H. Richman, Wykeham, Hants. *See* Charles Knight's *Half hours with the best Letter Writers and Autobiographers.*

NOBLEMEN, ETC.

Previous to the Civil Wars, boys of noble birth were in the habit of going to Eton as Commensals (*i.e.* Fellow Commoners), and in consequence taking their meals in Hall at the second table with the chaplain, usher and clerks. Though this privilege does not appear to have been revived, other privileges or distinctions are still to be met with in the eighteenth century. Thus it will be seen that it was a frequent habit to place peers at the head of their respective forms : but in this Eton never went quite to the length of Winchester, where in 1716 and 1717 the presence of the Duke of Hamilton and Brandon led to his being placed at the top of the whole school.

In the Eton List of 1678, but one nobleman appears, viz. Lord Alexander, who is at the top of Third Form. It should be noticed that his younger brother, Alexander *mi.*, has no " Mr. " prefixed to his name. In the next list (for 1698) we find the prefix " Mr. " used to designate an " Honourable," and this custom has prevailed ever since. We find the same custom existing at Winchester in the seventeenth century, and at Harrow nowadays.

Another peculiarity with regard to the names of noblemen is that occasionally we find such names as " Lord Charles " without any surname following. From this we may fairly infer that their companions called them by such titles as " Lord Charles " and thus forgot to add the surname when writing the list.

Further, in the most formal lists we find noblemen's names written in red ink. A similar practice, but considerably extended, will be found existing on the Winchester Long Rolls, where gilt, scarlet and blue are all occasionally used.

The system of placing peers at the heads of their forms seems to have varied at times, and perhaps was never very strictly enforced. But originally they seem to have figured at the head of every form ; in the next stage they are only at the head in Upper School and not Lower, with the exception of the First Form or Bible Class ; and in the final stage they are at the head only in the removes of Fourth Form. The list of 1767 is the last which continues the practice in its final stage.

Other privileges (not indeed figuring in these School Lists) which survived still longer were the practice by which noblemen occupied the stalls in chapel, and the custom of the highest nobleman of each nationality presenting the Head Master with a badge on St. Patrick's, St. David's and St. Andrew's Day, and perhaps on St. George's (if it fell in school-time), and of the other noblemen dining with the Head Master on those days.

ADDITIONS TO NAMES.

Besides the addition of *C.* to denote Colleger, the list for 1742 has *C. Prae.* and *C. P.* to show the College praepostor, and similarly *Op. Prae.* and *Op. P.* to denote the Oppidan praepostors; and in the Holbech list for 1789 it seems that *P.* is added to the names of the first seven Collegers with a similar object.

There are a few instances of initials being prefixed to the names, e.g. the various boys of the name of Lewis in the list for 1770. Again a few names have crosses placed against them, perhaps denoting the writer of them, e.g. Hubbald in 1707; several names in 1742, and Baker in 1765.

In one list, that for July 1780, dashes made after various names (which have not been reproduced in the printed list) are said to denote that such boys had been confirmed on July 8, 1780.

BROTHERS.

The practice of discriminating between brothers during the period covered by these lists was by the addition of *major, minor, minimus* in varying forms of abbreviation. In a good many of these lists, however, brothers are not distinguished in any way. In one list alone that I have seen is the Winchester method of *senior* and *junior* employed, namely in the list in the Eton College Library for 1754.

As early as 1706 we meet with the custom which lingered at least as late as 1780 of describing two brothers thus: "Hunts 2." In those days, when locomotion was more difficult than at present, brothers, if at all near each other in age, often entered the school at the same time and were naturally placed next each other in the school. Thus on October 1, 1762, three of the Loraine family were admitted together; in 1754 we find in First Form the entry "Hills 3." Similar customs prevailed in other schools: thus in the Westminster list for 1732 two brothers are thus described: "Pickering's *ambo.*" The record for brothers entering at the same time is as far as I know held by Rugby, where four brothers of the name of Wittewronge entered the school on January 13, 1707.

It is curious that the superlative *maximus* is scarcely ever used. It will be noticed in the list for 1771, and again in 1775 it occurs when out of six boys of the name of Fraser (or Frazer) two are designated *max. ma.* and *max. mi.*, and the other four, *max.*, *ma.*, *mi.* and *min.* In other cases where there are more than three brothers in the same list, either the fourth is not distinguished in any way, or else is styled *quartus* as in the list for 1742.

PRIVATE TUTORS.

There can be little doubt that all through the eighteenth century it was quite usual for the sons of wealthy parents t come to Eton attended by a private tutor. The custom indeed survived much later, and may not be entirely extinct even now. In later times, however, a boy has been compelled to have an ordinary tutor as well, which does not seem to have been the case in the eighteenth century. The most famous instance of a private tutor was Barnard, who acquired such renown as tutor to the three Townshends at Eton that he was appointed Head Master in 1753 without ever having been an assistant. There are but two lists that I have seen giving any record of private tutors, and as neither of these is among those printed in this volume, it may be worth while quoting them.

(1) In the list for 1781 printed in the *Gentleman's Magazine* for January 1832, after the Assistants come :

"Private Tutors to Noblemen and others, not assisting in the School :

Mr. Luxmoore (afterwards Bishop of St. Asaph)—to the E. of Dalkeith.

Mr. Kelly—to the Marq. of Huntley.

Mr. Kerr—to the E. of Downe.

Mr. Hand—Mr. Butler.

Mr. Plumptre, afterwards Dean of Gloucester—to the Hon. Mr. Bathurst.

Mr. Cole—to the Marq. of Blandford.

Mr. Bayley—to the Hon. Mr. Montagu.

Mr. Norbury jun."

No pupil is assigned to Mr. Norbury.

(2) In the list for 1788 (origin unknown) after the Assistants come :

"Private Tutors.

Rev. Mr. Luxmore $\left\{ \begin{array}{l} \text{Ld. Dalkeith.} \\ \text{— H. Montague.} \end{array} \right.$

Rev. Mr. Heslop, Honble. Mr. Stuart.

—— Hannington, Mr. Herbert.

—— J. Roberts, Ld. Morpeth.

—— Luxmore ju., Douglas's 2.

—— Hanger, Ld. Blantire and Mr. Stuart.

—— Hand, Liddell.

—— Freeman, Newcomen.

—— Norbury, Mr. Fitzmorris.

Mr. Walker, Ld. Tullibardine.

— Baker, Latouche's 2.

— Kitnar, Ld. Le Poer, and Mr. Beresford.

— Hayes, Ld. Brome."

EXTRA MASTERS.

In no instance are any masters teaching subjects that came to be called "Extras" to be found in the lists printed in this volume. For the fact that they existed, however, we have various evidence. Thus the parish register records the death of several persons who were writing masters.

Further, in "Nugae Etonenses," compiled c. 1766, we find the following list :*

Writing Masters.—Domine Evans, Hardy, Jem Jarrard.

French.—Lemoine, Porny.

Drawing.—Cozens.

Dancing.—Hickford.

Fencing.—Angelo.

Boxing.—The Nailor.

Jawing and Blackguard.—My Lord the Bargeman.

We shall probably be safe in assuming that the last two subjects were not included in the authorised school curriculum, and may restrict our attention to Writing, Drawing, French, Dancing and Fencing. Of these *Writing* had, no doubt, always been taught, and was indeed a necessary subject when boys came to school so young. When the other subjects first came to be taught cannot be said, but possibly Dancing was not taught until the Dancing School was built, *c.* 1750. This school became known successively as the Fencing School and the School of Arms, and was finally demolished in 1904.

These five subjects were probably the usual ones taught at public schools at this time: at any rate we find that at Rugby

* *Etoniana* (Magazine), No. 4, p. 61.

Saturday afternoon was a half-holiday, "and like other half-holidays is for writing, dancing, French, drawing, or even fencing."* Possibly, however, Thomas James imported some of these subjects from Eton.

At Harrow too, in the first list that survives, we find two writing masters, a dancing and a French master.

Extra masters were doubtless paid by extra fees, and we find a charge of £1 1s. for "Writing Master, half a year, May 24," charged in Walter Gough's Bill of 1725, and William Pitt charged £1 2s. for a similar period.

The list of 1788 (origin unknown) gives the following list:

Mr. Angelo, fencing master.
— Porny, French   ,,
— Hexter, writing   ,,
— Dore, dancing   ,,
— Cooper, drawing   ,,

and they are regularly included after the Assistants when the lists came to be printed.

French and Drawing still continue to be taught, but the Writing Master, who had developed into *Writing, Arithmetic and Mathematics*, appeared for the last time in 1842, the Dancing Master and the Fencing Master at Michaelmas 1864.

DAMES.

Since the days of William Paston, who mentions his "hostess" in 1479, the Oppidans lived in various houses kept by boarding dames (a practice to be found in old days at Westminster, Harrow and Rugby), and it is not till the end of the eighteenth century that we find much trace of Assistants holding boarding-houses. In the first list of dames that has been preserved, and which occurs at the beginning of Dr. Barnard's account-book, we find seventeen dames enumerated, all of the female sex, and the introduction of male "dames" or "domines," as they were sometimes called, was perhaps not recognised till later and may have been the first step towards Assistants becoming boarding-house keepers. Indeed in the eighteenth century there can have been little inducement for Assistants to keep boarding-houses, since the fees were only about 20 to 25 guineas a year, which can have left but a small margin for profit, especially as the school terms then lasted for forty-two weeks in the year, as against

* "Life and Letters of Samuel Butler," Vol. I. p. 27.

thirty-seven at the present day. Some of the Assistants, however, took in a few favoured pupils for considerable fees; thus we find W. H. Roberts receiving £130 in 1764 for a boy of the name of Sargent, and other fees of £100 apiece for Cecil and Chauvet. Occasionally too in the case of boys of noble birth, a separate house would be taken for them, where no doubt they were under the supervision of some private tutor: for instance, we find a small house opposite College let in 1757 to the Earl of Hertford,* and the house in Weston's Yard, next to Savile House, let to the Duke of Marlborough from 1747–58.†

The accommodation in the boarding-houses must have been scanty, if measured by latter-day requirements: in fact one may wonder how the 500 or more boys under Barnard were ever accommodated at all. A certain number of new houses, however, were built during the eighteenth century. Thus, we find Mrs. Slatter writing in 1754 that "Dr. Snape....about 20 or 30 years ago built 2 large Boarding-houses capable to receive and lodge a much larger number of children than there are there at present." ‡ The dates and initials on the water-heads shew that these two houses were Jordley's and Godolphin House, built in 1722. Further the house at the south-east corner of Keate's Lane, so long in the possession of the Prior family, must from its appearance have been built during this century, while the house previously on the site of the New Schools and Baldwin's End (burnt in 1903) date from this century, and about 1788 Keate House and the house at present occupied by Mr. Kindersley were erected.

Some of the houses must have been of very small size, in fact in Barnard's book we find the numbers vary from Mrs. Pote, wife of the bookseller, who had one boarder, to Mrs. Mary Young and Mrs. Frances Yonge, who each had about thirty boarders respectively in the Manor House and in Jordley's.

After Barnard's time, we find the next list of dames in *Nugae Etonenses*, written in 1766. There under "Boarding Houses" come "*Domine* Evans, Hardy, Harding: *Dame* Milward, Key, Ely, Harris, Young—old and new, Graham, Hurd, Tyrrel, Newton." Two of the "domines," Evans and Hardy, were writing masters.

* Document in Woods and Forests Department, quoted in *Etoniana* (Magazine), No. 1, p. 5.

† College Lease-books.

‡ *Etoniana* (Magazine), No. 1, p. 3.

Finally in a list for 1788 giving the boys' tutors and dames, we find some boys boarding with at least seven out of the nine Assistants. But as nine is the most that any one Assistant had, the practice may still have been the exception rather than the rule.*

HOLIDAYS.

In Malim's day (1561) the only holiday time when boys regularly returned to their homes was from Ascension Day to the eve of the feast of Corpus Christi, a space of three weeks. Work was suspended at Christmas time from the 20th of December to Epiphany, and at Easter from the Wednesday before Easter to the end of Easter week, but at neither of these times could boys leave the School. We have here however the germ of the present day system of holidays, although the summer holiday is taken now somewhat later in the year.

Sir Henry Wotton alludes to this holiday in a letter to Lord Cork, dated July 4, 1636 :†

...this time of our vacation, when our school annually breaketh up two weeks before Whitsuntide and pieceth again a fortnight after.

In 1766 when Thomas James wrote his account of Eton Discipline, holidays are given as follows :

The Vacations are three times in the year, Easter, Xstmas and August, vulgarly called Bartlemetide, a most strange corruption from St. Bartholomew's name. The Xstmas Holydays last a month and the school breaks up the 2d Monday in December. The Easter Holydays last a fortnight, and the school breaks up on the Monday before Easter Sunday. The Holydays at August begin the first Monday in August and last a month.‡

The change in the date of the summer holidays was probably an innovation of Dr. Barnard, for in 1754 when he became Head Master, his entry book shews boys arriving at Eton all through August, but this does not happen in subsequent years.

NOTE ON THE PRINTING OF THE LISTS.

The arrangement and spelling of the original lists has been retained, but in a few cases, where the real name has been much distorted, and where I have been quite certain of the true spelling, I have added the latter enclosed within square brackets.

* For a list of Dames, see *Etoniana* (Magazine), No. 2, p. 30.
† Lismore Papers, Letter 382.
‡ *Etoniana* (Magazine), No. 8, p. 114.

ETON COLLEGE LISTS
1678–1790.

A LIST OF ETON SCHOLARS IN 1678.

VIth Form

James [C.]
Adams [C.]
Edmonds [Eman C.]
Blake [C.]
Offley [C.]
Ogdin
Willis [C.]
Brabourne *ma.* [C.]

Vth Form Collegers

Pagitt [? Pate]
Burrell
Noyse
Barton
Davis
Stephens
Rutton
Norwood
Shipman
Johnson *ma.*
Cannon *ma.*
Mullington
Brabourne *mi.* [O.]
Palmer
Dwight
Willis *mi.*
Tash
Cannon *mi.*
Clarke

Vth Oppidanes

Price (Sr. John)
Meers
Perry
Biggs
Lamplugh
Pelham
Lloyd *ma.*
Harwood *ma.*
Fifield
James *mi.*
Dashwood (Sr. Rob.)
Bybee
Turner
Baldwin
Palmer *mi.*
Gregory
Fulham
Corsellis
Powell *ma.*

IV Form Collegers

Worthington
Woodward [O.]
Whitton
Astin *ma.* [Austen *ma.*]
Astin *mi.* [Austen *mi.*]
Glascock
Batty
Skynner
Farmore [Farmer]

B

Angelow *ma.* [Ingelo *ma.*]
Angelow *mi.* [Ingelo *mi.*]
Paxton
Christon [Christian]
Staples
Watkins *ma.*
Stills [Stile]
Rawson
Cook
Younger
Preston [O.]
Davis
Selwood
Coppleston
Meale, *alias* Moule
Baxter
Dwight *mi.*
Johnson *mi.*

IV Form Oppidanes

Croker
Tolmash
Powell *mi.*
Poyse [? Pope]
Conway (Sir John)
Weston
Harwood *mi.*
White
Watkins *mi.*
Bety [? Bery]
Hill
Matson
Frank
Smisston [? Simsston]
Nurse
Meverall
Woodecock
Wells
Mills
West
Jebb
Foster
Allen
Wild
Baynard
Cheas

Bowen
Lloyd *mi.*
Chennell
Whistler
Childe
Bradwell

IIId Form Coll:

Hawtrey
Llewelling
Martin
Pain [O.]
Butterfield
Bayly
Hildesley
Clinckard
Pilkington
Davers [Danvers]
Cheaney [Cheyne]
Cleaton [Clayton]
Burch
Russell
Rendall [O.]

IIId Form Oppid.

Ld. Alexander
Conway *mi.*
Cueston [? Cuerton]
Webb
Castell
Reeves
Llangley
Underhill
Raymund (Sr. Jemmatt)
Goores *ma.*
Goores *mi.*
Benskin
Angelow
Puliston (Sr. Rod.) [? Sir Roger]
Hull
Broome
Luttey [? Lutley]
Eyers
Veal

Davis
Laggatt
Moyle
Watts
Bookey
Colbourn
Cross
Yoldin [? Goldin]
Ransford
Robason
Stone
Needham
Hatton
Palling
Man
Rosewell
Roots
Elliott
Harwood *mi.*
Legg
Young
Shorthouse
Dee
Lauly

IId Form Collegers

Poole
Crouch
Landers [O.]
Coale [O.]
Sleech [O.]
Andrews [O.]
Berkinton [O.]
Hinton [O.]
Anglow *min.* [O.]

IId Form Oppidanes

Hull *mi.*
Herone

Walsingham
Pinckerich
Raymund *min.*
Boggs, *alias* Bogges
Feallowes
Johnson *min.*
Coderington
Littleton
Harding
Nowell
King
Osburne *ma.*
Osburne *mi.*
Hart
Martin
Sparks
Hull
Eyres
Goores
Jenny
Chauncey
Michell
Alexander *mi.*

Biblers Seat

Viner

Number about
—202—

Franklin   Palmer
Buller   Buckler
Rogers   Buckly
Barton
Fenwick
Gresham

[207]

[1706]

Reece [Rees C.]
Isoc [Isaac C.]
Hemming [C.]
Harris [C.]
Slatter [C.]
Podridge [Pordage C.]
Hawtry [C.]
Douty [C.]
Buckly [Bulkley C.]
Lamplue [C.]
Smith [C.]
Stamper [C.]
Thaccum [Thackham C.]
Croxall [C.]
Bilbe [C.]
Adams [C.]
Slatter [C.]
Britten [C.]
    6

Mr. Egerton
Mr. Finch

Windham
Foot
Baker

Gardiner [C.]
Whitton [C.]
Hetherington [C.]
Crow [C.]
Clarke [C.[
Bowpous [Burroughs C.]
Broom [C.]

Jenings [C.]
Hammond [C.]

Jones [C.]
Web [C.]
Weddall [C.]
Antrobus [C.]
Grant [C.]
Slatter [Shotter C.]
Harison [C.]
Hunt [C.]
Powell [Poole C.]
Wells [C.]
Carty [C.]
Lightenhouse [C.]
Glover [C.]
Green [C.]
Burton [C.]
Mr. Hyde
Mr. Lambart

Powel
Edes
Baker
Hays
Stracy
Baker
Hern
Unwin
Hill
Herbert
Raulinson
Haul
Powise [Powys]
Williams

Linely
Chetwin[d]
Snow
Cuff
Molineux
Austin
Marriot
Brown [C.]
Eaton [C.]
Whemmen [Wenman C.]
    5

Mr. Compton

Hunt
Aubry
Wudyer
Hodie
Turner
Hetherington
Bodneele
Caesar
Wanduper
Hooker
Burton

Wells mi. [C.]
Chapman [C.]
Ofley [C.]
Legg [C.]
Duck [C.]
Kemith [Kemeys C.]
Tempest [C.]
Thaccary [Thackeray C.]
Willatts [C.]
Baker [C.]
Nancy [Nanney C.]
Parrot [C.]
Glassup [C.]

Cook

Tipping   100

Writter [Wright]
Upton
Willoughby
Man
Pledwell
Fane
Pelham
Bevans
Husbands
Rhodes
Rowny
Edgley
Clare
Brockett

Curtis
Taubort [Talbot]
Hautry
Write
Fleethood [Fleetwood]
Spelman
Weston
Holt
Bradbury
Shooter
Greg
Cope
Lockett
Burrows
Hanccock
Eyre
Mountague
Fothall

Delves
Rogers
Series

Draper
Snow
Holcombe
St. John
Harbrow
Renison [Reynardson]
Jones

Pagiter [? Pargiter]
Dodwell
Keating
Herbert
Hern
Hythom [? Hysham]
 4

Ld. Burford
Ld. Seymours 2
Mr. Lumleys 2
Mr. Finch *mi.*
Mr. Egerton *mi.*

Nancy
Cole
Redman
Boles
Daws
Saunders
Richardson
Humphrys [C.]
Pittiward
Scawen
Yate
Upwatt
Buckworth
Brewer
Weel [Veel]
Nelham
Emile
Newcombe
Hetherington
Campbell
Lovett
Jacob
Hall
Hosier [C.]
Hopgood
Sedgick
Kinsman

Gardner
Frensham
Bavishet

Crockett
Luking [Luckin C.]
Strugnall
Cope
Maningham
Morse
Bettesson
Preston
Withers
Benson
Barnard [? Bernard C.]
Northy
Hatton
Benithon [Bonython]
Stroude   200

Evans [C.]
Micartie [? Macartney]
Phipps
Gregor [C.]
Armiger
Page
Eyre
Ashley
Smith
Skinner
Mountague
Win [Wynne C.]
Pratt
Snook

Turner [C.]
Mumbey

Pierce
Willoby [Willoughby]
Bertie
Gore
Dolbin
Dean
Harman
Quick
Garrard
Turton

Burton
Halsted [C.]
Flyer
Spelman
Cope
Burchitt
Austin
Atterbury
Pelham

Lucy [C.]
Baker
Whitton
Watton
Burton
Cooper
Blower
Fausett
Webley

Morison
Cary
Ivey
Air [? Eyre]
Archer
Mountague
Gravener [Grosvenor]
Clavering
Holcombe
Spelman
Devishier
Airt
Ashley [? Astly]
Marshe [March]
Giberne
Drax
Hubald
Capper
    3

Ld. Ross

Johnson
Sexton

Griffin
Pledwell
Tempest
Watson
Dean
Spencer [C.]
Car *mi.*
Rowlinson
Redman
Harvey
Moor
Car *ma.*
Good
Edwards
Mitchell
Napper
Currance
Nelson
Goldsborough
Hymor [Highmore]
Lovett
Thimblethope [? Themilthorp]
King

Jukes
Cotesworth
Reves
Web
Butts
Hopton [? Hopson]
Hicks
Kindsman
Man
Brockden
Moor
    [*erasure*]
Buckridge   300

Chiney [Cheney]
Curby
Herbert
Whitting
Ramshaw
    2

Ld. Dalkeith
Ld. Morphett [Morpeth]
Mr. Compton

———————

Molineux
Longland
Stevens
Pelham
Briver
Whetton
Chambers
Gibbs
Puleston
Heel *ma.*
Hetherington
Heel *mi.*
Almer [? Aylmore]
Burchitt
Nelson
Gardner
Hazard
Orme
Belomy
Warner
Turton
Peachey
Chornock
Phipps

———————

Mr. Howard

———————

Benson
Yate
Bowrous
Bow
Emiles 2
Hunts 2
Hubald *mi.*
Jacob
How
Cosley
Upton
Hitchcock
Perkins
Cornwallis
Shipman
Hook
Guer
Metcalfe

———————

353

———————

A copey of a list
sent to West by
Mr. Henry Drax:
1706

1707

Lamplugh, Collegers
Smith
Stamper
Thackham
Croxall
Bilby
Snape
Adams
Slatter
Bretton
Hetherington
Crow
Burroughs
Broom
Jennings
Baker
Jones
Webb
Weddall
Antrobus
Shotter
Harrison
Hunt
Elliott

———

Mr. Finch, Oppidents

———

Baker
Herbert
Rawlinson
Powys
Chetwind
Mollineux

———

6 form.

———

Pool, Collegers
Wells
Cartey

Lightonhouse
Glover
Green
Burton
Wenman
Chapman
Offley
Legg
Duck
Hawtrey
Keymish
Tempest
Gregg
Thackeray
Rees

———

Mr.
Compton, Oppidents
Mr.
West
Mr.
Dawnay

———

Austin
Marryott
Caesar
Hooker
Burton
Cook
Wright
Upton
Willoughby
Mann
Pelham
Walker
Bevans
Husbands
Rhodes
Rhowney

Edgly
Clare
Brockett
Curtis
Talbott
Wright
Fleetwood
Holt
Shootler
Burroughs
Eyre
Kynsman
Mountague
Tracey
Lockett, Collegers
Willats
Baker
Nanney
Paratt
Glassup
Hethrington
Crampbell [Campbell]
———

Delves
Loyd
Spellman
Fothall
Jones
Draper
St. John
Jones
Reynardson
Pargiter
Dodwell
Baker
Herne

Humphris, Collegers
Hosier
Frinsham
Luckyn
Capper
Evans
Gregor
———
Mr.
Dawnay

Mr.
Finch
———
Rogers
King
Longford
Hysham
Byam
Uthwatt
Veel
Redman
Cole
Costard
Daws
Pettiward
Bowles
Peacock
Yate
Buckworth
Nelham
Emelie
Jacob
Sedgwick
Hopgood
Richardson
Scawen
Short
Lovett
Hall
Maningham
Preston
Strugnell
Withers
Bonython
Mountague
Sherwood
Hatton
Mecartney
Froud
Page
Smith
Skinner
Ashly
Northy
Lee
Blake

4 form.

Ld. Burford	Spellman
Ld.	Dean
Seymours 2	Atterbury
Ld.	Burton
Morpeth	Hubbald ✠
Ld.	Herbert
Ross	Cope
Mr.	Drax
Lumbley	Ivie
Mr.	Eyre
Edgerton	Monson
Mr.	Mountague
Berkely	Burton
———	Quick
Gardner, Collegers	Webley
Wynn	March
Turner	Cary
Halstead	Bird
Sturges	Blower
Harman	Dean
Flyer	Clavering
Archer	King
Baker	Holcomb
Offley	Moore
Johnson	Grosvener
Spencer	Wheate
Jukes	Astly
———	Corrance
Armiger	Selfe
Benson	Sedgwick
Phipps	Crofts
Pratt	Saxon
Snook	Thomas
Munbey	Tempest
Turner	Kinsman
Austen	Redman
Burchett	Puleston
Willoughby	Hayes
Eyre	Brockden
Bertie	Buckeridge
Garrard	Hicks
Pelham	Harvey
Conwallis	Nelson
Hubbald	Napper
———	Devisher
Eyre	Sturt
Northlugh	Carr
Dolbin	Massey

Bernard
Highmore
Tate
Edwards
Castell
Good
Drake
Michell
Lovett
Reeves
Themilthorp
Goldsborough
Coatsworth
Hopson
Mann
Cheney
Clayton
Helyar
Rooksby
Whiting
Moore
Ramshaw
Butts
Stevens
Gandy
Heels 2
Nelson
Turton
Hare
Bateman
Pelham
Lingen

———

3 form.

———

Ld.
Dalkeith

———

Cranck
Young
Webb
Burchett
Aylmore
Chernock
Hitchcock
Lichere
Weston
Bateman

Hethrington
Bryver
Denham
Langton
Gardner
Chambers
Bowry
Mecanny
Rogers
Warner
Hunt
Hubbald
Phipps
Orme
Budgett
Burroughs
Handley
Bellimey
Emelie
Peachy
Perkins
Norton
Berney
Lee
Hestar
Benson
Mountague
Green
Orlebar
Hassard
Cooper
Medlicoat
Upman

———

2

———

Ld.   [? Ld. William
Buckcleare   Beauclerk]

———

Mr.
Compton
Mr.
Howard
Mr.
Bennett
Mr.
Berkely

———

Pukely
Pickering
Yate
Burroughs
Marriott
Elves
Emelie
Smith
Medcalf
Hatsell
Waller
Stiles
Hunt
Hook
How
Nash
Gear

Bacon
Jacob
Herring
Cartwright
Cooper
Massey
Lovells 2
Turner
Marryott
Marryott
Ball
Rutter
Peachey
Lawrence

_____

In all 357

A BILL OF ETON SCHOLE,

1718.

The Provost.	Mr. Burchet
	Mr. Willets
Dr. Godolphin	

Sixth Form.

Vice-Provost.	Humphreys [C.]
	Harding [C.]
Mr. Horne	Martin [C.]
	Smith [C.]
	Haynes [C.]
Fellows.	Kennedy [C.]
	Loshu [Lofting C.]
Dr. Richardson	Bankes [C.]
Dr. Weston	Heath [C.]
Dr. Hill	Sturges [C.]
Dr. Evans	Weston [C.]
Mr. Sleech	Abbot [C.]
Mr. Carter	Dishey [Disney C.]
	Redman [C.]
	Bullock [C.]
Upper Master.	Hancock [C.]
	Brown [C.]
Dr. Snape	Banks [C.]
	Jasper [C.]
	Pitman [C.]
Lower Master.	Mr. Townshend
	Mr. Lumley
Mr. Good	Summers
	Hume
	Walpole
Assistants.	Bartlett
	Bestland
Mr. Antrobus	Wilson
Mr. Snape	Child
Mr. Gilman	Child
Mr. Antrobus	Ansley [? Anstey]
	Wood
Mr. Thackeray	Philpot 33
Mr. Eliot	

Fifth Form.

Newbery [C.]
Burnaby [C.]
Mann [C.]
Lane [C.]
Morrell [Morral C.]
Croxall [C.]
Le Hunt [C.]
Batty [C.]
Par [C.]
Wessel [C.]
Fewis [Lewis C.]
Vincenti [Vincent C.]
Mr. Mildmay
Mr. Townshend
Mr. Foley
Clayton
Whaley
Powney
Lavibourn
Lee
Holder
Nuthall
Scrimpshire
Dale
Piggot
Corbet
Chadworth
Chadworth
New
Knowles
Chute
Clark
Crawley
Hascarot
Procktor
Clayton
Dawes
Fox
Fox
Newton
Kemble [? Hemble]
Gualher
Harding
Singleton
Pennant

Smith
Stevens   47

Remove.

Trimnell [C.]
Smith [C.]
Chase [C.]
Ianson [C.]
Goddard [C.]
Archer [C.]
Osborne [C.]
Nicholas [Nicholl C.]
Hume [C.]
Crawley [Cawley C.]
Bailey [C.]
Hickman
Sleech
Dell
Butler
Mandeville
Charlton
Chandler
Dongworth [? C.]
Graham
Worsam
Dixon
Noel
Naylor
Richardson
Lithieullier
Ld. Sidney
Mr. Stewart   28

Fourth Form.

Jones [C.]
Chapman [C.]
Ld. Graham
Ld. James
Ld. Brackley
Mr. Scot
Mr. North
Mr. Foley
Mr. Cornwallis
Trimnell
Chopping

Holder
Greenway
Rogers
Holcomb
Gordon
Lyme
Jenner
Long
Plaunceford [Pauncefort]
Herbert
Lound
Burgh
Banks
Brall
Holt
Seward
Coggin
Pearson [? C.]
Whitehall [C.]
Hughes [C.]
Lacey [C.]
Ewer [C.]
Broughton [C.]
Walters
Grice
Grigg [? Trigg]
Taylor
Shaw
Bacon
Corbet
Glyn
Bland
Wilkingon [? Wilkinson C.]
Towers [C.]
Norman [C.]
Clark
Patrick
Huxley
West
Sumner
Chester
Godolphin
Gascoigne
Hall
Perpoint
Hanbury
Poll
Prisick

Estwick
Douglass
Beal
Britton   63

Lower Schole.

Third Forme.

Gardner
Bryer [C.]
Banks
Mathew
Slingsly [? Slingsby]
Bly [C.]
How [C.]
Smith [? C.]
Buckworth
Fern
Walpole
Moxim
Godolphin
Nard
Clayton [C.]
Lock [C.]
Seward
Williams
Williams
Thickness [C.]   20

Lower Greek.

Vaughan
Thornicroft
Smith
Bateman
Richmond
Corrough
Hughes [C.]
Mr. More
Wise
Bromley
Huxley
Rhodes
Baly
Lenthall
Dillon
Smith

Windham
Pitt
Mr. St. John
Blackman
Banks
Sayer
Clarke
Shalton
Shalton
Long
Cowse
Winder [? C.]
Cowles
Archwood
Morralt [? Morral C.] 31

Jones
Wild
Medcalf
Holmes
Jenner
Acres
Blackall
Townshend
Broughton [C.]
Belchier [C.]
Mr. Charmichael
Roberts
Trevanion
Herbert
Ld. Charles
Hughes [C.]
Hodgekins
Husband
Philpot
Houghton
Temple
Burgh
Bambridge
Butler
Haydon
Jones
Laroche
Evelin
Barcroft
Bertie
Wise
Mr. Cornwallis

Pearse [? Peers C.]
Jackson
Folkes
Gough
Grape
Mills 38

Secd. Form.

Ld. Windsor
Mr. Foley
Mr. Lumley
Mr. Townshend
Mr. Fane
Cockrand
Bland
Daniel [C.]
Palmer
Parsons
Rogers
Bridgewater
Warring
Naylor
Belchier
Scot
Piggot
Scrimpshire
Mann
Colchester
Wood
Morris
Goddard
Showell
New
Cook
Knap
Johnson
Bennet
Haynes
Haynes
Crumpton 32

Lower Remove.

Clark
Holstone [? Rolstone]

c

Fry		Smith	
Crisp		Davenport	
Wells [C.]		Beckles	22
March			
Mann			
Taylor		**Bible Seat.**	
Herde			
Brown		Cross	
Clarke		Grey	
Hill	12	North	
		Philpot	
First Form.		Philpot	
		Merryweather	
Ld. Ganesborough		Merryweather	
Ld. William		Bradbury	
Mr. Windsor		Raven	
Mr. Cornwallis		Green	
Mr. St. John		Terry	
Sr. Peter Soames		Tyrwhit	
Beauman		Tyrwhit	
Holder		Hambleton	
Roberts		Fern	
Gough		Sibthorp	
Mellish		Shuttleworth	
Linwood		Grape	
Talbot		Hyett	
Pitt		Warf	
Dillon		Thibou	
Buckworth		Copley	
Meadows		Copley	
Udall		Buckridge	24
Hales			

353 [350]

LIST OF EATON SCHOOL
1725

July 1725.

Kent [C.]
Mountenny [Mountney C.]
Bowles [C.]
Lane [C.]
Burrough [C.]
Bland [C.]
Showell [C.]
Thickness [C.]
Parsons [C.]
Mountague [C.]
Chetwynd [C.]
Naylor [C.]
Goddard [C.]
Littleton
Wyndham
Trevanion
Pitt

6 form 17

Ld. Jersey
Ld. Windsor
Mr. Townshend
Mr. Vane
Sr. Hales
Sr. Grey
Sr. Smith
Payne
Gough
Mellish *ma.*
Belcher [C.]
Banister [C.]
Woodward [C.]
Beckles
Barton
Legrand *ma.*
Wood

Coventrye
Gibson
Layman [C.]
Buckeridge [C.]
Westley [C.]
Whalley [C.]
Taunton [C.]
Betham [C.]
Apthorp [C.]
Dorrington
Janssen
Mellish *ma.* [? *mi.*]
Hoblyn
Hammond
Chandler *ma.*
Chandler *mi.*
Simmonds
Copley
Kynaston
Barrowby [C.]
Ashby [C.]
Davis [C.]
Morland [C.]
Newton [C.]
Proctor [C.]
Powell [C.]
Colleton
Woodstock
Oldfield
Bredon
Lutterell
Boucher
Erskine

5 form 50

Mr. Needham
Mr. Herbert

Sr. Dashwood
Williams
Brooker
Brooks
Sleech
Warren
Turner
Newton
Trevellion
Kilderben [Kilderbee C.]

Remove 12

Johnston [C.]
Wilkes [C.]
Kynaston [C.]
Raynford [Raynsford C.]
Keen [C.]
Gwynn [C.]
Heaton [C.]
Price [C.]
Saunders [C.]
Harwood [C.]
Roydon [C.]
Howard [C.]
Armstrong [C.]
Hopkins [C.]

. . . .

Ld. Dorchester
Ld. Tichfield
Ld. Villiers
Mr. Windsor
Mr. Childe
Mr. Villiers
Mr. Sherley
Mr. St. John
Mr. Boscawen
Sr. Burgoyne
Waring
Gray
Brown
Copley mi.
Galward
Ruding ma.
Philpot
Shirley

Barton
Chambers
March
Musgrave
Barlowe
Erskine
Roderick
James
Goodman
Davenport
Fern
Dashwood
Green
Moor
Pennant
Hodges
Sandell

. . . .

Gore
Ruding mi.
Janssen
Tyrrwhitt mi.
Fortescue
Holmes
Hall
Boon
Wicker ma.
Bird ma.
Hackshaw
Grenville ma.
Grenville mi.
Lutley
Tyrrwhitt ma.
Talbot ma.
Bird mi.
Witmore
Smith [? C.]
Horton
Rouse
Smith ma.
Gascoigne
Macartny
Cross [C.]
Whitwick
Tilson ma.
Tilson mi.

Maul *ma.*
Maul *mi.*

. . . .

Ambrose
Allen
Fleetwoud
Brook *mi.*
Pott *ma.*
Vaughan
Gough *mi.*
Pott *mi.*
Plumtree
Palmer
Mills
Pratt
Weller
Adams
Gough
Cannon [C.]
Letchmore
Westley

4 form 98 [97]

Wetherell [C.]
Lethieullier
Hunt
Week
Keat [C.]
Vary
Goddard [C.]
Randall
Gilbert
Johnson
Charlton
Okeley
Turner
Currier
Sadleir
Loader
Smith
Colleton
Despard
Cheynell
Naish
Robinson

Britton
· Stainforth
Talbott *mi.*
Strode
Lutwych *ma.*
Hitchcock [C.]
Worsley
Hackshaw
Byrd
Herbert
Bridgman
Wicker
Windus
Busby [C.]
Cooper [C.]
Seraud [? Sarraud C.]
Midford
Sr. Bowyer
Talbot *mi.*
Moor
Eyre

. . . .

Lyttelton
Gale
Price
Ball
Shaw
James
Thompson
Holmes
Wakefield [C.]
Mountague
Mellicante
Farrant
Loyd
Timens
Sr. Humble
Cullen
Hale
Garlick
Fenwick
Dashwood
Herbert
Scudamore [C.]
Lyttelton *mi.*
Bellamy
Cracherode

Stonhouse
Goddard
Gibson
Darcy
Beasley
Green
Staples

. . . .

Stephens
Jackson
Shore
Cope
Wanley
Whalley
Pitt
Hayes
Dashwood *mi.*
Hale *mi.*
Mr. Villiers
Mountague
Beridge
Wood
Loyd *mi.*
Mr. Bathurst

3 form 91

Barker
Boat
Martin
Mr. Onslow
Legrand *mi.*
Mr. Cornwallis
Naish
Lutwych
Burwill
Samuell
Montague
Ld. Bute
Chaplin
Midford *mi.*
Merrick
Westbrook
Theed [C.]
Simmonds
Middleton

Mr. Corwallis [Cornwallis]
Lidwould
Wroughton
Timms
Wise
Mr. Boscawen
Ld. Andover
Adams
Topping
Sawyer
Dashwood
Pennyman
Ld. Sunbury
Bartlet
Mosley [C.]
Fortescue
Ld. G. Bentick
Mr. Windsor
Ld. Rockingham
Herbert
Rain
Gray
Jacomb
Green
James

2 form 44

Man
Cook
Edgcomb
Furnep [? Furness]
Western
Kendall
Smith
Talbott
Moor
Hathersal
Savage
Eley
Tonson [? Jonson]
Sleech
Tyrrell
Turner
Thompson

. . . .

Sr. W. Norwich
Ld. Turnbridge [Tunbridge]
Mr. Carey
Mr. Watson
Mr. Cornwallis
Mr. Watson
Mr. Childe
Broom
Wynne
Bodicot
Riggs
Micclesfield
Pott
Vernon
Mountague
Holmes
Frewen
Champion
Brown
Cook
Macket
Robinson
Cooper
Chaloner
Beesley
Hoper
Edwards
Cope
Cooke

Coulthrope
Monk
Lilly
Frever [? Trevor]
Taylor
Bouvirie
Gibson
Woulmington
Burton
Biddel
Moor
Tilson
Swan
Clinch
Mitchell
Kendall
Withers
Whitmore
Whitmore
Barnes
Noel

67

Upper School ... 176
Lower School ... 202

Total 378

A BILL OF ETON SCHOOL
Nov. 2d 1728.

Provost.

Dr. Godolphin

Vice Provost.

Dr. Carter

Fellows.

Dr. Sleech
Dr. Waddington
Dr. Richardson
Dr. Evans
Dr. Berryman
Mr. Lyttleton

Upper Master.

Dr. George

Lower Master.

Mr. Goode

Assistants Upper School.

Mr. Young
Mr. Dongworth
Mr. Ewer
Mr. Sumner

Lower School.

Mr. Elliot
Mr. Thackeray
Mr. Burchet
Mr. Sleech

[Collegers.]

Sixth Form.

Apthorp
Ashby
Davies
Moreland
Sleech
Cook
Keeble
Lang [Laynge]
Carter
Penwarn [Penwarden]
Chapman
Shrigley
Kilderby
Bradbourn
Roderick
Keen
Gwyn
Parry
Roydon
Maule

Fifth Form.

Howard
Barnes
Prat

Hopkins
Cannon
Anstey
Keate
Randall
West
Wetherelli [Wetherel]
Fletcher
Kelham
Sarraude
Dampier
Goddard
Payne
Berkely

Remove.

Cross
Jackson
Richards
Hitchcock
Windus
Trevannion
Farneworth
Phipps

Fourth Form.

Edwards
Wood
Warner
Whaley
Harwood
Clinch
Sherrard
Meese

Third Form.

James
Gilman
Amphlet
Savage
Sanders
Cole
Harrison

Mitchell
Penneck
Hodges
Lane
Thomson
Williams
Waterhouse
Wray
Sinclair
Cock
Poyntz

Oppidans.

Sixth Form.

Fenn
Musgrave
Heaton
Gill

5th Form.

Dashwood
Moore
Pennant
Gore
Grenville
Fortescue
Wicker
Byrd
Mr. Cartney [? McCartney]
Brown
Mills
Bean
Lethieulier
Steuart
Wooley
Lake
Vary
Milford
Gough
Wicker
Wightwick
Weeks
Currier

Loder
Smith
Naish
Fane
Gilbert
Charlton
Cheynell
Worsley
Moore
Shaw
Eyres
Darcey
Hale
Lanyon
Frampton
Mildmay
Philips
Talbot
Briton
Aubrey
Lutwich
Herbert
Burton

Remove.

Mr. Villiers
Mr. Bathurst
Timms
Loyd
Littleton
James
Staples
Goddard
Fenwick
Gale
Hammond
Jones
Gibson
Hale
Cope
Herbert
Hayes
Lutterel
Carter

Fourth Form.

Ld. Bute
Ld. Sherard
Ld. Castlecomer
Ld. Rumney
Ld. Sunbury
Mr. Child
Mr. Cornwallis
Mr. Howard
Mr. Onslow
Sr. Norwich
Stonehouse
Price
Oackley
Shawford
Whitby
Crackrode
Lloyd
Pit
Wanley
Stephens
Mountague
Dashwood
Mongomery
Mountague
Carter
Smith
Burwell
Boate
Sparks
Foot
Eaton
Hammersley
Wise
Chalconer
Ayscough
Bradbury
Borough
Medley
Balls
Mitford
Hoper
Grape
Simmonds
Sawyer
Ashe
Pit

Powel
Knight
Gilbert

Lower School.

Third Form.

Mr. Harvey
Boverie
Archdeckne
Timms
Mr. Boscawen
Merrick
Champion
Cholwell
Bullock
Ld. Rockinham
Rowland
Pennyman
Talbot
Westbrooke
Grenville
Edgecombe
Low
Bean
Johnson
Keeling
Wroughton
Levinz
Mr. Watson
Northlowe
Ld. Andover
Bentinck
Ld. George [? sc. Bentinck]
Tilson
Mr. Grimston
James
Bartlett
Swan
Mr. Townshends 2
Walpole
Sleech
Furnesse
Mr. Boscawen
Ducarell
Lilly

Mann
Page
Jonson
Jacomb
Holden
Gibbon
Whitmore
Western
Mr. Cornwallis
Ld. Euston
Bowyer
Noel
Payne
Rider
Witter
Mountague
Ducarel
Holderness
Firth
Talbot
Ld. Aug. Fitzroy
Hale
Medley
Grenville
Giffard
Rigs
Brown
Cholwel
Rayne
Wooley
Moore
Edwards
Penneck
Harvest
Mr. Grimston
Gray
Parry
Bradbury
Shoreditch
Cook
Turner
Ld. Tunbridge
Gibson
Noel
Ld. Hincinbrook
Potts
Trevor
Terrel

Philips
Calthorp
Coke
Webster

---

secd. Form.

Mountague
Berkley
Wilmot
Smith
Broome
Pitfeild
Moore
Carpenter
Grenville
Stephens
Bentley
Wenn
Wooley
Fuller
Serle
Barton
Mickfield
Short
Midwinter
Bidle
Cope
Aldworth
Hammersley
Mr. Watson
Whitmore
Elly
Wills
Hudson
Dalton
Hanbury
Frewin
Carpenter
Townshend
Kendal
Blackerby
Withers
Monk
Kendal
Staples
Dursley

Bishop
Salter
Crofts
Whitby
Meggot
Holden
Chudleigh
Plumptree
Smith
Powis
Bishop
Mitchell
Smith
Brand
Ducarell

First Form.

Barnes
Seewell
Baldwin
Gibbons
Barker
Davenport
Stretton
Whitby
Selwyn
Hyldyard
Atkins
Aubery
Jacomb
Dodd
Jennings
Allen

Bible seat.

Ld. Robt. Bertie
Mr. Mackenzie
Mr. Wentworth
Mr. Child
Sr. Hubard [? Sir John Huband]
Galliard
Hanson
Fortescue
Bernier

Wills

Boverie

Hale

Chetwynd

Green

Hamstead

Byfield

Guearin

Montelien

Bullock

Crowleys 2

Moneypenny

Walker

Read

———————————

Upper School ..173 [171]

———————————

Lower School ..205

———————————

    Total   ....378 [376]

———————————

BOYS AT ETON IN THE YEAR 1732.

Payne [C.]	Gilbert [C.]
Berkeley [C.]	Newey [C.]
Richards [C.]	Amphlett [C.]
Hayes [C.]	Gray
Carter [C.]	Hawest
Lyne [C.]	Hall
Phipps [C.]	Grenville
Asheton [C.]	Higgs
Hemming [C.]	Brown
Lord Sunbury	Smart
Clinch [C.]	West
Sparkes [C.]	Jephson
Bradbury [C.]	Noel
James	Barnard [C.]
Edgecombe	Giffard [C.]
Grenville	Balfour [C.]
Gilman [C.]	Newton
Lord Sandwich	Bowyer [C.]
Lord Tunbridge	More
Mr. Townshend	Parry
Lowe [C.]	Bradbury
Hall [C.]	Gibson [C.]
Wagstaffe [C.]	Cole [C.]
Princep [C.]	Hamersley
Lodington [C.]	Pennick [C.]
Hart [C.]	Fenton [C.]
Kelhan [C.]	Waterhouse [C.]
Ball [C.]	Cook [? Cock C.]
Gibbon [C.]	Hanmer [C.]
Bryant [C.]	Gretton [C.]
Reade [C.]	Plumptre [C.]
Walpole	Glyn [C.]
Allen	Berkeley
Sandys	Pennick

Trevor
Cambridge
Blisset
Montague
Cust
Burrough
Lord Conway
Mr. Conway
Mr. Howard
Mr. Stanhope
Mr. Townshend
Mr. Watson
Mr. Stanhope
Williams [C.]
Upton [C.]
Cox [C.]
Barford [C.]
Biddle
Aldworth
Piers
Tate
Bowden
Hammond
Parsons [C.]
Duquesne [C.]
Turner
Hanbury
Whitmore
Whitby [C.]
Whitby [C.]
Hudson
Cope
Selwyn
Ibbot
Terrent

Crowley
Gibbon
Crowley
Bishop
Allen
Willes
Pert [C.]
Canon
Gibson
Whitby [C.]
Milner
Aubrey

Pinner

Powis
Hamond
Chudleigh
Brereton
Green [? C.]
Ryder
Mr. McKenzie
Smith
Chetwynd
Moneypenny
Preston
Benson [? Banson C.]
Watford
Paxton
Clarges
Lawfield
Tilliard
Tonson
Fortescue
Marquess of Annandale
Lloyd [C.]
Lord Fitzwilliam
Dodd
Marquess of Granby
Lord George Johnstone
Lord Dursley
Lord Charles
Montilion
Blackett
Eldridge
Reynolds
Knightly
Fortescue
Broughton
Lord Dalkeith
Ambler
Rivers
Manby
Sleech
Bovery
Nason [C.]
Goodacre [? Goodere C.]
Norris [C.]
Grenville
Child
Kinsey

Burslem

Winder
Isaac
Richards [C.]
Wisher
Prior
Norris
Ward
Hanson
Pigot
Wells
Lord Robarts
Gallop
Ball [C.]
Chase
Jasper
Rivers
Williamson
Mr. Howard
Benson [? Banson C.]
Bowyer
Bather

Tyrrell

Mr. Howard
Reade
Edgecombe
Gours
Moneypenny
Harris
Mr. Townshend
Burder
Graham
Greene
Barrington
Fortescue
Fortescue
Taylor [C.]
Buller
Grover
Noel
Owen
Pinnell
Burton

[205]

THE NAMES OF THE BOYS IN ETON SCHOOL
DECEMBER 21st, 1742.

Captain
Taylor C. Prae.
Anstey C.
Potenger C. P.
Browne C. P.
Norbury C. P.
Young *ma.* C. P.
Pagett C. P.
Carter C. P.
Green C.
Talbot C.
Graham *ma.* C.
Champion C. Op. P.
Stephens C.
Brereton C.
Barclay *ma.* C.
Festing C.
Bever *ma.* C.

VI Form.

Mr. Cholmondly
Walker *ma.* C.
Jacques C.
Burrough C.
Carrington C
Evans C
Dinham C.
Richardson C.
Prior Op. Prae.
Sandys Op. P.
Macartney O. P.
Drax Op. Prae.
Coventry O. P.
Graham *mi.* C.

Cooper C.
Searle C.
Lewis *ma.* Op. P.
Ashenhurst *ma.*
Ashenhurst *mi.*
Dalrymple *ma.*
Wright *ma.*
Frank ✕

Hodson C.
Young *mi.* C.
Henley *ma.* C.
Moseley C.
Buchanan C.
Moody C.
Pratten C.
Templeman *ma.* C.
Cust C.
Sclater C.
Way
Walpole
Parkhurst
Noel
Kingscote
Vansittern
Calvert
Blount *ma.*

Howard C.
Somner C.
Becher C.
Williams *ma.* C.
Templeman *mi.* C.
Harris *ma.* ✕

D

Mainwaring
Russell
Taylor *ma.*
Newport
Woodyere
Tyrrwhit *ma.*
Trenchard
Pratt
Ascough
Hallum

V. Form.

Mr. Vaughan
Bruch C.
Banson C.
Cole C.
Lane C.
Walker *mi.* C.
Bullock *ma.* C.
Steavens
Wight
Egerton *ma.*
Ashurst
Elletson
Trevanion
Wright *mi.*
Playdell *ma.*
Cardale ×

Remove, 1742.

Ld. Charles
Ld. Downe
Mr. Bennett
Mr. Walpole
Sir Thos. Stapleton
Launder C.
James C.
Silke C.
Duck C.
Acton C.
North *Coll.*
Tollit C. [O.]
Waller *ma.*
Bowles *ma.*
Egerton *ma.* [*mi.*]

Bartlott
Long

Berkley C.
Pemberton C.
Knapp C.
Lewis C.
Foster
Myddleton
Blencoe *ma.*
Pote *ma.*
Hare
Weston
Townshend
Wyatt

Reade C.
Bennett C.
Smith *ma.* C.
Edwards C.
Bull C.
Dawnay *mi.*
Egerton *min.*
Whitehead
Whitmore
Hale
Lewis *mi.*
Tyrrhwit *mi.*
Clarke *ma.*

IV Form.

Lower School 153

Captain
III Form.

Burchitt C.
Taylor *mi.*
Boone *ma.*
Boone *mi.*
Mr. Brodrick
Blount *mi.*
Daw

Ld. Adams [? Ld. Adam Gordon]
Maiden C.
White *ma.*
Dalrymple *mi.*
Wogan *ma.*
Carrier C.
Harding *ma.*
Harding *mi.*

Glegg
Cranmer C.
Sr. Jno. Shaw
Lovejoy
Mr. Howe *ma.*
Stapleton
Buckworth
Richards
Barclay *mi.*
White *mi.*
Lockyear *ma.*
Hodges *ma.*
Bradyll *ma.*
Onslow
Dawes

Martin
Wilson
Bever *mi.*
Winnington
Hatch
Marsham C.
Mr. Bromley
Thibou
Amscotts
Thackeray *ma.*
Waller *mi.*
Wingfield
Heywood
Haslam *ma.*
Mason *ma.*
Hunter

Williams *mi.* ×
Sayer
Harwood

Furbar
Simpson
Ld. Plymouth
Day
Wright *min.*
Mordaunt *ma.*
Mordaunt *mi.*
Yate
Grice
Connor
Plumbe　　　×
Blencoe *mi.*
Mitchell *ma.*
Lee
Lloyd *ma.*

Lewis *min.*
Murray
Mr. North
Leeson
Young *ma.*
Young *mi.*
Bradbury
Lloyd *mi.*
Pytts *ma.*
Cornwall
Mr. Howe *mi.*

II Form.

Strugnell
Eldridge
Bullock *mi.*
Bullock *min.*
Capper
Naylor
Webb
Chapman C.
Ld. Burford
Smith *mi.*
Clarke *mi.* C.
Cowper C.
Henley *mi.*
Thoyts
Samson
Herring *ma.*

Hill   ×
Barker
Hammond
Bradyll *mi.*
Smith *min.*
Pytts *mi.*
Herring *mi.*
Pleydell *mi.*
Strong
Hodges *mi.*
Garden
Neugent
Mr. Calvert
Mitchell *mi.*
Lewis *quar.*
Wooton
Smyth *quar.*
Mason *mi.*
Mr. Chetwynd
Hind
Bowles *mi.*
Pote *mi.*
Foley
Lemoine
Gill *mi.*
Montagu
Colchester *ma.*
Fell

I Form.

Wogan *mi.*
Thackeray *mi.*
Thackeray *min.*
Reynolds *ma.*
Piggot
Jennings
Warren
Shafto
Blackwell
Wedgborough
Reynolds *mi.*
Holland
Herd
Colchester *mi.*
Ingram
Mordaunt *min.*
Harris *mi.*

Lumley
Hall
Tullie
Hayward
Chalton

Bible-Seat.

Paxton
Tyrrell
Wright *quartus*
Bullock *quartus*
Lockyear *mi.*
Wade
Waller *min.*
Marshall
Wynne
Whitter *ma.*
Whitter *mi.*

Provost.
Dr. Bland

Fellowes.
Dr. Carter
Dr. Berriman
Mr. Sleech
Dr. Harris
Mr. Golding
Mr. Burton
Mr. Reynolds

Head Master.
Dr. George

Assistants.
Mr. Cooke
Mr. Layng
Mr. Plumtree

Lower Master.
Mr. Somner

Assistants.
Mr. Apthorpe
Mr. Barnes & Mr. Reade

In the 6th Form No. 17
„ „ 5 „ „ 56
„ „ Remove „ 16
„ „ 4 Form „ 42
—

In the Upper
School are 131
scholars.

3 Form 75
2 „ 45 [44]
1 „ 22
Bible Seat 11

In ye Lower School
153 [152]

The total sum
amounts to
284 [283] Scholars.

JOHN NORTH,

December 21,

MDCCXLII.

BILL OF ETON COLLEGE & SCHOOL 1745.

1745.

Visitor.
Dr. Thomas

Provost.
Revd. Dr. Bland

Vice Provost.
Revd. Dr. Carter

Fellows.
Revd. Dr. Berriman
,, Mr. Sleech
,, Dr. Harris
,, Mr. Golden
,, Mr. Burton
,, Mr. Reynolds

Upper Master.
Revd. Mr. Cooke

Lower Master.
Revd. Dr. Sumner

Upper Assistants.
Mr. Dampier
,, Plumbtree
,, Purt

Lower Assistants.
Mr. Apthorp
,, Barnes
,, Reade

Conducts.
Mr. Bostock
,, Hudgate [Hugget]

Collegers.

Sixth Form.

Graham *ma.*
Brereton
Barckley
Prior
Evans
Richardson
Graham *mi.*
Cowper
Frank
Hudson [Hodshon]
Young

Fifth Form.

Henley
Moody
Pratten
Cust
Sclater
Howard
Sumner
Harris
Beecher
Templeman
Hallam
Cole
Lane
Walker
Bullock
Cardale
James

Silk
Acton
Forster [Foster]
Blincowe
Barckley *mi.*
Knapp
Hill
Lewis
Reade
Vanburgh
Briddall [Brydall]
Bennett
Smith
Burchett
Okes
Marshall

Remove.

Gibson

Fourth Form.

Parkhurst
Marsham
Thackeray
Waller
Sayer
Williams
Lee
Slade
Pratt
Elkington
Plumbe
Chapman

Third Form.

Clarke
Kendall
Cowper
Loveden [Loveday]
Lavours [Savours]
Hill
Millward

Barker
Gordon [Garden]
Roberts
Denue [Denne]

Second Form.

Price
Holland   70

Oppidans.

Fifth Form.

Lord Walpole
Mr. Vaughan
Mr. Barrington
Mr. Broderick
Taylor
Tyrwhit
Elletson
Wright
Jones
Egerton
Hare
Weston
Pemberton
Townshend
Egerton *mi.*
Hole [? Hale]
Sotheron
Pote
Tyson
Wyatt
Taylor *mi.*
Boons [? 2]
Wutmore [Whitmore]
Carr
Ekins

Remove.

St. Shaw [Sr. Shaw]
Waller
Dawes

Buckworth
Stapleton
Richards
Barckley *min.*
Onslow
Hodges
Locker
Martin
Price
Humberstone

Fourth Form.

Lord Plymouth
Lord Lumley
Mr. North
Mr. Hope
Sir Strickland
Key
Wilson
Heywood
Amcotts
Mason
Hunter
Hawtrey
Deane
Manfield
Harwood
Simpson
Day
Wright
Mordaunts [? 2]
Damer
Yate
Furbar
Mitchell
Blincowe
Pitts
Foster
Youngs 2
Dobins
Lloyd *ma.*
Murray
Lloyd *mi.*
Naylor
Frasier

Roberts
Bogdany

Third Form.

Rebow
Loveday *ma.*
Leeson
Capper
Bullock
Churchill
Curwen
Lord Burford
Henley
Herrings 2
Bullock
Hammond
Braddyle
Axtell
Pytts
Pledwell
Strong
Hodges *mi.*
Fox
Nugent
Mitchell *mi.*
Mountague
Estwick
Goleborne
Kelly
Mr. Calvert
Mason
Dimmock
Howards [? 2]
Smyth
Tyrrell
Elliott
Grante
Hinde
Pote *mi.*
Colchester
Wogan
Soames
Foly
Nell
Thackeray
Shafto

Reynolds
Pigott
Newman

Second Form.

Pennings 2 [Jennings 2]
Wettam
Smith
Lumley
Hall
Vassell
Parkers [? 2]
Charlton
Harris
Browne
Hird
Tully
Mordaunt
Ingram
Marshall
Wynne
Astley
Colchester *mi.*
Simpson
Hasted
Pacey
Wade
Sir Bridges
Cherry
Bullock
Waller

First Form.

Thackeray
Sclater
Whitter
Lownes
Brereton
Kimber
Ireson *min.* [? Leeson *mi.*]
Fletcherd
Small
Millington
Lockyer

Bible Seat.

Crispigny
Stronge
Buckworth
Lovill
Poccock
Hollis
Scott
Short
Thackeray
Small
Eade
Horn
St. Legers 2
Smith
Morrell   [244]

A BILL OF ETON ~~COLLEGE~~ SCHOOL [1747–8].

Provost.	*Collegers.*
Dr. Sleech	
	Harris
	Hallam
Vice Provost.	Acton
	Foster
Dr. Harris	Berkly *ma.*
	Knapp
	Hill
	Pote
Fellows.	Bridall
	Ekins *ma.*
Dr. Berryman	Burchett
Mr. Reynolds	Oakes
Mr. Burton	Berkly *mi.*
Mr. Cook	~~Gibson~~
Mr. Sturges	
Mr. Ashton	
	Marsham
	Thackeray *ma.*
Upper Master.	Manfield
	Pitts
Dr. Sumner	Waller
	Ekins *mi.*
	Sayer
	Arden
Lower Master.	Lee
	Slade
Mr. Dampier	Williams
	Elkington
	Bones
Assistants.	Bogdani
	Gach [Gaches]
Mr. Plumtree	Walker
Mr. Purt	Neal
Mr. Reap	Kendall
Mr. Apthorp	Bullock
Mr. Barnes	Churchill
Mr. Sleech	

Pemberton *ma.*
Mountague

___

Savours
Pemberton *mi.*
Garden
Templeman
Smith
Roberts
Morgan
Tew
Preston
Jepson
Thackeray *mi.*

___

Raiment
Browne
Skynner
Wilmott
Richards
Trion
Horne
Benwell
Round
Stevenson
Hollis
Humphrys

___

Durnford
Belchier
Heal [Heald]
Tickell
Scott
Fletcher

___

Leicester
Whistler
Lewis
Patterson

___

Oppidants.

___

Tyrrhwitt
Taylor
Wyatt
Nicholas

___

Ld. Burford

Ld. Plimouth
Mr. North
Mr. Bromly
Offly
Wright
Younge
Loyd
Nailor
Blagdon
Rebowe
Leeson
Townsends 2
Stillingfleet
Henly
Herring
Bullock
Bradyl
Hey
Ld. Herbert
Mr. St. John
Mr. Calvert
Lee
Smith
Cranford

___

Cavendish
Pledwell
Mountague
Fox
Nugent
Pitts
Mitchell
Earl
Long

___

Smith
Mason
Elliot
Dymock
Offly
Newnham
Russel
Williams
Soams
Scott
Edwards
Laroche
Hill

Glass
Hind
Colchester
Wogan
Milington
Foly
Evelyn
Soame
Hume
Penn
Parmer
Barlett

Harris
Parker *ma.*
Reynolds
Whetham
Shafto
Piggott
Lumly
Vassall
Pointz 2
St. Legers 2

Chetwood *ma.*
Townsend
Chetwood *mi.*
Morritt
Charlton
Hird
Smith
Mordaunt
~~Richards~~
Bathurst
Parker *mi.*
Wynn
Ingram
Jeaferson
Hasted
Simpson
Ellison
Matthew
Sedly
Sr. Pole
Sr. Armytage
Fenwick
Donellan
Pugelas

Stevenson
Tombs
Seewell
Pacy
Kimber
Hall *ma.*
Hewett *ma.*
Greenly
Jennings 2
Walpole

Cambell
Sr. Bridges
Hulse
Crespigny
Chetwood *min.*
Waller
Sloper
Ld. Blanford
Thackeray *min.*
Mr. Archer
Randyl
Morris
Ld. Brudenel
Meredith
Laroche

Bayly
Turnour
Craster
Hall *min.*
Bullock
Creswick
Witer
Kemmish
Armytage
Loundes
Humphrys
Marsh
Leeson
~~Holles~~
Davies
Windham
Eld
Ld. Milsington

Mr. St. John
Lovell

King	Mr. Howard
Holeford	Stevenson
Brereton	Topham
Chesshire	Dusalis
Pocock	Turnour
Hewett *mi.*	Yarp
Warren	Farnaby
Sheels	Wright
Dusalis	Pacy
Mitchell	Blackewell
Ld. Charles [sc. Spencer]	Pearson
	Dawes
Jeaferson	Barrell
Howitt	Barritt
Witters 2	Crespigny
Smith	
Cotterell	Martin
Eaton	Gale
	Needham
Ld. Newbattle	Harden [250]

A BILL OF ETON SCHOOL, JAN^{ry} 30th, 1753.

6th Form.
Collegers.

Roberts
Soame
Edwards
Brooke
Tew
Jepson
Palmer
Brandfoot
Harris
Thackeray
Richards

Oppidants.

Mason
Townshend

5th form.
Collegers.

Howes
Hawtrey
Warre
Cant
Sewell
Eyre
Ellis *ma.*
Chamberlayne
Stevenson
Davies
Ellis
Colton

Oppidants.

Ld. Blandford
Ld. Milsingtown
Mr. Cornwallis
Mr. Archer
Morris
Welby
Lovell
Leigh
Hugenson
Lynch
Leicester
Taylor
Morgan.
Eld
Byron
Bromfield
Knight

Remove.
Collegers.

Heald
Dealtry
Scott
Tickell
Waller

Oppidts.

Mr. St. John
Wyndham
King
Holford

James
Clarke
Brereton
Girdler
Orlebar

4th form.
1st Remove.
Collegers.

Stevenson
Eaton
Lamb
Whichcot
Sturges
Chamberlayne

Oppidts.

Ld. Charles [sc. Spencer]
Ld. Percival
Desalis
Pacey
Lucas
Marten
Desalis
Harvest
Brown
Byam
Willes
Russell
Sheeles
Maddox

2d Remove.
Collgs.

Blackwell
Baker
Leicester
Horne
Davers
Munday
Leicester
Blomberg
Jones

Oppidts.

Heath
Dalby
Cotterell
Simpson
Courtenay
Elison
Tighe
Addams
Burgoyne
Dawes
Clayton
Gally

3d Remove.
Collgs.

Leicester
Rugge

Oppidts.

Ld. Fordwich
Ld. Newbattle
Mr. Howard
Bourne
Walker
Desalis
Beauclerke
Clarke
Haughton
Gale
Sandys
Farnaby
Williams
Whalley
Post

Upper School
114

3rd form.
1st Remove.
Collegrs.

Lewis
Davies

Oppidts.

Mr. Cornwallis
Bransby
Jenner [? Fenner]
Fonnereau
Walker
Jones
Vaughan
Campbell
Hill
Harrison
Potter
Hales
May
Turner
Moore
Wingfield
Garnier

2d Remove
Collgrs.

Morgan
Pindar

Oppidents.

Mr. Bouverie
Mr. Percival
Sr. Jno. Loyd
Day
Wright
Wyndham
. Whichcot
Heywood
Hunter
Needham
Ratcliffe
Russell
Dillon

3rd Remove.
Collgrs.

Grosvenor
Farnham
Crane

Oppidts.

Ld. Gainsborough
Heywood
Whichcot
Wynne
Bostock
Style
Crofts
Way
Kemp
Williams
Ratcliffe
Grape
Dundass
Rushout

4th Remove.
Collrs.

Fenoughlet
Taylor

Oppidts.

Sir. Wm. Fowler
Sumner
Hatch
Pote
King
Knowles
Tighe
Warden
Arcedeckne
Hodges
FitzThomas
Clarke
Chatfield
Harding
Collins
Osborne
Dod
Berrige

5th Remove.
Collgrs.

Glasse

Oppidts.

Ld. Beaumont
Ld. Walkworth
Mr. North
Mr. Cornwallis
Basset
Rashleigh
Byron
Greive

6th Remove.
Collgrs.

Rugge
Henson
Williamson

Oppidts.

Burgh
Timberlake
Berrige
Herbert
Lucas
Williams
Maidman
Jones
Patterson
Pearson
Buckle
Terry
Vandeput
Allen
Lukin
Clough
Laverick
Ellis

2d Form.
1st Remove.
Collgrs.

Clough
James
Manistree

Oppidts.

Ld. Hinchinbrooke
Ld. Hamilton
Howard
Baker
Waterhouse
Brinkman
Sharp
Carter
Breedon
Howard
Gregory
Stert

2d Remove.
Collgrs.

Cleaver
Nightingale

Oppidts.

Pacey
Hill
Pearson
Hill
Ottewell
Fulham
Addair
Allen
Moore
Millar
Sommers
Hughes
Herbert
Newton
Salter

1st Form.
Collgrs.

Nartlow
Newman

Oppidts.

Ld. Howard
Ld. Spencer

E

Mr. Percival
Mr. Cornwallis
Mr. Bennet
Mr. Noel
Timberlake
Terry
Coates
Adderly
Barnard
Powell
Duer
Haynes
Clayton
Addair
Chetwynd
Croftes
Blair
Cope
Millar
Moore
Humphreys

Chetwynd
Dadyly
Sumner
Cambridge
Hales
Broderick
Boucher
Batten
Stone
Cassmajor
Burch
Boscawen

Lower School
170

In all 284.

ETON COLLEGE [DECEMBER 1753].

Provost.

Dr. Sleech

Vice Provost.

Dr. Burton

Fellows.

Mr. Reynolds
Mr. Ashton
Mr. Cooke
Mr. Hetherington
Mr. Lyne
Mr. Southernwood

Upper Master.

Dr. Sumner

Lower Master.

Mr. Dampier

Assistants.

Dr. Apthorpe
Mr. Sleech
Mr. Norbury
Mr. Young
Mr. Graham
Mr. Sumner

Sixth Form Collegers.

Jepson
Palmer
Branfoot
Harris
Richards
Howes
Hawtrey
Warre
Sewell
Ellis
Chamberlane
Stevenson
Davies
Ellis   :: in all 14

Fifth Form Coll:

Bromfield
Colton
Heald
Scott
Tickell
Waller
Stevenson
Eaton
Harvest
Sturges
Chamberlane
Heath
Whichcot
Keate
Baker
Leycester
Horne
Davers

Monday
Blomberg
Jones :: 21

Remove College.

Leycester
Rugge :: 2

Fourth Form College.

Lewis
Davies
Lewes
Olliver
Morgan
Pindar
Hanson
Farnham
Grosvenor
Crane :: 10

Third Form College.

Fenoulhet
Taylor
Rolt
Rugge
Williamson
Clough
Maidman
Manistre
Brougham
James
Cleaver :: 11

Second Form Coll:

Somers
Nartloo
Gibbs
Newman
Stack

Welstead
Basill · :: 7

First Form Coll.

More
Dudley [Dadley]
Stone
Burch :: 4

. . . .

. . . .

Sixth Form Oppidans.

Lord Blanford
Lord Milsington
Lord Brome
Mr. Archer
Morgan
Eld
Byron
Knight

Fifth Form Opp.

Lord Charles Spencer
Lord Percival
Mr. St. John
Wyndham
King
Holford
Dealtry
James
Orlebar
Desalis
Pacey
Lucas
Desalis
Browne
Byam
Willis
Russel
Sheeles

Maddox
Portman
Dalby
Cotterell
Simpson
Courtnay
Ellison
Tighe
Burgoyne
Clayton
Gally
Cotsford

Remove Oppidans.

Lord Fordwich
Lord Newbattle
Mr. Howard
Skipwith
Walker
Leycester
Desalis
Beauclerk
Sandys
Farnaby
Williams
Whalley
Post
Ridding
Bransby

Fourth Form Opp :

Lord Gainsborough
Mr. Cornwallis
Mr. Bouverie
Sr. Loyd
Fonnereau
Walker
Vaughan
Campbell
Hill
Harrison
Potter
May

Turner
More
Hales
Winfield
Garnier
Pepys
Sturges
Monoux
Wright
Wyndham
Whichcot
Haywood
Hunter.
Needham
Ratcliff
Dillon
Barrell
Russel
Blechynton [Blechynden]
Chamberlane
Bowles
Haywood
Whichcot
Wynne
Bostock
Style
Crofts
Way
Williams
Ratcliffe
Grape
Keck
Dundas
Clarke
Rushout
Beridge
Davies
St. John
Leonard
Jones

Third Form Opp :

Kemp
Sumner
Hatch
Pote

King
Knowles
Tighe
Warden
Archdecne
FitzThomas
Sr. Wm Fowler
Clarke
Chatfield
Harding
Colins
Osborne
Algood
Dodd
Taylor
Chetwynd
Timberlake
Crawford
Byron
Lord Warkworth
Basset
Rasleigh [Rashleigh]
Lord Boumont
Mr. Cornwallis
Mr. North
Vandeput
Herbert
Grieve
Carver
Williams
Burgh
Lukyn
Clough
Terry
Allen
Lucas
Pearson
Locock
Breedon
Jane
Buckle
St. John
Jones
Baker
Edwards
Laverick
Combes
Lee·

Maynards 2
Haywards 2
Stert
Sharp
Lord Hinchinbrook
Massey
Chetwynd
Gregory
Carter
Pacey
Howard
More
Fulham
Timberlake
Gunning
Batt
Hayward
Cambridge
Herbert
Thomas
Hill
Pearson
Ottiwell
Adair
Miller
Hughes
Lord Spencer Hamilton
Salter
Duer
Revely
Kennit
Harvey

Second Form Opp :

Lord Dunkellin
Morrice
Mr. Perceval
Howard
Allen
Radcliffe
Newton
Croftes
Mr. Noel
Terry
Archbold
Hatch

Adair

Beauclerk
Aderley

Thomason
Hales

Hill
Blair

Boucher
Henly

Palmer
Barnard

Broderick
Powell

Fuller
Clayton

Mosely
Lord Ossulston

Dampier
Lord Howard

Farnaby
Mr. Cornwallis

Rasleigh [Rashleigh]
Mr. Mashams 2 [Marsham]

Coke
Millar

Forester
Marten

Sharpless
Farrell

Sumner
Boscawen

Clough
Cotes

Wrights 2
Wright

Hanbury
Casamajor

Hill
Mason

Layton
Gower

Duckworth

Taylor

Mr. Boverie

First Form Opp.

Calder

Snows 2

Lord Ashbrook

Sumner

Lord Greville

Cope

Oppidants	257
Collegers	69
	326

Newnham

A BILL OF ETON SCHOOL 1754.

[*Provost.*
Dr. Sleech

Vice-Provost.
Dr. Burton

Fellows.

Mr. Reynolds
Mr. Cook
Mr. Ashton
Mr. Hetherington
Mr. Lyne
Mr. Southernwood

Upper Master.
Mr. Barnard

Lower Master.
Mr. Dampier

Assistants.

Dr. Apthorpe
Mr. Sleech
Mr. Norbury
Mr. Younge
Mr. Graham
Mr. Sumner
Mr. Forster
Mr. Ekins]

6th Form Collegers.

Richards
Howes
Hawtrey
Warre
Sewell
Ellis *ma.*
Chamberlayne
Stevenson
Davies
Ellis *mi.*
Bromfeild
Colton
Heald   : :   13

5th Form.

Tickle
Scott
Waller
Stevenson
Eaton
Harvest
Sturges
Chamberlayne
Heath
Keate
Baker
Leycester
Horne
Davers
Munday
Blomberg
Jones
Smith
Rugge   : :   19

Remove.

Padwyn [Paddon]
Lewis
Davies
Sturges　　　:: 4

4th Form.

Lewis
Oliver
Morgan
Pindar
Hanson
Stevenson
Hawtrey
Farnham
Grosvenour
Crane
Fenoulhet
Taylor
Rolt　　　:: 13

3 Form.

Rugge
Williamson
Clough
Maidman
Manistre
Brougham
James
Cleaver
Nartlou
Stack　　　10

1 and 2 Form.

Sommers
Gibbs
Hales
Wealsted
Newman
Basil
Moore
Stone
Burch　　　:: 9

In all 68
Collegers.

6 Form
Oppidents.

Ld. Milsington
Ld. Broome
Elde
Byron
Knight
Wyndham
Holford
Dealtry
James

5 Form.

Orlebar
Ld. Perceval
Ld. Charles Spencer
Ld. Fordwich
Mr. Howard
Brown
Byam
Russell
Sheeles
Maddox
Portman
Cotterell
Tighe
Burgoyne
Galley
Cotsford
Skipwith
Walker *ma.*
De Salis
Beauclerke
Sandys
Farnaby
Williams
Whalley
Post
Redding
Bransby

Remove.

Mr. Cornwallis
Sr. Lloyd
Pepys

Fonnerau
Walker *mi.*
Vaughan
Cambell
Hill
Harrison
Potter
Turner
Hales
Garnier
Wyndham
Radcliff
Blechynden

4 Form.

Ld. Gainsborough
Mr. Boverie
Sr. Fowler
Monnoux
Wright
Whichcoate
Haywood
Hunter
Needham
Dillon
Russell
Chamberlayne
Bowles
Whichcoate
Wynne
Bostock
Crofts
Style
Way
Radcliff
Keck
Dundas
Rushout
Berrigde [Beridge]
Davies
St. John
Leonard
Grenville
Kemp
Sumner
Hatch
Pote

King
Knowles
Tighe
Warden
Archdeckne
Fitzthomas
Chatfeild
Hardinge
Collins
Osbourn
Allgood
Dodd
Taylor
Chetwynd
Crawfurd
Timberlake
Byron
Travaille
Griffiths
Averne

3rd Form.

Vandeput
Mr. Cornwallis
Mr. North
Clerk
Ld. Warkworth
Basset
Rashleigh
Ld. Bowmont
Herbert
Ld. Beauchamp
Carver
Greive
Lukin
Burgh
Clough
Lee
Williams
Alen
Baker
Terry
Lucas
Breedon
Pearson
Locock
Williamson

St. John
Jeane
Buckle
Jones
Edwards
Laverick
Chetwynde
Combes
Revelay
Dobbs
Maynard *ma.*
Gunning
Sharp
Moore
Fulham
Massey
Carter
Batt
Hayward
Maynard *mi.*
Pacey
Ld. Hinchinbrook
Howard
Hayward 2
Gregory
Grenville
Timberlake
Stert
Thomas
Crawley
Bonnin
Cambridge
Herbert
Kennet
Pearson
Ottiwell
Duer
Addair
Hill
Hughes
Miller
Ld. Spencer [sc. Hamilton]
Mr. Conway
Calvert
Salter
Harvey
Ld. Dunkellin
Morrice

Allen
Mr. Noel
Radcliffe
Crofts
Howard *mi.*
Newton
Archbold
Henley
Taylor
Blair
Rainsford
Pepys
Shreyer
Eliot
Buckerigde
Corryton
Salmon
Mugrove [Musgrove]
Cooper
Wentworth

2 Form.

Rogers
Mr. Perceval
Terry
Baker
Adair
Adderley
Powell
Barnard
Hatch
Hales
Clayton
Ld. Ossulstone
Ld. Howard
Newnham
Mr. Cornwallis
Mr. Marsham *ma.*
Miller
Mr. Marsham *mi.*
Sumner
Martin
Farrell
Boscowen
Wright
Welstead
Cotes

Casmajor
Gower
Mason
Beauclerck
Duckworth
Cope
Boucher
Moseley
Snow
Thomason
Moore .

1st Form.

Ld. Dursley
Ld. Ashbrook
Ld. Greville
Mr. Duburgh
Mr. Boverie
Hill
Broderick
Martin
· Neville
Farnaby
Forester

Cook
Sumner
Clough
Coxs 2
Snow
Hawke
Rawling
Hymore
Sharpless
Collins
Rashleigh
Legge
Layton
Hills 3
Haywood
Hanbury
Blackwell
Colder [Calder]
Stockley
Wrights 2
Boscowen
Fauquier
Dampier
Storer
Yonge   325   [342]

A BILL OF ETON COLLEGE AND SCHOOL IN AUGST. 1756.

Provost.	*Eton S[c]hool.*
Dr. Sleech	6th Form Colle.
Vice Provost.	Waller
	Scot
Dr. Burton	Stevenson
	Eaton
Fellows.	Harvest
	Sturges
Mr. Reynolds	Chamberlayne
Mr. Ashton	Heath
Mr. Cook	Keate
Mr. Hetherington	Baker
Mr. Lyne	
Mr. Southernwood	5th Form Colle.
	Davers
Upper Master.	Jones
	Rugge
Dr. Bernard	Cotsford
	Paddon
Lower Master.	Lewes
	Davies
Dr. Dampier	Grosmith
	Oliver
Assistants.	Morgan
	Pindar
Dr. Apthorpe	Hanson
Mr. Sleech	Russell
Mr. Norbury	Farnham
Mr. Younge	
Mr. Graham	Remove Colle.
Mr. Sumner	
Mr. Foster	Chamberlayne
Mr. Ekins	Stevenson

Hawtrey
Taylor
Baskett

4th form Colle.

Rolt
Harrison
Rugge
Avarne
Jones
Watts
Clough
Maidman

3d form Colle.

Stack
Brougham
Cleaver
Jeames
Reynolds
Langford
Cameron
Allen
Gibbs
Evans
Berdmore
Farrel
Welstead
Mosely
Adderly
Burch

2nd form Colle.

Sharpless

1st form Colle.

Smith

6th Form Oppi.

Maddox
Tighe
Burgoyne

Gally
Skipwith
De Salis
Beaucklerk
Ld. Fordwich
Sandys
Wally [Whalley]
Mr. Howard
Post

5th form Oppi.

Ld. Gainsborough
Mr. Boverie
Sr. John Eden
Sr. Js. Macdonald
Ridding
Bransby
Pepys
Fonnerau
Walker
Vaugham
Harrison
Turner
Garnier
Blechynden
Lewes
Monoux
Whitchcote
Haywood
Needham
Boles
Whitchcote
Wynne
Croftes
Way
Williams
Bostock
Grape
Keck
Dundas
Rushout
Beridge
St. John
Bates
Fabean

Remove Oppi.

Grenville
Sumner
Hatch
Knowles
Tighe
Archdecne
FitzThomas
Chatfield
Hardinge
Collins
Ranby
Dod
Crawfurd
Byron
Travel
Griffiths
Ward
Harris
Powys
Horne

4th form Oppi.

Duke of Roxburghe
Ld. Walkworth
Ld. Beauchamp
Ld. Hinchenbrook
Mr. Conway
Mr. North
Mr. Conwallis
Mr. Damer
Vandeput
Clarke
Herbert
Carver
Rashleigh
Grieve
Lukin
Clough
Lee
Pollen
Burgh
Spencer
Drew *ma.*
Drew *mi.*
Wyke

Wake
Wanley
Napier
Baker
Burrough *ma.*
Edwards
Breedon
Burrough *mi.*
Terry
Lucas
St. John
Jeane
Jones
Buckle
Combes
Laverick
Reivly
Dobs
Kennet
Robinson
Maynard
Akehurst
Penton
Rutherford
Skipp
Williams
Sharp
Fulham
Musgrave
Taylor
Batt
Peyps
Calvert
Stert
Hayward *ma.*
Hayward *mi.*
Hayward *min.*
Grenville
Knitly
Pacey
Massey
Cooper
Hamond
Smith
Rigby
Hilbert [Ilbert]
Whish

3rd form oppi.

Duer
Weston
Crawley
Henley
Hill
Cambridge
Ottivell
Hughes
Adair
Ld. Spencer [sc. Hamilton]
Wake
Dutton *ma.*
Phipps
Corryton
Grover
Meadows
Radcliffe
Harvey
Williams

Banks
Ld. Dunkellen
Morrice
Rainsford
Mr. Noel
Croftes
Newton
Howard
Sparrow
Blair
Archbould
Rogers
Buckeridge
Smith *ma.*
Smith *mi.*
Mr. Petty
Gulstone
Wainman *ma.*
Wainman *mi.*
Clayton
Hawkins *ma.*
Newnham
Salter
Jener
Williams
Hyliade [Hildyard]

Bonnin
Ld. Howard
Mr. Perceval
Baker
Adair
Barnard
Ld. Ossulstone
Martin
Mr. Marsham
Miller
Clough
Adderly
Powel
Mr. Damer
Fry
Lake *ma.*
Byam *ma.*
Neville
Lee
[B]ailey
[F]ox
Rous
Hatch
Thornton
Strickland
Moreland *ma.*
Boscawen
Wright
Cotes
Cass *ma.* [Cassmajor]
Gore
Haywood
[D]uckworth
[Sn]ow
Crawfurd
Beauclerk
Hawke
Dutton
Collins
Sumner
Wentworth
Boucher
Vanneck
Coke
Redwood
Norton
Farley
Mr. Wallop *ma.*

Mr. Wallop *mi.*
Glyne

Jodrell *ma.*
Byam
Cope
Ld. Ashbrook
Martin
Thomason
Mason
Rashleigh
Hill *mi.*
Forester
Mr. Deburgh
Mr. St. John
Hawkins *mi.*

Williams
Moreland *mi.*
Farrer
Goodenough
Hodgins
Byngham
Osborne
Cotton

Ld. Berkeley
Scott
Cox *ma.*
Willimott
Flemin
Hanson
Horton
Orde

2d form oppi.

Cook
Mr. Boverie
Highmoore
Suter
Dalby
Storer
Finch
Stanly
Hanbury
Farnaby

Hill
Chaloner
Lamb
Dampier
Snow
Legge
Lycester

Bell
Sumner
Isherwood
Green
Layton
Coxe
Taylor
Lake
Wright
Younge
Vanneck
Blackwell
Hanmer
Brougham
Hill
Twining

1st form oppi.

Ld. Milton
Ld. Mahone
Ld. Lestly
Ld. Kerr
Ld. Morpeth
Mr. Damer
Mr. Howard
Mr. Lestly
Mr. Piercy
Wright *ma.*
Boscawen
Knitly
Davidson
Fauquier
Calvert
Smith
Meade
Perrin
Clarke
Stone

F

Foster

Fulham

Tyson

Fry *mi.*

Ibbetson

Ford *ma.*

Ford *mi.*

Tuder *ma.*

Tuder *mi.*

Bog

Shepherd *ma.*

Shepherd *mi.*

Grey

Gunthorpe

More

Goldwin

Joddrell *mi.*

Manners

Hawke *mi.*

Howard *mi.*

Tracey

Finch *mi.*

Tash

Farrer

Reaves

Sergent

Lister

Sidney

Owen

Tomkins

Medlicote

Clifton

Hughes

Adderly

Dampier   402 [403]

A BILL OF ETON SCHOOL IN AUGST. 1757.

[*Provost.*

Dr. Sleech

Vice-Provost.

Dr. Burton

Fellows.

Mr. Reynolds
Mr. Ashton
Mr. Cook
Mr. Lynne
Mr. Hetherington
Mr. Southernwood

Upper Master.

Dr. Bernard

Lower Master.

Dr. Dampier

Assistants.

Dr. Apthorpe
Mr. Sleech
Mr. Norbury
Mr. Young
Mr. Graham
Mr. Sumner
Mr. Foster
Mr. Ekins]

6th Form Coll.

Waller
Scott
Stevenson
Eaton
Harvest
Sturges
Chamberlayne
Heath
Keate
Baker
Davers
Jones
Rugge
Cotsford
Ridding

5th Form Coll.

Paddon
Grosmith
Oliver
Morgan
Bates
Pindar
Farnham
Stevenson
Fabian
Chamberlayne
Hawtrey
Bostock
FitzThomas
Hatch
Taylor
Russell
Rolt
Harrison

F 2

Avarne
Rugge
Jones

Remove Coll.

Watts
Burrough *ma.*
Burrough *mi.*
Robinson
Laverick
Maidman

4th Form Coll.

Wish
Rigby
Cameron
Smith
Stack
Akehurst
Jeames
Brougham
Reynolds
Langford
Cleaver
Allen
Evans
Williams

3d Form.

Berdmore
Farrell
Welsteade
Mosely
Stone
Stanley
Sharpless
Davidson

2d Form.

Jemmett

Smith

1st Form.

Tudor *ma.*
Tudor *mi.*

Oppits.

6th Form.

Burgoyne
Gally
Beaucklerk
Pepys
Fonnerau
Garnier
Bowles
Whichcote

5th Form.

D. of Roxburghe
Ld. Gainsborough
Ld. Beauchamp
Ld. Walkworth
Mr. North
Mr. Conwallis
Sr. John Eden
S. James Macdonald
Wynne
Croftes
Way
Williams
Keck
Davies
St. John
Grenville
Sumner
Tighe
Archdecne
Chatfield
Hardinge
Collins

Ranby
Dodd
Crawfurd
Travell
Griffith
Byron
Harris
Powys
Horne
Clarke
Herbert
Carver
Rashleigh
Greive
Lukin
Clough
Pollen
Spencer
Rutherford

Remove.

Mr. Damer
Drewe
Wyke
Wake
Wanley
Napier
Baker
Edwards
Breedon
Lucas
St. John
Jones
Revely
Dobbs
Kennett
Nicholls
Pigott

4th Form.

Ld. Hinchenbrook
Ld. Spencer
Ld. Dunkellen
Mr. Noel

Mr. Conway
Mr. Petty
Penton
Skipp
Williams
Sharpe
Fulham
Musgrave
Taylor
Batt
Pepys
Calvert
Haywards 2
Grenville
Knightly
Hammond
Ilbert
Needham
Kendall
Duer
Weston
Henley
Phipps
Crawley
Cambridge
Wake
Grover
Hughes
Adair
Dutton
Corryton
Radcliffe
Williams
Clayton
Harvey .
Pemberton
Sparrow
Morris
Salter
Banks
Buckeridge
Rainsford
Rogers
Hawkins
Lee
Archbould
Blair
Fox

Newton
Smiths 2
Wainmans 2
Hyliade [Hildyard]
Gulstone
Foote
Popham
Stedmans 2
Jones
Heathe

3rd Form.

D. of Beaucleu
Ld. Howard
Ld. Ossulstone
Ld. Ashbrooke
Ld. Berkeley
Ld. Bellacey
Mr. Scott
Mr. Percevail
Mr. Marsham
Mr. Damer
Mr. Wallops 2
Mr. Deburgh
Mr. St. John
Mr. Boverie
Mr. Noel
Sr. John Nelthorpe
Baker
Bonnin
Neville
Adair
Miller
Barnard
Martin
Clough
Adderly
Fry
Byam
Baily
Thornton
Rouse
Hatch
Moreland
Butler
Farley

Davidson
Foister
Brickenden
Faukener
Delves
Boscawen
Wright
Cass *majr.* [Casamajor]
Gore
Duckworth
Snow
Crawfurd
Beaucklerk
Hawke
Dutton
Collins
Jodrell *ma.*
Sumner
Ventworth
Coke
Redwood
Strickland
Glynne
Farrer
Leigh
Boucher
Norton
Parry
Haywood
Grisdale
Grymmes
Gundrey
Hanson
Goodenough
Cope
Forrester
Rashleigh
Mason
Williams
Hill
Thomason
Martin
Dixon
Beaucher
Osborne
Hawkins
Scott
Cox *ma.*

Willimott
Orde
Finch .
Storer
Hanbury
Lambe
Cook
Highmoore
Suter
Farnaby
Steward
Cotton
Williams
Byngham
Hodgins
Smart
Verchilds 2
Baker
Hill
Calvert
Chaloner
Dampier
Dalby
Legge
Leycester
Knightly
Snow
Churchill
Bell
Clifton
Meade
Sumner
Coxe *mi.*
Frye
Green
Isherwood
Churchill
Lake
Taylor
Brougham
Hanmer
Wright
Wright
Twining
Lister
Layton
Blake
Boyd

Hambley
Manley
Davidson

2d Form

Ld. Fitzwilliams
Ld. Mahoon
Ld. Kerr
Ld. Morpeth
Mr. Damer
Mr. Howard
Duckworth
Fauquier
Tyson
Hill
Foukes
Young
Wright
Boscawen
Clarke
Fords 2
Finch
Jodrell *mi.*
Gunthorpe
Knightly
Moore
Foster
Hughes
Fulham
Owen
Davis
Doble
Baker
Shepherd
Sargeant
Bogge
Tomkins

1st Form.

Ld. Cranburn
Mr. Scott
Mr. Piercy
Shepherd
Honeywood

Goldwin
Stannier
Dashwood
Farrer
Brudnall
Tash
Tracey
Manners 2
Rashleigh
Storer
Reives
Fielding
Medlicote
Davies
Howard
Prayd
Nisbitt
Sidney
Wilson
Harris

Cook
Grape
Adderly
Pottenger
White
Stones 2
Bateman
Windham
Douty
Ambrose
Martin
Carrington   409 [407]

Cromfield [? Crownfield]
Grave [? Grieve]
Harris
Manly

Jones
Hayley

A BILL OF ETON SCHOOL IN AUGT. 1758.

6th Form.

Chamberlayne
Heath
Keate
Jones
Rugge
Cotsford
Ridding
Pepys
Garnier
Paddon
Grosmith
Oliver
Morgan
Bates
Pindar
Bowles
Croftes
Ld. Gainsborough
Keck
Sr. Jms. Macdonald
Davies
Grenville *ma.*

5th Form.

Duke of Roxburgh
Ld. Henchinbrook
Ld. Walkworth
Ld. Beauchamp
Mr. Conway
Mr. North
Mr. Conwallis
Mr. Damer
Sr. John Eden
Russell
Bostock
Grape
FitzThomas
Stevenson
Fabian
Chamberlayne
Hawtrey
Sumner
Taylor
Tighe
Archdecne
Chatfield
Hardinge
Collins
Ranby
Dodd
Byron
Powys
Horne
Rolt
Harrison
Avarne
Rugge
Jones
Clarke
Herbert

Carver
Rashleigh
Grieve
Lukin
Clough
Pollen
Robinson [C.]
Wyke
Wake
Wanley
Baker
Edwards
Breedon
Lucas
St. John
Jones
Buckle
Revely
Kennet
Nicholls
Piggott
Cameron [C.]
Watts [C.]
Burrough *ma.* [C.]
Burrough *mi.* [C.]
Penton
Skipp
Williams
Sharpe
Fulham
Musgrave
Taylor
Batt
Pepys
Calvert
Hayward *ma.*
Hayward *mi.*
Grenville *mi.*
Knightly
Hammond
Needham
Kendall
Ottley

Remove.

Ld. Spencer

Whish
Rigby
Smith
Akehurst
Grover
James
Brougham
Langford
Cleaver
Duer
Weston
Henley
Phipps
Crawley
Cambridge
Wake
Addair
Dutton
Foote
Williams
Clayton
Harvey
Perrin
Keck

4th Form.

Duke of Gordon
Ld. Dunkellin
Ld. Howard
Ld. Ossulstone
Ld. Wm. Gordon
Mr. Petty
Mr. Percival
Mr. Marsham
Mr. Damer
Mr. Grey
Mr. Littleton
Allen [C.]
Evans [C.]
Williams [C.]
Pemberton
Sparrow
Morrice
Banks

Rogers
Rainsford
Buckeridge
Hawkins
Lee
Newton
Wainman *ma.*
Wainman *mi.*
Foxe
Hildyard
Gulstone
Popham
Stedman *ma.*
Jones
Stevens
Heath ⎫
Hayley ⎪
Berdmore ⎬
Hatch ⎭
Baker
Neville
Addair
Bernard
Miller
Bonnin
Martin
Clough
Adderly
Stedman *mi.*
Foyster
Frye
Byam
Thornton
Rouse
Farley
Butler
Davidson
Brickenden
Faulkner
Jodrell
Delves
Treacher
Yeo
Murray
Gould
Kirshaw
Cust
Woodward

Boscawen
Gore
Duckworth
Snow
Collins
Cassamajor
Farrel [C.]
Boucher [C.]
Welsteade [C.]
Griesdale [C.]
Crownfield [C.]
Salter [C.]
Crawfurd
Beauclerk
Hawke
Sumner
Wright
Coke
Norton
Parry
Leigh
Glynne
Farrer
Haywood
Grimes
Monday
Wentworth
Daultry
Iremonger
Dashwood

3d Form

Duke of Buccleugh
Ld. Ashbrook
Ld. Berkeley
Ld. Bellaesye
Ld. Fitzwilliams
Mr. Gordon
Mr. Wallop *ma.*
Mr. Wallop *mi.*
Mr. Boverie
Mr. Deburgh
Mr. St. John
Mr. Scott

Mr. Noel
Mr. Damer
Mr. Howard
Ld. Mahon
Mosely ⎫
Jones ⎬
Stone ⎪
Manley ⎭
Dutton
Gundry
Goodenough
Cope
Mason
Forrester
Dixon
Hanson
Thomason
Martin
Beacher
Foxe
Wormley
Hill
Williams
Savage [C.]
Stanley [C.]
Rashleigh
Osbourne
Hawkins
Scott
Coxe
Wilmott
Orde
Storer
Finch
Hanbury
Lamb
Cooke
Farnaby
Cotten
Highmoore
Suter
Williams
Smart
Ottley
Walker
Nicholls
Thorpe
Sharpless

Hodgins
Horton
Verchild *ma.*
Knightly
Verchild *mi.*
Baker
Chaloner
Calvert
Dampier
Legge
Leycester
Bell
Dalby
Blake
Boyde
Hill
Churchill
Snow
Browne
Nicolls
Davidson [C.]
Jemmitt [C.]
Fielding [C.]
St. John
Scott
Sumner
Clifton
Meade
Coxe
Green
Frye
Lake
Taylor
Brougham
Hanner [Hanmer]
Twining
Lister
Wright
Isherwood
Churchill
Sr. Jno. Nelthorpe
Dawson
Duckworth
Fauquire
Tyson
Moore [C.]
Smith [C.]
Ottley

Parsens
Douglass
Ibbetson
Foulks
Hill
Wright
Younge
Boscawen
Ford *ma.*
Ford *mi.*
Finch *mi.*
Jodrell
Honeywood
Gunthorpe
Manners
Layton
James
Amyant *ma.*
Clarke
Tracey
Hughes
Brudenall
Foster
Fulham
Ld. Kerr
Ld. Morpeth
Owen
Tighe
Williams
Davis *ma.*
Doble
Sarjeant
Sheppard *mi.*
Sheppard *ma.*
Hambly
Stannyer
Manners
Clarke *ma.*
Clarke *mi.*
Bailey
Gray

2d Form

Mason
Grieve

Baker
Tomkyns
Bogg
Mr. Piercy
Wilson
Hambly
Ld. Cranbourn
Hanbury.
Parsens
James
Tash
Praed
Medlicote
Davies
Goldwin
Farrer
Dashwood
Nisbett
James
Storer
Reives
Pote
Grape
Adderly
Cooke
Gore *mi.*

1st Form.

Ld. George Gordon
Stone *mi.*
Howard
Rashleigh
Sidney
Cope
White
Browning
Windham
Douty
Pottenger
Liddel
Jones
Strudwich
Jones
Jennings

Ambrose
Carrington
Twining
FitzHugh
Younge
Foulkes
Cary
Martin
Foster
Newland
Amyant *mi.*
Wilson
Vincent
Christian *ma.*

Christian *mi.*
Peachy
Stone
Willis
Hanbury
Heath *ma.*
Heath *mi.*
Savage
Hanmer
Farrer
Times
Coats
Poole
Leycester   443

A BILL OF ETON SCHOOL AT XTMAS 1759.

Provost.

Dr. Sleech

Vice-Provost.

Dr. Burton

Fellows.

Mr. Cooke
Dr. Ashton
Mr. Hetherinton
Mr. Southenwood
Mr. Lyne
Dr. Apthorpe

Upper Master.

Dr. Bernard

Lower Master.

Mr. Dampeir

Assistants.

Mr. Sleech
Mr. Norbury
Mr. Young
Mr. Graham
Mr. Sumner
Mr. Foster
Mr. Ekins
Mr. Edwards

6th form Collegers.

Ridding
Paddon
Morgan
Bates
Pindar
Bostock
Grape *ma.*
Stevenson
Hawtrey
Chamberlayne
Fabian
Sumner *ma.*

5th form Coll.

Taylor
Harrison
Avarne
Rugge
Jones
Robinson
Burrough *ma.*
Burrough *mi.*
Whish
Grover
Langford
Cleaver
Akehurst
James
Brougham *ma.*
Evans
Allen
Salter
Reynolds
Barnes
Heath

Hayley
Berdmore

Remove Coll.

Jones
Clough
Crownfield
Duckworth
Munday

4th form Collegers.

Murray
Bouchir
Jones
Manley
Mosely
Stone
Savage
Stanley
Bromely
Parr *ma.*
Parr *mi.*
Walker
Davidson
Sharpless

3d form Coll.

Jemmet
Brougham *mi.*
Hanmer
Gough
Fielding
Moore
Foulkes
Shepherd *mi.*
Shepherd *ma.*

2d Form Coll.

Wilson
Cleeve

Reeves
Beauchamp

1st form Coll.

Haskins
Smith

6th form Oppidants.

Archdecne
Harding
Ranby
Byron
Powis
Horn
Mr. Conwallis
Mr. North
Herbert
Ld. Beauchamp
Mr. Damer *ma.*
Wake *ma.*
Baker *ma.*
Breedon
St. John *ma.*
Buckle
Revely

5th form Opp.

Duke of Gordon
Ld. W. Gordon
Ld. Ossulstone
Ld. Howard
Mr. Conway
Mr. Lyttleton
Mr. Marsham
Mr. Grey
Mr. Damer *mi.*
Nichols
Penton
Taylor
Batt
Fulham *ma.*
Pepys

Calvert
Hayward *ma.*
Hayward *mi.*
Knightley *ma.*
Hammond
Needham
Otley *ma.*
Wakefield
Duer *ma.*
Weston
Henley
Wake *mi.*
Foot
Perrin
Byrne
Crawley
Cambridge
Adair
Dutton *ma.*
Keck *ma.*
Eden
Morrice
Hawkins *ma.*
Lee
Hilyard
Stedman
Pemberton
Banks
Buckeridge *ma.*
Raynsford
Newton
Foxe *ma.*
Gulstone *ma.*
Popham
Stevens
Baker *mi.*
Neville
Barnard
Miller
Bonnin
Martin
Adderly *ma.*
Thornton
Rouse
Farley *ma.*
Butler
Davison
Brickendon

Faulkener
Jodrell *ma.*
Yeo
Collins
Kirshaw

Remove Opp.

Mr. Gordon
Delves
Cust
Woodward
Boscawen
Gore *ma.*
Snow *ma.*
Cassamajor
Hawke
Beauclerk
Norton
Parry
Leigh
Farrer
Grimes
Yorke
Wise
Macdonald

4th form Oppidants.

Duke of Bucleugh
Ld. Ashbrook
Ld. Berkely
Ld. Bellacyse
Mr. Wallop *ma.*
Mr. Wallop *mi.*
Mr. St. John
Mr. Bouverie
Mr. Scott
Mr. Noel
Wentworth
Dealtry
Ironmonger
Blake
Elwis
Duer *mi.*
Raymond

G

Dutton *mi.*
Gundry
Goodenough
Dixon
Hanson
Martin
Cope
Mason *ma.*
Wormely
Foxe *mi.*
Smith
Williams
Cunningham
Lane
Floyer
Scott
Storer *ma.*
Finch *ma.*
Osborne
Coxe *ma.*
Willmott
Orde
Williams
Hawkins *mi.*
Rashleigh *ma.*
Lamb
Cooke *ma.*
Hanbury
Smart
Farnaby
Cottin
Highmoore
Williams
Otley *mi.*
Walker
Nichols
Tharpe
Whitehorn
Weston
Ford
Hulse *ma.*
Hulse *mi.*
Benyon
Osborne
Hull
Ascough
Acourt
Holder *ma.*

Layng
Churchill
Fortescue
Verchild *ma.*
Verchild *mi.*
Baker *mi.*
Knightley *mi.*
Chaloner
Calvert
Dampeir *ma.*
Legge
Leycester *ma.*
Bell
Douglas
Blake
Hill
Churchill *ma.*
Nichols
Dawson
Brown
Snow *mi.*
Scott
Price
Gardiner

3d form Oppidants.

Ld. Ophaly
Ld. Carlisle
Ld. Ker
Ld. Fitzwilliams
Ld. Mahoon
Ld. Cranbourn
Mr. Damer
Mr. Piercy
Mr. FitzGerald
Mr. Howard
Sr. John Nelthorpe
Scott
Sumner *mi.*
Fauquier
Tyson
Parnel
Green *ma.*
Frye
Coxe *mi.*
Wright *ma.*

Clerk
Grey
Husbands
Parsons *ma.*
Spence
Horton
Scott
Priescott
St. John
Thompson
Mead
Tracy
Gunthorpe
Isherwood
Clifton
Jodrell *mi.*
Wright *mi.*
James *ma.*
Churchill *mi.*
Tighe
Ford *ma.*
Finch *mi.*
Otley
Boscawen
Ford *mi.*
Ibbetson
Hill
Gooch *ma.*
Baker *min.*
Hughes
Sargent
Manners
Hodges
Layton
Young
Amyand *ma.*
Clerk
Fulham *mi.*
Owen
Williams
Hamly
Manners
Bayley
Hume
Chambers
Irby *ma.*
Fettyplace
Pitt

Tompkins
Grimstone
Cowley
Foster
Gregory *ma.*
Gregory *mi.*
Bromfield
Pledwell
Grieve
Hanbury
Buckeridge *mi.*
Strudwick
Bogg
Parsons *mi.*
Medlicote
James *mi.*
Prade
Cope
Tash
Griffin
Farrer
Mason *mi.*
Browning
Davis
Vincent
Points
Christian *ma.*
Williams
Longe
Sumner *min.*
Baker
Gibbons
Rickets
Nisbet
Pote
Cooke *mi.*
Newland
White
James *min.*
Storer *mi.*
Adderly *mi.*
Sidney
Jones *ma.*
Smallman
Holder *mi.*
Hanbury
Jennings
Murphy

Drew
Aglionby
Bambridge

Not placed.

Collins
Ross

2d form Oppidants.

Mr. Chulmondely
Mr. Mountague
Keck *mi.*
Savage
Birt
Cary
Grape *mi.*
Rashleigh *mi.*
Gore *mi.*
Green *mi.*
Dampeir *mi.*
Croftes
Weston
Doughty
Howard
Poole
Salkill
Twining
Amyand *mi.*
Ambrose
Leycester *mi.*
Gulstone *mi.*
Lovibond *ma.*
Fitz Hugh
Hatch
Pottenger
Martin
Aldsworth
Irby *mi.*
Jodrell *min.*
Windham
Quarrell
Carrington
Hanmer
Smith

Folkes
Liddle
Christian *mi.*
Jones *mi.*
Wilson
Foster
Jeffreson
Peachy
Spencer
Crawford *ma.*
Lovibond *mi.*
Tims
Willis
Benson

1st form Oppidants.

Ld. George Gordon
Mr. Aylmore
Redwood
Farley *mi.*
Cotes
Young
Vincent
Lane
Heath *ma.*
Heath *mi.*
Irwin
Antony
Lander
Chulmondely
Farley *min.*
Halliday *ma.*
Bartelot
Palmer
Kelly *ma.*
Skelton
Martyr
Webb
Cotes
Goach *mi.* [Gooch *mi.*]
Williams
Kelly *mi.*
Lewis
St. John
Halliday *mi.*
Willis

Waldegrave *ma.*
Waldegrave *mi.*
Crawford *mi.*
Smith
Brookland
Hall *ma.*
Hall *mi.*
Brown
Bridges

Loft
Blake

Finis

Total & Exact at
Xtmas 1759, all
amounting to 472

[Election] 1760   A LIST OF ETON SCHOOL.

The Provost.

Dr. Sleech

V. Provost.

Dr. Burton

The Fellows.

Dr. Ashton
Mr. Cooke
Mr. Hetheringtn.
Mr. Southernwd.
Mr. Lyne
Dr. Apthorpe

Uppr. Master.

Dr. Barnard

Lowr. Master.

Dr. Dampier

The Assistants.

Mr. Younge
Mr. Graham
Mr. Foster
Mr. Roberts
Mr. Sleech
Mr. Norbury
Mr. Ekins
Mr. Edwards

Mr. Prior
Mr. Davis

The 6 Form : C.

Bostock
Grape
Stevenson
Hawtrey
Chamberlayne
Fabian
Sumner
Taylor
Harrison
Rugge
Jones

5th Form : C.

Robinson
Burrough
Wish
Grover
Langford
Cleaver
Akehurst
James
Evans
Allen
Reynolds
Barnes
Heath
Hayley
Berdmore

Jones
Clough
Duckworth
Munday

Remove : C.

Crownfield
Jones
Moseley

4th Form : C.

Manley
Savage
Stanley
Bromley
Parr
Walker
Sharpless
Davidson
Jemmet
Brougham
Hanmer
Gough
Sheppard

3d Form : C.

Fielding
Moore
Foulk's
Sheppard
Wilson
Cleave
Reeves
2d Beauchamp
Haskins
Smith

6 Form Oppts.

Hardinge
Ranby

Mr. Cornwallis
Mr. Damer
Baker
Breedon
Penton
Mr. Conway
Fulham
Taylor
Batt
Pepys
Calvert

5th Form Oppts.

D. of Gordon
Ld. Wm. Gordon
Ld. Ossulstone
Ld. Howard
Mr. Littleton
Mr. Marsham
Mr. Damer
Haywards 2
Hammond
Needham
Wakefield
Duer
Weston
Henley
Wake
Foote
Perrin
Byrne
Crawley
Keck
Eden
Morrice
Hawkins
Hildyard
Stedman
Raikes
Pemberton
Buckeridge
Raynsford
Newton
Popham
Baker
Neville

Barnard
Miller
Martin
Adderley
Thornton
Rouse
Butler
Davidson
Brickendon
Fawkner
Joddrell
Delves
Kirshaw
Collins
Yeo
Tomkinson
Boscawen
Woodward
Cust
Gore
Snow
Cashamajor
Beauclerk
Hawke
Norton
Parry
Farrer
Grimes
Macdonald
Wise
Yorke
Lawrence

Remove Opts.

Ld. Berkley
Ld. Ashbrooke
Mr. Wallops 2
Dealtrey
Iremonger
Blake
Duer
Raymond
Dutton
Gundrey
Goodenough
Dickson

Martin
Cope
Wormley
Fox
Williams
Smith

4th Form Opts.

Ld. Bellacyse
Mr. St. John
Mr. Bouverie
Cunningham
Lane
Floyer
Scott
Finch
Coxe
Willmott
Orde
Williams
Hawkins
Rashleigh
Lamb
Cooke
Gardiner
Hanbury
Farnaby
Cotten
Highmoor
Williams
Ottley
Walker
Nicholls
Tharpe
Whitehorne
Weston
Ford
Hulse
Benyon
Ossborne
Hull
Ayscough
A'Court
Holder

Fortescue

D. Beaucleugh
Mr. Scott
Mr. Noell
Layng
Churchill
Verchilds 2
Baker
Knightley
Chaloner
Calvert
Dampier
Legge
Leycester
Bell
Douglas
Blake
Hill
Churchill
Nicholls
Dawson
Snow
Price

Ld. Staverdale
Mr. Damer
Sr. Jn. Nelthorpe
Hulse *mi.*
Scott
Sumner
Fauquier
Parnell
Green
Coxe
Wrighte
Gray
Spence
Frye
Husbands
Horton
Scott
Prescott
Thompson
Mead
Tyssen
St. John
James
De Gray
Alkin

Mole
Prime
Onslow
Blake

3d Form Opts.

Tracey
Mr. Howard
Ld. FitzWilliams
Isherwood
Clifton
Ld. Carlile
Joddrell
Ld. Ophaley
Wrighte
Churchill
Ford
Tighe
Finch
Ottley
Boscawen
Ford
Ibbetson
Gooch
Hughes
Sargent
Hill
Baker
Manners
Hodges
Layton
Gunthorpe
Yonge
Amyand
Fulham
Ld. Rt. Kerr
Hambley
Bayley
Owen
Williams
Ld. Mahon
Manners
Hume
Chambers
Irby
Fettyplace

Pitt
Hanbury
Tomkins
Grimstone
Cowley
Foster
Gregory *ma.*
Pledwell
Gregory *mi.*
Browning
Mr. Conway
Aglionby
Adams
Bromfield
Greive
Mr. Percy
Buckeridge
Strudwick
Ld. Cranborne
Parsons
Tash
Christian
Medlycott
James
Mason
Williams
Farrer
Poyntz
Bogg
Prayde
Griffin
Longe
Cooke
Willmot
Vincent
Davis
Sargent
Cope
Mr. Monctons 2
Talbot
Hinchcliff
Murphy
Baker
Gibbons
Pote
James
Sumner
Ricketts

Nisbett
Storer
Newland
Mr. Fitz-Gerald
White
Jones
Smallman
Holder
Hanbury
Jennings
Hoar
Sidney
Johns
Hulse
Bambridge
Chambers
Dampier
Savage
Rashliegh
Mr. Cholmondl'y
Gore
Weston
Doughty
Leycester
Windham
Grape
FitzHugh
Greene
Salkield
Twining
Pool
Aldsworth
Drew
Keck
Howard
Isted
Reeves
Jefferson
Athill
Spencer
Pess [?]
Mitchell
Perry
Newnham
Paterson
Neve
Inglis
Wootton

Stroud
Sr. M. Fleming

2nd Form Opts.

Amyand
Crottes
Birt
Gulstone
Lovibond
Irby
Jodrell
Young
Quarrell
Thorold
Hanmer
Martin .
Hatch
Potenger
Foister
Smith
Carrington
Foulks
Liddell
Christian
Jones
Crawford
Cary
Benson
Redwood
Peachy
Willis
Lovibond
Wilson
Timms
Farley
Lane
Anthoney
Hanbury
Cotes
Mr. Montague
Mr. Aylmer
Irving
Halliday
Death
Haeth [Heath]
Snowden

Farley
Heath
Willis
Cotes
Skelton
Martyr
Ross
Cholmondley
Webb
Kelly
Bartelott
St. John
Williams

1st Form Opts.

Ld. Ge. Gordon
Vincent
Spotswoods 2
Palmer
Gooch
Lewis
Lander
Coxe
Brown
Crawford
Mordaunt
Curtis's 2
Brookland
Tyley
Loft
Farrer
Williams
Waldegraves 2
Halls 2
Blake
Piggott
Bridges
Clifton
Watts
Rich
Jarvis's 2
Backwell
Boscawen
Whitehorne
Gray

Key
Garrick
Charters's 2
Constant
Metham
Dutton
Hair

Newlands 2
Gordon
Sr. W. Compton
Davy
Toppin

_____

484 [486]

A LIST OF ETON SCHOOL
August 1761.

1761.

The Provost.
Dr. Sleech

The V. Provost.
Dr. Burton

The Fellows.

Dr. Ashton
Mr. Cooke
Mr. Hetheringtn.
Mr. Lyne
Mr. Southernwd.
Dr. Apthorpe

Upr. Master.
Dr. Barnard

Lowr. Master.
Dr. Dampier

Assistants.

Mr. Young
Mr. Graham
Mr. Foster
Mr. Roberts
Mr. Davis
Mr. Sleech
Mr. Norbury
Mr. Ekins
Mr. Prior
Mr. Edwards

6 Form Collrs.

Hawtrey
Chamberlayne
Rugge
Sumner
Taylor
Harrison
Jones
Burrough
Whish
Grover
Langford
Cleaver

5th Form Coll.

Akehurst
Pemberton
Reynolds
Barnes
Heath
Hayley
Berdmore
Jones
Clough
Duckworth
Mundy
Crownfield
Jones
Moseley
Manley
Cox
Savage
Stanley
Bromley
Hare

Remove Coll.

Parr
Walker
Davidson
Sharpless

4th Form Coll.

Jemmett
Brougham
Cox
Hanmer
Gough
Sheppard
Topping
Blake
Fielding
Foulkes
Sheppard
Wilson
Newland
Beauchamp
Jesse
Haskins
Reeves
Morrice
Banbrigge
Newland
Smith
Clifton
Cleeve

6 Form Oppts.

Mr. Damer
Penton
Fulham
Mr. Conway
Needham
Wakefield
Duer
Weston
Henley
Foote
Perrin

Byrne
Crawley
Keck
Eden
Morrice
Hawkins
Hildyard
Stedman

5th Form Oppts.

Raikes
Raynsford
Mr. Littleton
Nevile
Martin
Mr. Marsham
Mr. Damer
Thornton
Butler
Davidson
Brickendon
Faulk'ner
Joddrell
Delves
Kirshaw
Collins
Tomkinson
Boscawen
Gore
Snow
Beauclerk
Hawke
Norton
Grimes
Wise
Lawrence
Dealtrey
Iremonger
Duer
Raymond
Dutton
Ld. Ashbrook
Gundry
Goodenough
Mr. Wallop
Dixon

Ld. Berkley
Martin
Wormley
Fox
Smith
Manistre
Floyer
Scott
Ld. Bellacyse
Mr. St. John
Cunningham
Lane
Finch
Gardiner
Wilmot
Orde
Mr. Bouverie
Williams
Hawkins
Rashleigh
Lamb
Cooke
Hanbury
Farnaby
Cotton
Highmore
Williams
Ottley
Walker
Nicholl
Whitehorne
Weston
Hulse
Benyon
Osborne
Hull
Ayscough
A'court
Holder
Weston

Remove.

D. of Buccleugh
Mr. Scott
Mr. Noel
Storer

Lang
Churchill
Verchilds 2
Baker
Knightley
Chaloner
Calvert
Dampier
Legge
Leycester
Bell
Hill
Churchill
Snow
Nicholls
Dawson
Price
Calley
James

4th Form Oppts.

Mr. Damer
Sr. Jon. Nelthorpe
Ld. Stavordale
Mr. Howard
Ld. FitzWilliams
Ld. Ophaley
Ld. Carlisle
Ld. Robt. Kerr
Ld. Mahon
Mr. Irby
Mr. Conway
Sr. Samp. Gedon
Scott
Sumner
Fauquier
Green
Wright
Grey
Fry
Spence
Husbands
Horton
Scott
Tompson
Mead

St. John
Tyssen
De Grey
Alkin
Mole
Rime
Onslow
Toote [Foote]
Price
Tracey
Gunthorpe
Isherwood
Clifton
Jodrell
Wright
Tighe
Finch
Hughes
Sargant
Hill
Baker
Churchill
Ford
Sr. Jas. Ibbetson
Boscawen
Gooch
Manners
Hodges
Aglionby
Layton
Bigland
Jackson
Hanbury
Young
Amyand
Fulham
Hambley
Bailey
Owen
Manners
Hume
Chambers
Fettiplace
Pitt
Tomkins
Grimstone
Cowley
Foster

Gregory's 2
Browning
Clive
Murphy
Butcher
Adams
Mitchell
Greathead
Johnson
Rishton
Hudson
Brabazon

3d Form Opts.

Davy
Williams
Bromfield
Grieve
Mr. Percy
Pleydell
Buckeridge
Strudwick
Ld. Cranborne
Parson
Tash
Christian
Medlycott
James
Mason
Williams
Poyntz
Wilmot
Prade
Farrer
Long
Cooke
Davis
Bogg
Vincent
Sargeant
Hinchliff
Perry
Griffin
Grimes
Dodwell
Blake

Talbott
Storer
Mr. Monctons 2
Pote
Baker
Jones
Hanbury
Holder
Ld. Wm. FitzGerald
Sidney
Hulse
Gibbons
Sumner
Ricketts
Hoare
Nisbett
White
Jennings
Dampier
Stroud
Grant
Gordon
Johns
Smallman
Hunter
Holbech
Wotton
James
Chambers
Gore
Leycester
Wyndham
Aldsworth
Savage
Green
Salkeld
Twining
Drew
Athill
Newnham
Rashleigh
Mr. Cholmond'ley
Weston
Doughty
Fitzhugh
Pool
Jefferson
Isted

Keck
Spencer
Allen
Woodroffe
Frankland
Lane
Grape
Neeve
Ambrose
Birt
Amyand
Croftes
Gulstone
Lovibond
Mr. Irby
Jodrell
Young
Quarrell
Foster
Hanmer
Hatch
Howard
Smith
Benson
Anthoney
Crawford
Farley
Kelly
Burwell
Paterson
Hunter

———————

Thurold
Grimes
Reylor [Paylor]
Redwood
Halliday
Lane
Lloyd
Sr. M. Fleming
Carrington
Jones
Liddell
Foulkes
Peachy
Willis
Metham
Inglis

H

Willis
Wilson
Lovibond
Mr. Mountague
Cotes
Mr. Aylmer
Hanbury
Skeet
Farley
Lewis
Smith
Dighton
Sr. W. Compton
Martin
Budworth
Taylor
Parry
Cameron

2d Form Opts.

Cary
Timms
Heath *ma.*
Skelton
Irving
Death
Heath *mi.*
Cotes
Cholmondeley
Williams
Bartelot
Vincent
Cox
Palmer
Pigott
Ld. Geo. Gordon
Holborn
Ross
Kelly
Martyr
St. John
Lewis
Spotswoods 2
Jones
Mordaunt
Webb

Lander
Williams
Curtis's 2
Crawford
Jones
Tyley
Halls 2
Lofft
Cooke
Whitehorne
Boscawen
Bridges
Cotes
Gooch
Husbands
Dutton

1st Form Opts.

Brown
Jervis's 2
Rich
Brookland
Blake
Simmons
Baker
Waldegraves 2
Chesshyre
Charters's 2
Stanley
Harding
Saunders
Prade
Cooke
Constant
Hoblin
Talbot
Arabin
Lasscells
Watts
Key
Webley
Backwell
Ashton
Ellison
Garrick
Roberts

Beauchamp
Winfield
Milbanke
Boyfield
Davies
Mr. Berk'ley
Mr. Townshend
Rowlls
Dawson
Adamson
Burrel

Williams
Motte
Barrington
Hamilton
Collier
Calley
Tuffnell
Blagrove

Total 505

[? JULY] 1762.

[*The Provost.*	6th form Colls.
Dr. Sleech	Sumner
	Harrison
V. Provost.	Rugge
	Jones
Dr. Burton	Burrough
	Whish
	Grover
The Fellows.	Langford
	Cleaver
Dr. Ashton	Akehurst
Mr. Cooke	Pemberton
Mr. Hetheringtn.	Reynolds
Mr. Lyne	Barnes
Mr. Southernwd.	Heath
Dr. Apthorpe	
Upper Master.	5th form Colls.
Dr. Barnard	
	Berdmore
Lowr. Master.	Jones
Dr. Dampier	Clough
	Duckworth
	Crownfield
Assistants.	Jones
	Moseley
Mr. Young	Manistre
Mr. Graham	Coxe
Mr. Foster	Savage
Mr. Roberts	Stanley
Mr. Davis	Bromley
Mr. Sleech	Hare
Mr. Norbury	Hayter
Mr. Ekins	Parr
Mr. Prior	Walker
Mr. Edwards]	Davidson
	James

Jammett
Brougham
Coxe
Hanmer
Gough
Sheppard

Remove Colls.

Topping
Blake
Hayter
Foulkes

4th form Colls.

Sheppard
Wilson
Newland
Cleeve

3d form Colls.

Bainbridge
Reeves
Beauchamp
Jesse
Smith
Haskyns
Hanmer
Wilson
Wigsell
Newland
Morrice

1st form Colls.

Davis

6th form Opps.

Penton
Fulham
Weston
Foote
Eden

Hawkins
Raikes
Mr. Marsham
Mr. Damer
Thornton
Neville
Butler
Davidson
Brickendon
Fawkener
Jodrell
Delves
Kirshaw
Collins
Tomkinson

5th form Opps.

Gore
Snow
Hawke
Beauclerck
Norton
Grime
Wise
Lawrence
Iremonger
Duer
Dutton
Ld. Ashbrooke
Gundry
Goodenough
Mr. Wallop
Dixon
Lord Berkeley
Wormley
Foxe
Floyer
Scott
Ld. Bellasyse
Mr. St. John
Cunningham
Lane
Finch
Gardiner
Willmot
Orde
Mr. Bouverie

Williams
Hawkins
Rashleigh
Lamb
Cooke
Hanbury
Highmore
Williams
Walker
Nicoll
Whitehorn
Weston
Hulse
Benyon
Osborne
Ayscough
Acourt
Weston
Storer
Layng
Churchill
Verchild *ma.*
Verchild *mi.*
Baker
Challoner
Dampier
Legge
Leycester
Duke of Buccleugh
Bell
Mr. Scott
Hill
Mr. Noel
Churchill
Nichols
Dawson
Snow
Price
Calley
Floyer
Allcock
Scott
Sumner
Fauquier
Mr. Damer
Green
Thompson
Wrighte

Grey
Spence
Fry
Husbands
Scott
Ld. Stavordale
De Grey
Mole
Onslow
Mr. Howard
Ld. FitzWilliams
Ld. Carlisle
Tracey
Delgardno
Johnson
Prime
Brabazon
Mead
Tyssen
St. John

Remove Opps.

Sr. Jno. Nelthorpe
Ld. Ophaley
Sr. Js. Ibbetson
Alkin
Price
Foote
Gunthope
Isherwood
Jodrell
Wrighte
Tighe
Finch
Hughes
Sargent
Hill
Baker
Churchill
Ford
Gooch
Manners
Hodges
Aglionby
Jackson
Sr. Sampson Gideon

Hanbury
Greathead

4th form Opps.

Ld. Kerr (Robt.)
Ld. Mahon
Mr. Conway
Young
Amyand
Fulham
Hamby [Hambly]
Owen
Manners
Hume
Fettyplace
Pitt
Tomkyns
Grimstone
Cowley
Forster
Gregory
Butcher
Browning
Murphy
Adams
Mitchell
Rishton
Hudson
Johnson
Layton
Bigland
Mr. Percy
Ld. Cranborne
Greive
Bromfield
Parsons
Medlycott
Christian
Williams
Poyntz
Dodwell
Grimes
Tash
James
Mason
Willmott

Praed
Cooke
Farrer
Bogge
Vincent
Sargent
Buckeridge
Perry
Griffin
Pleydwell
Graves
Fidell
Johnson
Gunman
Mr. Monckton *ma.*
Mr. Monckton *mi.*
Ld. Wm. Fitzgerald
Davy
Long
Talbot
Storer
Baker
Jones
Holder
Hulse
Hanbury
Nisbett
White
Dampier
Strode
Sumner
Dewberry
Pote
Johns
Gordon
Grant
Hunter
Gibbons
Ricketts
Jennings

Lower School.

3rd form Opps.

Hoare
Holbeche

James
Gore
Leycester
Aldsworth
Windham
Savage
Green
Salkeld
Twyning
Drew
Athill
Doughty
Mr. Cholmondeley
Newnham
Weston
Fitzhugh
Jefferson
Isted
Keck
Spencer
Alleyne
Woodroffe
Frankland
Lane
Martin
Mr. Grimstone
Pool
Rashleigh
Blake
Parry
Birt
Amyand
Gulstone
Mr. Irby
Jodrell
Young
Quarrell
Foster
Benson
Anthony
Crawford
Farley
Kelly *ma.*
Lovibond
Hatch
Smith
Grape
Burwell

Tredcroft
Cameron
Hunter
Inglis
Neve
Brown
Willis
Sr. Mich. Fleming
Parry
Crofts
Paylor
Lane
Lloyd
Baker
Grymes
Thorold
Redwood
Halliday
Metham
Mr. Montague
Lovibond
Skeete
Farley
Lewis
Budworth
Cotes
Piggott
Hanbury
West *ma.*
West *mi.*
Mr. Aylmer
Wharton
Carrington
Jones
Folkes
Willis
Cary
Heath *ma.*
Irving
D'aeth
Heath *mi.*
Cotes
Skelton
Kelly
Cholmondeley
Williams
Bartelott
Vincent

Coxe
Ld. G. Gordon
Holbourne
Dighton
Taylor
Liddell
Mott
Ross
Timms
Palmer
St. John
Lewis
Crawford
Jones *ma.*
Jones *mi.*
Hall *ma.*
Williams
Hall *mi.*
Laught [Lofft]
Cooke
Curtis
Tyley
Dutton
Lander
Talbot
Vanderpool
Mr. Leslie
Pigott
Barry
Pemberton
Dalrymple

2nd form Opps.

Spotswood *ma.*
Mordaunt
Hawkins
Martyr
Cotes
Boscawen
Eden
Hoblyn
Curtis
Husbands
Bridges
Simmonds
Baker

Webb
Hatch
Whitehorn
Spotswood *mi.*
Gooch
Rich
Sanders
Harding
Stanley
Cheshyre
Arabin
Waldegrave
Constant
Brookland
Brown
Blake
Collyer
Charters *ma.*
Charters *mi.*
Jarvis *ma.*
Jarvis *mi.*
Cooke
Waldegrave
Ashton
Ld. Roose
Barrington
Sr. Walter Compton
Key
Garrick
Watts
Webley
Rice
Milbank

1st form Opps.

Backwell
Donaldson
Wingfield
Delancey
Praed
Adamson
Ellison
Blaygrove
Mr. Townsend
Mr. Berkeley
Pott

Price	Knowles *mi.*
Tunstall	Gibson
Beauchamp	Finch
Roberts	Lord Binning
Tuffnall	Mr. Stanhope
Williams	West
Rowles	Knowles *min.*
Dawson	Pollard *ma.*
Reed	Pollard *mi.*
Burwell	Nares
Smith	Doughty
Boyfield	Mr. Clive
Nibbs	Finch
Wigsell	Kent
Thorpe	Collyer
Calley	Chartres *min.* [503]
Knowles *ma.*	

[ELECTION] 1763.

[*Provost.*	6th forms Colls.
Dr. Sleech	Akehurst
	Pemberton
Vice-Provost.	Reynolds
Dr. Burton	Barns
	Heath
	Clough
Fellows.	Duckworth
Dr. Ashton	Jones
Mr. Cooke	Manistre
Dr. Apthorpe	Coxe
Mr. Hetherington	
Mr. Southernwood	
Mr. Lyne	
	5th form Colls.
Upper Master.	Orde
Dr. Bernard	Highmore
	Stanley
	Bromley
Lower Master.	Hare
Dr. Dampier	Hayter *ma.*
	Lange [Layng]
	Davidson
Assistants.	Leycester
Upper School.	Parr
	James
Mr. Graham	Brougham
Mr. Roberts	Coxe
Mr. Foster	Gough
Mr. Davis	Shepperd *ma.*
Mr. Heath	Topping
	Blake
Lower School.	Hayter
	Foulkes
Mr. Sleech	Crownfield
Mr. Prior	Savage
Mr. Ekins	Shepperd *mi.*
Mr. Norbury	Foster
Mr. Edwards]	

Remove Colls.

Willson
Sparkes

4th form Colls.

Cleave
Pulteney
Johnson
Howe
Salkeld
Spencer
Beauchamp
Smith

3rd form Colls.

Haskins
Willson
Wigsell *ma.*
Newland
Morris

2nd form Colls.

Leigh
Capstack
Lampard
Hill

1st form Colls.

Wigsell *mi.*
Boyfield
Seymour

6th form Opps.

Mr. Damer
Butler
Fawkener
Joddrell

Gore *ma.*
Hawke
Grimes
Wise
Duer
Gundry
Mr. Wallop
Dixon

5th form Opps.

Scott
Mr. St. John
Cunningham
Lane
Finch
Willmott
Mr. Bouverie
Williams
Hawkins
Rashleigh
Cooke
Nicholl
Weston
Osborne
Asyscough
A'Court
Weston
Storer
Verchild
Dampier
Legge
D. of Buccleugh
Hill
Mr. Noel
Nichols
Dawson
Price
Calley
Alcock
Scott
Thompson
Sumner
Fauquier
Mr. Damer
Greene
Wright

Grey
Husbands
Spence
Scott
De Grey
Ld. Stavordale
Mole
Prime
Onslow
Tracey
Ld. Ophaley
Ld. FitzWilliam
Ld. Carlisle
Frye
Mead
St. John
Turner
Sr. Jno. Nelthorpe
Price
Aulkin
Gunthorpe
Joddrell
Wright
Finch
Hughes
Sargent
Hill
Baker
Hanbury
Churchill
Greathead
Sr. Sampson Gideon
Ackland
Ld. Ker
Mr. Irby
Mr. Conway
Palmer
Ingles
Jackson
Younge
Amyand
Fulham
Hambly
Owen
Tomkyns
Hume
Grimstone
Cowley

Gregory
Browning
Butcher
Hudson
Adams
Rishton
Johnson
Duberry
Woolcombe

Remove Opps.

Mr. Percy
Ld. Cranbourne
Lutterell
Cave
Bromfield
Parsons
Medlicott
Christian
Williams
Poyntz
Dodwell
Grimes
Tash
Willmott
Praed
Cooke
Farrer
Bogge
Vincent
Sargent
Buckeridge
Perry
Griffin
Graves
Pleydwell
Johnson
Layton
Pointer

4th form Opps.

Mr. Monckton *ma.*
Mr. Monckton *mi.*
Gunman

Long
Talbott
Storer
Baker
Hulse
Hanbury
Ld. W. FitzGerald
Nisbett
White
Sumner
Strode
Gibbons
Pote
Johns
Hunter
Ricketts
Holder
Jennings
Phipps
Dulaney
Duer
Mr. Grimston
Digby
Leycester
Gore
Windham
Savage
Jefferson
Doughty
Fitzhugh .
Alleyne
Penn
Prideaux
Hoare
Holbeche
Nevill
Athill
Weston
Isted
Mr. Cholmondeley
Woodroffe *ma.*
Belt
Hunter
James
Frankland
Greene
Martin
Mr. Irby *mi.*

Young
Brown
Forster
Pool
Keck
Birt
Amyand
Gulston
Joddrell
Quarrell
Crawford
Farley
Benson
Anthony
Kelly
Neve
Inglis
Hunter
Cameron
Custance
Smith
Tredcroft
Burrell
Milles
Williams
Post
Woolcombe

Lower School.

3rd form Opps.

Willis
Parry
Piggot
Rashleigh
Lane
Mr. Montague
Gough
Skeete
Crofts
Payler
Metham
Lewis
Halliday
West
Dalrymple

Johnson
Sr. W. Lorraine
Denny
Winnington
Grimes
Cotes
Redwood
Thorold
Farley
Mr. Montague
Mr. Strangeways
Lloyd
Baker
Rawlins
Sr. Mich. Fleming
Kelly
West
Falkner
Dutton
Wharton
Skelton
Vincent
Dighton
Cholmondeley
Campbell
Cotes
Mr. Aylmer
Munday
Piggot
Coxe
Williams
Carrington
Taylor
Baker ×
Folkes
Ld. G. Gordon
Jones
Carey
Vilett
Bartelott
Willis
D'aeth
Heath *ma.*
Heath *mi.*
Liddell
Webster
Ford
Holbourne

Mott
Ross
Palmer
Crawford
Lewis
Hall
Curtis
Vanderpool
Hanbury
Pemberton
Champain
Agnew
Mr. Villiers
Gally
Hornby
Jones
Ross *mi.*
Younge
Irvin
Lander
Talbot
Jones
Elvin
Lofft
Parker
Hesse
Mappe
Barry
Hall
Cotes
Husbands
Baker
Stanley
Bridges
Eden
Curtis
Boscawen
Martyr
Hoblyn
Hawkins
Harding
Simmons
Cooke
Saunders
Whitehorne
Townly
Webb
Spotswood

Wilkinson
Skene
Calvert
Reese
Hayes
Northey
Hatch
Cheshyre
Delancy
Spotswood
Cooke
Ashton
Constant
Arabin
Milbank
Jarvis
Jarvis
Charters
Blagrove
Waldgrave
Barrington
Blackwell
Ld. Roose
Dawson
Finch
Smith
Blake
Brown

Unplaced.

Pelham
D. of Hamilton
Ld. Douglass
Thomas
Anderson
Croft
Lord Clinton
Mr. Clinton
Barton
Smith
Seaton
Willson
Mr. Byron
Forster
Townsend

2nd form Opps.

Burgh
Keen
Pott
Charters *mi.*
Garrick
Rice
Watts
Collier
Ripley
Ellison
Waldgrave *mi.*
Tunstall
Price
Mr. Berkeley
Brookland
Key
Webley
Bishop
South
Moore
Festin *ma.*
Praed
Baker
Adamson
Knowles
Pigott
Nibbs
Smith
Rowles
Wood
Reid
Tuffnell
Beauchamp
Knowles *mi.*
Calley *mi.*
Roberts
Charters *min.*
Willis
Woodroffe *mi.*
Dawson
Thorpe
Gibson
Pollard *ma.*

1st form Opps.	Byam
	Irish
Best	Davis
Cutler	Colthurst
Rice	Elvin
Lorain	Lemoine
Lorain	Simmons
Burrell	Earle
Brookland	Collier
Doughty	Ottley
Nares	Layton
Pollard *mi.*	Knowles
Lord Binning	Knowles
Husbands	Kent
West	Cooke
Warburton	Harrison
Paxton	Lander
Gibbons *mi.*	Allen
Corbett	Mr. Monson
Harding	Piggott
Harding	Garrick
Mr. Clive	Lark
Richardson	Douglass
Ld. Mahon	Gibbons *mi.*
Stevens	Mr. Manners
Chute	Manners [513]

AUG. 1, 1764.

[*Provost.*

Dr. Sleech

Vice-Provost.

Dr. Burton

Fellows.

Dr. Ashton
Dr. Lyne
Mr. Cook
Dr. Apthorp
Mr. Hetherington
Mr. Southernwood

Upper Master.

Dr. Barnard

Lower Master.

Dr. Dampier

Assistants.

Mr. Sleech
Mr. Graham
Mr. Foster
Mr. Roberts
Mr. Davies
Mr. Heath
Mr. Prior
Mr. Norbury
Mr. Ekins
Mr. Edwards]

6th Form.

Clough C.
Duckworth C.
Jones C.
Gundry
Mr. Fox
Lane
Manister C.
Coxe C.
Orde C.
Mr. Bouverie
Williams
Crownfield C.
Cooke [C.]
Highmore C.
Rashleigh *ma.*
Nicoll
A'court
Hare C.
Hayter C.
Storer
Legge
Hill
Calley
Scott
Fauquier

5th form.

Stanley C.
Layng C.
Davidson C.
Dampier [C.]
Leycester C.
Parr C.
James C.
Sumner [C.]
Mr. Damer
Brougham [C.]

Coxe C.
Husbands
Spence
Sheppard C.
De Grey
Ld. Stavordale
Mole
Prime
Ld. FitzWilliams
Ld. Carlisle
Turner *ma.*
Price
Alkin
Topping C.
Blake C.
·Gunthorp
Hayter C.
Joddrell *ma.*
Finch
Sargent *ma.*
Hill
Hanbury
Foulkes C.
Greathead
Ackland
Palmer
Inglis C.
Jackson C.
Amyand
Fulham
Owen
Hume
Mr. Irby *ma.*
Tomkyns
Grimston
Cowley
Foster C.
Gregory
Mr. Conway
Browning
Butcher
Adams
Rishton
Hudson
Johnson
Woolcomb *ma.*
Russell
Cave

Broomfield
Ld. Cranborn
Parsons
Williams
Poyntz
Dodwell
Wilson C.
Willmott
Praed *ma.*
Farrer
Sargent *mi.*
Buckeridge
Perry
Griffin
Pledwell
Graves
Johnson

Remove.

Mr. Moncktons 2
Sparkes [C.]
Pointer [C.]
Gunman
Long
Talbott *ma.*
Baker
Cleeve C.
Hulse
Hanbury Williams
Nesbit
White
Strode
Gibbons *ma.*
Duer
Dulaney
Holder
Johnes
Pote C.
Hunter
Rickets
Phipps
Whish
Johnson [C.]
Pulteney C.
Digby
Auberey

4th form.

Ld. Malpas
Mr. Grimston *ma.*
Hunter [C.]
Leycester [C.]
Salkeld C.
Spencer C.
Beauchamp [C.]
Smith C.
Penn [C.]
Prideaux
Hoare
Holbeche
James
Gore
Neville
Wyndham
Savage
Frankland
Jefferson
Green
Athill
Doughty
Weston
Fitzhugh
Isted
Woodroffe *ma.*
Martin
Dimsdale
Haynes
Kerrick
Grenville *ma.*
Carlyon
Brown

Mr. Irby *mi.*
Anthony C.
Woolcombe *mi.* C.
Fleet C.
Young
Foster
Pool
Keck
Birt
Amyand
Joddrell *mi.*
Quarrell

Benson
Kelly
Neve
Cameron
Inglis
Custance
Hunter
Tredcroft
Burwell
Milles *ma.*
Williams
Maule
Trapier
Plummer
Hughes
Jenner
Mr. Mountagues 2
Mr. Strangeways
Sr. W. Lorraine
Haskins C.
Jeffreys
Jesse
Willis
Piggott
Rashleigh *mi.*
Gough
Skeete
Crofts
Paylor
Lloyd
Metham
Lewis
Halliday
Winnington
Johnson
Dalrymple
Grimes
Cotes
Redwood
Budworth
Thorold
West
Baker
Southcote
Baker
Wilson C. [? O.]
Sr. Mich. Fleming
Mr. Aylmer

Mr. Fortescue
Ld. Windsor
Mr. Windsor
Kelly
Fawkener
Dutton *ma.*
Wharton
Skelton
Vincent
Campbell
Cotes
Mundy
Piggott
Williams
Taylor
Baker
Jones
Folkes
Cary
Heaths 2
Webster
Churchill
Liddell
Cholmondeley
Cox
D'aeth
Willis
Vilett
Manners
Gibbs
Egerton
Moreshead
Maynard
Milles *mi.*
Knott
Turner *mi.*
Lynch
Emly
Randolph

3rd Form.

Dighton
Ld. G. Gordon
Bartelott
Ford

Holbourne
Ross *ma.*
Lewis
Hall *ma.*
Curtis *ma.*
Vanderpool
Pemberton
Mr. Villiers
Gally
Jones's 2
Ross *mi.*
Young
Skene
Talbott *mi.*
Jones
Elvin *ma.*
Loft
Parker
Hesse
Mapp
Brookes
Mott
Ld. Clinton
Hornby
Barry
Hall *mi.*
Cotes
Husbands
Stanley
Boscawen
Hawkins
Harding
Saunders
Whitehorn
Wilkinson
Hayes
Northey
Hoblyn
Simmons
Cooke
Calvert
Barton
Martyr
Webb
Baker
Bridges
Reese
Thomas

Pelham
Owen
. . . .
Townley
Kynaston
Mr. Grimston
Raynsford
Hatch
Delancey
Ashton
Cooke
Charters *ma.*
Barrington
Ld. Roose
Cheshire
Constant
Danby
Milbank
Blagrove
Jervis
Arabin
Backwell
Dawson
Finch
Smith
Irvin
Festin
Sparkes
Wades 2
Moore
Ellis
Edwards
Grenville *mi.*
Blake
. . . .
Ld. Chewton
Brown
Chichester
Ld. Lumley
Mr. Clinton
Duke Hamilton
Burgh
Keene
Pott
Garrick *ma.*
Rice
Watts
Collier

Ripley
Ellison
Mr. Waldegrave
Tunstall
Mr. Berkeley
Brookland
Key
Charters
Webley
Bishop
Darolles
Smith
Drake *ma.*
Macpherson
Stone
. . . .
Drake *mi.*
South
Mr. Townsend
Townsend
Praed *mi.*
Baker
Adamson
Knowles *ma.*
Pigott
Nibbs
Smith
Wood
Rowles
Reid
Knowles *mi.*
Tufnell
Roberts
Calley
Dawson
Garforths 2
Corbet
Mr. Byron
Plummer
Champain C.
Newland C.
Morris [C.]
Foster [C.]
Leigh C.
Hill C.
Lucas
Darby *ma.*
Thompson

Pottinger
. . . .
Lewis
Massey
Monck
Burslem
Rowe
Cecil
Cartwright
Cole
Cooke

2nd Form.

Wilson
Croft
Beauchamp *
Willis
Woodroffe *mi.*
Pollard *ma.*
Morant
Ld. Binning
Thorp
Ld. Douglass
Gibson
Rice
Burrell
Harding *ma.*
Cutler
Best
Doughty
Lorraines 2
Festin
Anderson
Colthurst
Sr. G. Beaumont
Darby *mi.*
Lewis
Husbands
Warburton
Brookland
Harding *mi.*
Nares
Peirce
Irish
Richardson
Chute

Byam
Pollard *mi.*
Paxton
Stevens
Seaton
Mr. Clive
Lloyd
Davis
Gibbons *mi.*
Dutton *mi.*
Ottley
Allen
Wigsell C.
Lemoine
Earl
Simons
Feesey
Thompson
Yeamans 2

1st Form.

Cooke
Carket
Kingscote
Collier
Molineaux
Mr. Monson
Piggott
Wilkes
Boyfield C.
Knowles *min.*
Harrison
Elvin *mi.*
Garrick *mi.*
Lark C.
Croft
Best *mi.*
Knowles
Harding
Douglass
Dampier
Mr. Manners
Mr. Clinton
Mr. Townsend
Newman
Gregory

Pott
Seymours 2
Keppell
Rowland
Reads 2
Sampson
Delavaux

Oxendon
Reeves
Taylor
Darby *min.*
Cooke [513]
[? Arden]

AUG. 1765.

Provost.	6 form.
Dr. Sleech	Orde C.
	Crownfield C.
V. Provost.	Cooke *ma.* C.
	Highmoor C.
Dr. Burton	Hare C.
	A'Court
	Hayter *ma.* C.
Fellows.	Layng C.
	Davidson C.
Dr. Ashton	Dampier *ma.* C.
Dr. Cooke	Leycester *ma.* C.
Mr. Hethrington	Parr C.
Dr. Lyne	James C.
Mr. Southernwood	Sumner C.
Dr. Apthorp	Mr. Damer
	Spence
	De Grey
Masters.	Mole
	Prime
Upper Dr. Bernard	Turner *ma.*
Lower Dr. Dampier	Price
	Finch
	Sargent *ma.*
Assistants.	
	5 form.
Mr. Graham	
Mr. Foster	Brougham C.
Mr. Roberts	Sheppard C.
Mr. Davis	Topping C.
Mr. Heath	Hayter *mi.* C.
	Hill
Mr. Prior	Hanbury
Mr. Sleech	Foulkes C.
Mr. Norbury	Greathead
Mr. Ekins	Palmer
Mr. Edwards	Ingles C.

Jackson C.
Amyand
Fulham
Hume
Mr. Irby *ma.*
Tomkyns C.
Foster C.
Browning C.
Mr. Conway
Hudson
Woolcombe *ma.*
. . . .
Cave
Ld. Cranborne
Parsons
Williams
Poyntz
Dodwell
Wilson C.
Willmott *max.*
Praed *ma.*
Vincent
Sargent *mi.*
Buckeridge
Johnson
. . . .
Sparkes C.
Digby
Pointer C.
Talbot *ma.*
Long
Mr. Monckton
Baker *ma.*
Cleeve C.
Hulse
H. Williams
Nisbet
White
Strode
Gibbons *ma.*
Pote C.
Johns
Hunter *ma.*
Ricketts
Phipps
Whish C.
Aubery
Longley

Johnson C.
Pulteney C.
Dymoke
Jenner
. . . .
Prideaux
Hunter *ma.* C.
Hoare
Holbeche
James
Gore
Leycester *mi.* C.
Neville
Wyndham
Savage
Frankland
Jefferson
Green
Salkeld C.
Athill
Doughty
Ld. Malpas
Weston
Spencer C.
Woodroffe *ma.*
Martin
Smith C.
Mr. Grimston *ma.*
Penn C.
Dimsdale
Haynes
Stanhope
Kerrick
Grenville *ma.*
Carlyon
Brown
Ashwood

Remove.

Isted
Young *ma.*
Pool
Birt
Mr. Irby *mi.*
Anthony C.
Neve
Cameron

Hunter *mi.*
Inglis
Custance
Milles *ma.*
Woolcombe *mi.* C.
Fleet C.
Maule C.
Trapier
Plummer *ma.*
Hughes
Jefferies
Willis *ma.*
Mr. Mountague
Gough
Skeete
Crofts
Dalrymple
Johnson
Winnington
Sr. W. Loraine
Mr. Montague
Southcote
Holt

---

4 form.

Kelly *ma.*
Tredcroft
Rashleigh
Payler
Metham
Halliday
Grymes
Redwood
Budworth
Mr. Strangeways
Baker
Wilson C. [? O.]
Thorold
Baker
Kelly *mi.*
Sr. Mich. Fleming
Dutton *ma.*
Wharton
Skelton
Vincent
Campbell

Cotes
Munday
Pigott
Mr. Aylmer
Williams
Taylor
Baker ×
Folkes
Cary
Heaths 2
Webster
Churchill
Cholmondeley
Cox
D'aeth
Vilett
Manners
Egerton
Gibbs C.
Maynard
Milles *mi.*
Mr. Fortescue
Knott
Turner *mi.*
Lynch
Ld. Windsor
Tickles 2
Grady
Emly C.
Randolph C.
Cornwall
Andrews
Plumtre
Lewis *ma.*
Dighton
Ld. G. Gordon
Bartelott
Ford
Holbourne
Ross *ma.*
Lewis *ma.*
Hall *ma.*
Vanderpool
Pemberton
Mr. Villiers
Galley
Jones's 2
Ross *mi.*

Skeene
Talbot *mi.*
Newland C.
Morris C.
Elvin
Loft
Parker
Hesse
Mapp
Brooks
Ld. Clinton
Wentworth
Pool
Purvis
Barton
. . . .
Mr. Arbuthnott
Hanbury
Young
Hornby
Hayes
Husbands
Boscawen
Cotes
Hawkins
Harding
Hoblyn
Simmons
Wilkinson
Barry
Eden
Cooke
Barton
Forster C.
Bridges
Stanley
Owen
Thomas
Pelham
Hall *mi.*
Froud
Foyster
Northey
Whitehorne
Calvert
Martyr
Webb
Greathead

Willmott *ma.*
Davenant
Milles *min.*
Mr. Ward
Sr. T. Clarges
Hunter
Brown

------

3 form.

Reese
Townley
Kynaston
Mr. Grimston *mi.*
Raynsford
Cooke *mi.*
Ashton
Delancey
Charters *ma.*
Barrington
Ld. Roose
Danby
Cheshyre *ma.*
Blagrove
Finch
Backwell
Smith
Leigh C.
Irvin
Sparkes
Wades 2
Moor
Ellis
Grenville *mi.*
Hatch
Edwards
Dawson
Milbank
. . . .
Jarvis
Festin *ma.* C.
Arabin
D. Hamilton
Ld. Lumley
Burgh
Keene
Pott *ma.*

Ripley
Brown
Chichester
Garrick *ma.*
Watts
Collier *ma.*
Tunstall
Ellison C.
Dayrolles
Bishop *ma.*
Smith
Stone
Grape
Mr. Clinton
Mr. Waldegrave
Key
Charters *mi.*
Henniker
Mr. Stanley *ma.*
Wood
Forest
Sr. Ch. Watson
. . . .
Rice
Brookland *ma.*
Webley
Drake *ma.*
Mr. Berkeley
Lewis *mi.*
Mr. Walpole
Drake *mi.*
South
Mr. Townsend *ma.*
Baker
Townsend
Adamson
Reid *ma.*
Knowles *ma.*
Roberts
Garthforths 2
Plummer *mi.*
Lucas C.
Darby
Pigott
Rowles
Corbett
Mr. Stanley *mi.*
Praed *mi.*

Thompson
Pottinger
Calley
Mr. Hanger
Mr. Grimston *min.*
Tufnell
Mr. Byron
Smith
Campbell
Rice
. . . .
Pollard *ma.*
Mr. Hyde
Willis *mi.*
Colthurst
Sr. Davd. Carnegie
Beauchamp
Ld. Douglass
Dawson
Knowles *mi.*
Anderson
Lorraines 2
Woodroffe *mi.*
Cecil
Doughty
Sr. G. Beaumont
Nibbs
Cornwalls 2
Cheshyre *mi.*
Hill [C.]
Cole
Burslem C.
Mr. Fortescues 2
Massey
Ireland
Trower *ma.*
Willmotts 2
. . . .
Wilson
Reid *mi.*
Weller *ma.*
Carkett
Lewis *mi.*
Shard *ma.*
Rowe
Morant
Gibson
Burrell

Hopkins
Cutler
Lewis
Husbands *mi.*
Warburton
Festin *mi.* C.
Irish
Richardson
Seaton
Paxton
Stevens
Mr. Clive
Dutton *mi.*
Williams
Nares
Thorp
Brookland *mi.*
Mr. Monson *ma.*
Mr. Watsons 2
. . . .
Buxton
Ackland *ma.*
Lutterel
Davis
Ogleby
Brown
Salter
Leigh
Carew
Moore
Dobbs

----

2 form.

Best
Jones
Harding *ma.*
Chute
Pierce
Byam
Harding *mi.*
Pollard *mi.*
Lloyd
Davis
Gibbons *mi.*
Ottley
Cartwright

Donaland
Way
Earle
. . . .
Wigsell C.   .
Lark C.
Baker
Weller *mi.*
Molineux
Johnston
Lemoine
Simons
Yeamans
Cooke *min.*
Delavaux
Pigott
Pott *mi.*
Rowlands 2
Collyer *mi.*
Kingscote
Wilkes
Sampson
Knowles *min.*
Reeves C.
Seymour *ma.*
Shard *mi.*
Harrison
Croft
Talbott
Heywood
Mr. Townsend
Knowles
Seymour *mi.*

----

1 form.

Newman
Forrest
Gregory
Oxendon
Best *mi.*
Dampier *mi.*
Ld. Graham
Hatch
Pott
Baker
Monk

Taylor

Cooke *mi.*

Keppell

Garrick *mi.*

Bishop *mi.*

Bishop *min.*

Trower *mi.*

Mr. Manners

Mr. Monson *mi.*

Mr. Monson *min.*

Simeon

Douglass

Reid *ma.*

Reid *mi.*

Reid *min.*

Hall *mi.*

Aclands 2

Paxton [? Pogson]

Parker

Beckwith

Croft *mi.*

Johnston

Wogan

Ellis

Parker

Saunders

6	23	
5	92	272
Rem.	31	
4	126	
3	166	
2	46	250
1, &c.	38	
	522	

The number at Xtmas 1765 was 527.

A LIST OF ETON SCHOOL,
ELECTION 1766.

The Provost.
Dr. Barnard

The V. Provost.
Dr. Burton

The Fellows.

Dr. Ashton
Dr. Cooke
Dr. Lyne
Mr. Hetheringtn.
Mr. Southernwd.
Dr. Apthorpe

Upper Master.
Dr. Foster

Lower Master.
Dr. Dampier

Assistants.

Mr. Graham
Mr. Roberts
Mr. Davis
Mr. Heath
Mr. Edwards
Mr. Sleech
Mr. Norbury
Mr. Prior
Mr. Langford
Mr. Hawtrey

The 6th Form C.

Layng
Davison
Dampier
Leycester
Parr
James
Sumner
Brougham
Sheppard
Topping
Hayter
Inglis
Tomkins

The Fifth Form C.

Foster
Browning
Wilson
Poynter
Pote
Whish
Johnson
Poulteney
Leycester
Savage
Salkeild
Spencer
Smith
Anthony
Woolcomb
Fleet
Maule
Holt
Stanhope
Gibbs

Remove Coll.

Emley
Randolph
Newland
Morris

The 4th Form C..

Forster *mi.*
Leigh
Froud
Charters *ma.*
Ellison
Charters *mi.*

The 3d Form C.

Beauchamp
Burslem
Reeves
Hill
Wigsell
Larke
Simons

2nd F. { Sampson / Monk }

1st F. Ellis

The 6th Form Op.

Mole
Mr. Irby *ma.*
Hudson
Woolcomb
Poyntz
Wilmott
Praid
Sargent

The 5th Form.

Buckeridge
Johnson

Hulse
Hanbury
White
Hunter *ma.*
John's
Phipps
Longley
Aubury
Prideaux
Holbech
Gore
Neville
Frankland
Doughty
Weston
Woodroffe
Mr. Grimstone *ma.*
Grenville
Carlyon
Ashwood

Isted
Gough
Young
Pool
Birt
Mr. Irby *mi.*
Hunter *mi.*
Custance
Mills *ma.*
Plummer
Hughes
Jeffries
Willis
Mr. Montague
Skeete
Dalrimple
Johnson
Sr. Wm. Loraine

Piggot
Budworth
Mr. Strangways
Wilson
Dutton
Wharton
Vincent
Campbell

K

Cotes
Munday
Piggot
Mr. Aylmer
Williams
Cholmondeley
Baker
Foulk's
Cary
Webster
Churchill
Sutton
Egerton
Maynard
Mills *mi.*
Mr. Fortescue
Nott [Knott]
Turner
Lynch
Grady
Ld. Windsor
Tickles 2
Ford
Vanderpool
Pemberton
Mr. Villiers
Gally
Freeman
Manners

The Remove, Op.

Thorold
Baker
Ld. Clinton
Andrew
Cornwall
Plumptre
Lewis
Bartelot
Dighton
Holbourn
Lewis
Hall *ma.*
Jones's 2
Ross
Talbot

Lofft
Wentworth
Pool
Purvis
Barton
Harris
Davenant
Browne
Simcoe
Young
Hornby
Pemeroy [Pomeroy]

4th Form Oppts.

Mr. Arbuthnot
Mr. Ward
Sr. Thos. Clarges
Hay's
Husbands
Cotes
Boscawen
Hawkins
Harding
Butler
Hoblin
Simmons
Barry
Eden
Barton
Brydges
Thomas
Hall *mi.*
Stanley
Owen
Northy
Whitehorn
Calvert
Martyr
Webb
Greatheed
Mills *min.*
Sleech
Fitzhurbert

Ld. Roos
Mr. Grimstone

Reese
Townley
Kynaston
Rainsford
Cooke
Delancy
Barrington
Danby
Chesshyre
Blagrove
Finch
Backwell
Smith
Irvin
Sparke
Wades 2
Ellis
Grenville
Hatch
Dawson
Milbank
Shubrick
Lewis

D. Hamilton
Ld. Lumley
Mr. Stanley
Mr. Clinton
Ld. Middle[ton]
Sr. Chas. W[atson]¹
Burgh
Keen
Pott
Ripley
Chicester
Garrick
Watts
Collyer
Stone
Wood
Hanniker
Bishop *ma.*
Dayrolls
Jarvis
Grape
Key
Forrest *ma.*

Lewis
Bramston
Rotherforth
Topham
Bagnall
Batiscombe
Ennis
Stricland
Hayter
Hare

The 3d Form Op.

Rice
Brookland *ma.*
Webley
Mr. Walpole
Mr. Townsend
Mr. Berkeley
Adamson
Garforths 2
Plummer
Piggot
Mr. Stanley
Thomson
Mr. Hanger
Mr. Grimstone [*mi.*]
Tuffnell
Ireland
South
Baker
Knowles
Roberts
Darby
Rowles
Praid
Cally
Rice
Fanshawe
Mr. Byron
Mr. Broderick
Mr. FitzWilliams

Corbett
Smith
Pottenger

¹ The paper has been torn here.

Pollard *ma.*
Mr. Hyde
Willis
Colthurst
Ld. Douglas
Loraines 2
Doughty
Campbell
Nibbs
Cornwalls 2
Wilmotts 2
Trower
Hand
Powell *ma.*
Sr. D. Larnige [Carnegie]
Anderson
Woodroffe
Cecil
Sr. Geo. Beaumo*t.*
Chesshyre
Mr. Fortescue
Ogilvy
Moore
Lewis
——— —— ———
Davison
Cole
Carew
Wilson
Weller
Carkett
Dutton
Shard *ma.*
Cutler
Richardson
Rowe
Paxton
Brookland *mi.*
Mr. Monson [*ma.*]
Mr. Watson's 2
Lewis
Mr. Clive
Reed
Lewis
Fahies's 2
Egerton
Husbands
Warburton

Downing
Morant
Gibson
Burrell
Stevens
Irish
Powell
Best [*ma.*]
Acland
Lutterell
——— —— ——
Buckeridge
Campbell
Hopkins
Williams
Thorpe
Simeon
Harding
Peirse
Cartwright
Donnellan
Earle
Wey
Hinchley
Davis's 2
Dobbs
Gibbons
Verdon
Monk
Mr. Cathcart
———————
Cooke
Wool'y
Leigh
Buckston
Jones
Chute
Ottley
Baker
Lloy'd
Browne
Wingfeild
Byam
Molineaux
Weller
Lemoine
Yeamons
Coke

Delavaux
Pott
Rowlands
Wilkes
Shard *mi.*
Ld. Graham
Harding
Croftes
Mr. Vaughan
Brice

Unplaced.

Frere
Parriot
Parker
Mills
Jarvis
Milner
Taylor
Mitcham
Hervey
Barno [Barlow]
O'Brien
Hill
Cruttenden
Woodhouse
Barstard *ma.*

The 2nd Form.

Pollard *mi.*
Twigg
Buckley
Johnson
Knowles
Collyer
Blagrove
Salter
Kingscoat
Harrison
Talbott
Heywood
Mr. Townshend
Oxendon
Forrest *mi.*

Gregory
Newman
Dampier *mi.*
Johns *mi.*
Pott
Trower
Bishop *mi.*
Norbury
Hatch
Knowles
Mr. Monson *mi.*
Garrick *mi.*
Praid
Aclands 2
Cooke
Mr. Manners
Best *mi.*
Douglas
Simeon
Montgomery
Bishop *min.*
Shubrick
Baker
Buck
Buckeridge
Mr. Villiers

The 1st Form Op.

Saunders
Pogson
Hall *min.*
Butler
Cotterell
Chamberlayne
Manning
Brereton
Parker *ma.*
Langrishe
Mr. Monson
Parker
Beby
Gascoine
Beckwith
Angelo
Shuvet [Chauvet]
Simpson

Ld. Lindsey
Johnson
Duke
Scudamore
Pott
Croft
Hanson
Luard
Ennis

Holesworth
Barstard *mi.*
Mr. North
Sr. Thos. Carew
Hanbury
Griffith

498 [487]

A BILL OF ETON COLLEGE,
AUGUST 1767.

Provost.

Dr. Barnard

Vice Provost.

Dr. Burton

Fellows.

Dr. Cooke
Dr. Apthorpe
Dr. Ashton
Mr. Hetherington
Mr. Southernwood
Dr. Dampier

Upper Master.

Dr. Foster

Lower Master.

Mr. Sleech

Upper Assistants.

Mr. Roberts
Mr. Edwards
Mr. Davis
Mr. Heath
Mr. Sumner

Lower Assistants.

Mr. Norbury
Mr. Prior
Mr. Hawtry
Mr. Langford
Mr. Jepson

6th Form Collegers.

Inglis
Tomkins
Foster
Browning
Poynter
Pote
Johnston
Pulteney

5th Form Collrs.

Leycester
Savage
Salkeld
Spencer
Smith
Anthony
Woolcombe
Fleet
Maule
Holt
Baker
Stanhope
Gibbs
Emly
Randolph

Morris
Barton
Foster
Froud

Remove & 4th Form
    Collegers.

Charters *ma*.
Leigh
Ellison
Charters *mi*.
Battiscomb
Hayter
Furlow
Ireland
Reeves
Knap
Doughty
Beauchamp

3d Form Collrs.

Buslem [Burslem]
Hinckly
Hill
Simons
Wigsell
Lark
Wooley
Sampson
Monk

2d Form Collrs.

Hanson
Ellis
Simpson

Oppidans
6th Form.

Mr. Irby *ma*.
Wilmot

Sargent
Hulse
Phipps
Aubrey
Longley
Prideaux
Neville
Frankland
Weston
Grenville *ma* .
Young

5th Form Ops.

Poole
Birt
Mr. Irby *mi*.
Milles *ma*.
Jeffreys
Willis *ma*.
Mr. Montagu
Gough
Skeete
Pigot *ma*.
Mr. Strangeways
Dutton *ma*.
Wharton
Vincent
Campbell
Cotes *ma*.
Munday
Pigot *mi*.
Williams
Baker
Webster
Churchill
Cholmondeley
Sutton
Egerton
Maynard
Mills *mi*.
Mr. Fortescue
Turner
Ld. Windsor
Ford
Pemberton
Gally

Freeman
Tickell *ma.*
Tickell *mi.*
Thorold
Andrews
Plumtree
Dighton
Smith
Lewis
Hall *ma.*
Ross
Talbot
Ld. Clinton
Loft
Pole [Pool]
Barton
Purvis
Davenant
Brown
Simcoe
Hornby
Pomeroy
Yates
Hayes
Husbands
Boscawen
Cotes *mi.*
Hawkins
Butler
Hoblyn
Simmons
Barry
Eden
Bridges
Hall *mi.*
Owen
Thomas
Northey
Calvert
Martyr
Webb
Greatheed
Milles *min.*
Mr. Ward
Sr. Thos. Clarges
Choldwich
Sleech
Fitzherbert

Rennels
Hawes

——— ———— ———

Remove Opps.

———

Townley
Kynaston
Mr. Grimston
Cooke
Barrington
Ld. Roos
Danby
Chesshyre
Blagrove
Finch
Backwell
Irving
Sparkes
Wade *ma.*
Wade *mi.*
Ellis
Grenville *mi.*
Dawson
Milbank
Lewis
Shubrick
Lewis
Topham
Ld. Kilwarlin
Cole

4th Form Opps.

———

Duke Hamilton
Ld. Lumley
Mr. Stanley
Ld. Petersham
Ld. Middleton
Sr. Chas. Watson
Mr. Stanhope
Mr. Clinton
Burgh
Keene
Pott
Ripley
Chichester

Garrick
Watts
Collyer [ma.]
Stone
Bramstone
Rutherford
Bagnall
Coward
Wood
Henniker
Jarvis
Bishop
Dayrolles
Grape
Key
Ennys [ma.]
Hare
Strickland
Forrest

Mr. Walpole
Mr. Townshend
Mr. Stanley
Mr. Hanger
Mr. Grimston
Mr. Broderick
Mr. Fitzwilliams
Brookland
Webley
Adamson
Garforth ma.
Garforth mi.
Plumer
Pigot
South
Baker
Knowles
Praed
Roberts
Rowles
Cawley [Calley]
Rice
Fanshaw
Hutchinson
Huger
Walpole
Leonard
Tufnell

Moore
Plumtree
Pomeroy

Mr. Hyde
Sr. David Carnegie
Ld. Douglas
Sr. George Beaumont
Mr. Fortescue
Mr. Fox
Corbet
Smith
Potenger
Pollard
Willis mi.
Colthurst
Wilmot
Powell
Cornwall ma.
Cornwall mi.
Hand
Woodroffe
Moore
Fahie
Cecil
Jacob
Nibbs
Trower
Anderson
Campbell
Pigot
Agar ma.
Lewis
Thompson
Omahara
Featherstone
Petley
Porter

3d Form Opps.

Mr. Fortescue
Lewis
Chessyre
Davison
Cole
Carew

Weller
Carket
Dutton
Shard *ma.*
Rowe
Paxton
Brookland
Mr. Monson [*ma.*]
Mr. Watsons 2
Mr. Clive
Lewis
Husbands
Warburton
Gibson
Burrell
Ackland *ma.*
Luttrell
Manby
Egerton
Taylor
Mr. Waldegrave
Plumbe

Cutler
Richardson
Morant
Powell
Milles
Irish
Buckeridge *ma.*
Simeon *ma.*
Peirse
Gibbons
Monk
Harvey
Mitchel
Freer
Mr. Cathcart [*ma.*]
Campbell
Williams
Scot
Donnellan
Way
Hopkins
Davies
Dobbs
Davis
Walcot

Cartwright
Coote
Harding
Booker
Kynaston
Downing

Otley
Barlow
Leigh
Buxton
Jones
Chute
Wingfield
Coke
Delavaux
Pott
Ld. Graham
Croft
Verdon
Cooke
Weller
Baker
Cooke
Shard *mi.*
Gwyn
Farhill
Woodhouse
Molyneux
Rowlands
Brice
Lloyd
Brown
Parker
Lemoine
Mr. King
Cole
Hayes

Wilkes
Mr. Vaughan
Twigg
Buckley
Collier *mi.*
Mr. Townshend
Butcher

Pott
Johnston
Salter
Kingscoat
Harrison
Talbot
Johnes
Bastard *ma.*
Heywood
Oxendon
Obrien
Ackland *mi.*
Pigot
Harding
Newman

Blagrave
Praed
Forrest
Milner
Jarvis
Smith
Cruttenden
Gregory
Dampier
Shubrick
Pott
Trower
Bishop
Norbury
Chauvet
Hatch
Mr. Monson [*mi.*]
Garrick
Ackland *min.*
Cooke
Phipps
Buck
Hill
Ld. Tullibardin

Unplaced Opps.

Corbet
Llywellyn
Ld. J. Murray

St. Leger
Goodall

2d Form Opps.

Mr. Manners
Mr. Villers
Mr. North
Ld. Lindsey
Baker
Montgomery
Bishop
Best
Butler
Simeon *mi.*
Buckeridge *mi.*
Beeby
Cottrell
Saunders
Douglas
Sr. Thos. Carew

Brereton
Chamberlayne
Fuller
Pogston
Parker
Manning
Griffith
Langrish
Hanbury
Angelo
Mr. Monson [*min.*]
Bastard *mi.*
Scudamore
Beckwith
Fitter
Naylor
Duke *ma.*
Parker
Leward
Simeon
Potts 2
Brown

1st Form Opps.
———

Gascoigne
Ld. Cantaloupe
Mr. West
Mr. Catchcart *mi.*
Croft *mi.*
Duke *mi.*
Coote
Hutchinsons 2
Gunthorpes 2.

St. Legers 3
Melson
Greyhurst
Agar *mi.*
Ennys *mi.*
Coventry
Holdsworth
Neville
Allen
Repkombe
Campbell   469 [474]

A BILL OF ETON COLLEGE,
AUGUST 1768.

Provost.

Dr. Barnard

Vice Provost.

Dr. Burton

Fellows.

Dr. Cooke
Dr. Ashton
Dr. Apthorpe
Mr. Hetherington
Mr. Southernwood
Dr. Dampier

Upper Master.

Dr. Foster

Lower Master.

Mr. Sleech

Upper Assistants.

Mr. Roberts
Mr. Edwards
Mr. Davis
Mr. Heath
Mr. Sumner

Lower Assistants.

Mr. Norbury
Mr. Prior
Mr. Hawtrey
Mr. Jephson
Mr. Langford

Collegers 6th Form.

Pote
Johnston
Pulteney
Leycester
Savage
Smyth
Anthony
Woolcombe
Fleet

5th Form Collrs.

Maule
Holt
Stanhope
Baker
Gibbs
Emly
Randolph
Plumtree
Butler
Barton
Foster
Froud
Rennell
Charters

Leigh
Cole
Reeves
Ellison
Charters
Battiscombe
Hayter
Furlow
Ireland
Knapp

4th Form Collrs.

Beauchamp
Burslem
Paxton
Hinckley
Hill
Simons
Wigsell
Lark

3d Form Collrs.

Wooley
Rowlands
Cole
Sampson
Wilson
Monk
Goodall
Butler
Hanson
Paddy

2d Form Collrs.

Naylor
Duke *ma.*
Simpson
Duke *mi.*

1st Form Collrs.

Berry
Canning

Oppidans 6th Form.

Grenville *ma.*
Milles *ma.*
Willis *ma.*
Mr. Montague
Skeete
Wharton
Vincent
Pigot
Baker

5th Form Opps.

Webster
Cholmondeley
Sutton
Egerton
Milles *mi.*
Maynard
Mr. Fortescue [*ma.*]
Ld. Windsor
Tickell *ma.*
Tickell *mi.*
Gally
Freeman
Andrews
Smith
Loft
Barton
Davenant
Brown
Simcoe
Hayes *ma.*
Husbands *ma.*
Boscawen
Cotes
Hawkins
Hoblyn
Simmons
Eden

Bridges
Calvert
Milles *min.*
Mr. Ward
Sr. Thos. Clarges
Sleech
Fitzherbert
Cholwich
Hawes
Townley
Kynaston
Cooke *ma.*
Mr. Grimston
Barrington
Danby
Cheshire
Ellis
Blagrave [? Blagrove]
Backwell
Sparkes
Grenville *mi.*
Dawson
Shubrick
Topham
Lewis
Ld. Kilwarlin
Lawrence
Delabere
Webb
Ld. Lumley
Keene
Pott
Ripley
Chichester
Garrick *ma.*
Watts
Collier *ma.*
Stone
Mr. Stanley [*ma.*]
Ld. Petersham
Ld. Middleton
Rutherforth
Bagnall
Coward
Wood
Henniker
Jarvis
Dayrolles

Sr. Chas. Watson
Mr. Stanhope
Ennys *ma.*
Strickland
Hare
Key
Willis

———

Remove Opps.

——

Brookland
Webley
Mr. Walpole
Mr. Townsend
Adamson
Garforth *ma.*
Garforth *mi.*
Plumer
Pigott
Mr. Stanley *mi.*
Mr. Hanger
Mr. Grimston
South
Baker
Knowles
Roberts
Rowles *ma.*
Calley
Rice
Fanshaw
Mr. Broderick
Sr. David Carnegie
Cornwall *ma.*
Mr. Fitzwilliams
Hutchinson *ma.*
Moore
Plumtree
Edmonson
Petley
Jenner
Bartelot
Portal
Huger
Leonard

4th Form Opps.
———

Lewis
Corbet *ma.*
Smith
Pollard
Mr. Hyde *ma.*
Willis *mi.*
Colthurst
Wilmot
Powell *ma.*
Doughty
Cornwall *mi.*
Hand
Woodroffe
Moore
Faie [Fahie]
Cecil
Jacob
Nibbs
Trower *ma.*
Anderson
Sr. Geo. Beaumont
Agar *ma.*
Lewis
Thompson
Omeara
Featherston
Galloway

———

Mr. Fortescue *mi.*
Lewis
Chessyre
Davison
Cole
Weller *ma.*
Carket
Dutton
Shard *ma.*
Rowe
Brookland *mi.*
Mr. Monson *ma.*
Mr. Watson *ma.*
Mr. Watson *mi.*
Mr. Clive
Lewis
Husbands *mi.*
Warburton

Gibson
Burrell
Ackland *ma.*
Luttrell
Cutler
Richardson
Manby
Egerton
Taylor
Mr. Waldegrave
Mr. Clinton
Plumbe
Mr. Fox
Sumner
Cator
Fenton
James
Wilson
Rous
Brotherton *ma.*
Gilpin
Cox
Manley
Morant
Powel *mi.*
Best *ma.*
Mills
Irish
Buckeridge *ma.*
Simeon *ma.*
Peirse
Gibbons *ma.*
Monk
Harvey
Mitchell
Frere
Cambell *ma.*
Scott
Way
Davis
Dobbs
Cartwright
Coote *ma.*
Walcot
Hardinge *ma.*
Booker
Kynaston *mi.*
Downing

L

Adam
Mr. Legge
Dyson
Freeman
Snow
Maynard
Fleete
Ld. Ludlow
Leigh
Burgh
Gibbons *mi.*

3d Form Opps.

Donnellan
Otley
Barlow
Leigh
Buxton
Jones
Chute
Wingfield
Coke
Delavaux
Pott
Ld. Graham
Croft *ma.*
Cooke
Weller *mi.*
Baker
J. Cooke
Shard *mi.*
Woodhouse
Molyneux
Brice
Lloyd
Parker
Lemoine
Browne
Mr. King
Hayes *mi.*

Wilkes
Mr. Vaughan
Twigg
Buckley
Collier *mi.*
Blagrave

Mr. Townshend
Johnston
Bastard *ma.*
Johnes
Heywood
Oxendon
Pole
Salter
Kingscoat
Obrien
Pigot
Hardinge
Newman
St. Leger
Newport
Lawry
Walker

Praed
Milner
Jarvis
Smith
Cruttenden
Gregory
Dampier
Pott
Shubrick
Bishop *ma.*
Trower
Norbury
Chavet [Chauvet]
Hatch
Ld. Tullibardin
Mr. Monson *mi.*
Ackland
Cooke
Mr. Phipps
Shutz
Smith
Buck
Jones
Oliver

Mr. Manners
Mr. Villers
Mr. North
Ld. Lindsay
Baker
Montgomery

Bishop *mi.*
Simeon *mi.*
Buckeridge *mi.*
Beeby
Cottrell
Sr. Thos. Carew
Manning
Sanders
Best *mi.*
Milward

Garrick
Brereton
Fuller
Parker
Chamberlayne
Langrishe
Bastard *mi.*
Hanbury
Angelo
Pogston
Mr. Monson [*min.*]
Scudamore
Emblyn
Gascoigne
Estwick
Llewellyn
Skerret
Brotherston *mi.*
Griffith
Newnham

Hodges
Shipton
Hurt
Sheppard
Stratfield
Swinnerton
Rowles *mi.*

2d Form Opps.

Ld. Murray
Beckwith
Fitter
Brown
Leward
Coote *mi.*

Simeon *min.*
Greyhurst
Pott
Corbet *mi.*
Parker
Hutchinson *min.*
Ld. Cantaloupe
Mr. West
Gunthorpe *ma.*
Garforth *min.*
Brown
Lane *ma.*
Croft [*mi.*]
St. Leger
Pott
Gunthorp *mi.*
Hamilton
Holdsworth
St. Leger
Agar *mi.*
Coventry
Nevill
St. Leger
Melson

1st Form Opps.

Campbell
Allen
Ryan
Sparkes
Barrow
Hale
Lane *mi.*
Manby
Langston
Mr. North
Mr. Bennet
Mr. Marsham
Repkombe
Spendlove
Dennis
Scott
Dominiceti
Gordon
Leigh *ma.*
Leigh *mi.*

A BILL OF ETON COLLEGE,
AUGUST 1769.

Provost.

Dr. Barnard

Vice Provost.

Dr. Burton

Fellows.

Dr. Cooke
Mr. Hetherington
Mr. Southernwood
Dr. Apthorpe
Dr. Ashton
Dr. Dampier

Upper Master.

Dr. Foster

Lower Master.

Mr. Sleech

Upper Assistants.

Mr. Roberts
Mr. Edwards
Mr. Davis
Mr. Heath
Mr. Sumner

Lower Assistants.

Mr. Norbury
Mr. Prior
Mr. Jephson
Mr. Hawtry
Mr. Langford

Collegers 6th Form.

Leycester
Savage
Smyth
Woolcombe
Maule
Holt
Stanhope
Baker
Gibbs

5th Form Collrs.

Emly
Randolph
Plumtree
Butler
Barton
Foster
Froud
Rennell
Cooke
Charters
Lee
Cole
Reeves
Ellison

Hayter
Key
Charters
Furlow
Ireland
Knapp
Beauchamp

Remove & 4th Form

Hinkley
Symons
Wigsell
Larke
Fleet
Paddon
Wingfield
Wolley
Cole
Sampson
Wilson

3d Form Collrs.

Monk
Goodall
Butler
Mitchell
Hanson
Paddy
Naylor
Sympson
Hunt

2d Form Collrs.

Duke
Lee
Berry

1st Form Collrs.

Dominiceti
Lee

Oppidans 6th F.

Willis
Wharton
Baker
Sutton
Maynard
Milles
Mr. Fortescue
Ld. Windsor
Freeman
Loft
Davenant

5th Form Opps.

Hayes
Husbands
Boscawen
Eden
Calvert
Webb
Milles
Mr. Ward
Sr. Thos. Clarges
Fitzherbert
Cholwich
Hawes
Kynaston
Barrington
Ld. Roos
Danby
Ellis
Cheshire
Blagrove
Backwell
Grenville
Ld. Kilwarlin
Delabere
Ld. Lumley
Keene
Ripley
Chichester
Garrick
Collier
Stone
Mr. Stanley

Ld. Middleton
Rutherford
Bagnall
Ld. Petersham
Sr. Chas. Watson
Ennys
Strickland
Mr. Stanhope
Willis
Mr. Townshend
Mr. Walpole
Adamson
Garforth *ma.*
Garforth *mi.*
Plumer
Mr. Stanley
Mr. Hanger
Mr. Grimston
South
Baker
Rowles
Calley
Rice
Fanshaw
Sr. David Carnegie
Cornwall
Mr. Broderick
Mr. Fitzwilliams
Hutchinson
Walpole
Moore
Plumptree
Edmondson
Jenner
Bartelot
Welsh
Corbet
Smith
Pollard
Mr. Hyde
Willis
Colthurst
Wilmot
Doughty
Cornwall
Hand
Woodroffe
Faye [Fahie]

Cecil
Jacob
Sr. George Beaumont
Agar
Omara
Featherston
Galloway
Tripe
Portal
Ward

—

Remove Opps.

Anderson
J. Lewis
H. Lewis
Cheshire
Davison
Mr. Clive
Weller
Carkett
Dutton
Mr. Monson
Mr. Watson *ma.*
Mr. Watson *mi.*
Husbands
Gibson
Burrell
Ackland
Luttrell
Manby
Egerton
Taylor
Mr. Waldegrave
Ld. J. Clinton
Plumb
Mr. Fox
Cator
Fenton
Gilpin
Wilson
Rous
Paterson
Booker
Clapp

4th Form Opps.

———

Warburton
Sumner
Cox
Manley
Cutler
Richardson
Morant
Powell
Best
Irish
Buckeridge
Simeon
Peirse
Gibbons
Monk
Harvey
Mitchell
Freer
Scott
Way
Davies
Dobbs
Coote
Walcot
Harding
Kynaston
Adam
Mr. Legge
Dyson
Maynard
Snow
Ld. Ludlow
Lee
Luxmore
Thoroton
Otley
Barlow
Leigh
Buxton
Jones
Chute
Coke
Delavaux
Pott
Ld. Graham
Croft

Cooke
Weller
Baker
J. Cooke
Woodhouse
Molineux
Brice
Lloyd
Parker
Lemoine
Browne
Hayes
Luxmore
Stewart
Colby
Battine
Andrew

———

Gibbons
Sutton
Donnellan
Wilkes
Mr. Vaughan
Twigg
Collier
Blagrave
Mr. Townshend
Johnson
Bastard
Johnes
Heywood
Oxendon
Pole
Newport
Kingscoat
Obrien
Hardinge
St. Leger
Lawrie
Swinerton
Newman
Maynard
Walpole
Hawkins
John
Haggit
Lowndes
Burton

3d Form Opps.
————

Horton	Barnard
Praed	Amyatt
Milner	Saunderson
Jarvis	Wells
Smyth	Raper
Gregory	————
Monk	Garrick
Dampier	Brereton
Pott	Fuller
Shubrick	Parker
Trower	Langrishe
Bishop	Bastard
Norbury	Hanbury
Chauvet	Angelo
Ld. Tullibardin	Mr. Monson
Hatch	Scudamore
Mr. Monson	Brotherson
Ackland	Wilmot
Buck	Emblyn
Jones	Gascoigne
Oliver	Estwick
Bosanquet	Llewellyn
Dury	Pogson
Rives *ma.*	Skerrit
Rives *mi.*	Griffith
Robinson	Newnham
Musgrave	Kynaston
Mr. Broderick	Hodges
Wright	St. Leger
	Hutchinson
	Molesworth
Mr. Manners	Dodd
Mr. Villers	Hurt
Mr. North	Beckwith
Ld. Lindsey	Fitter
Baker	Browne
Montgomery	Coote
Bishop	Greyhurst
Simeon	Gunthorp
Buckeridge	Simeon
Beeby	Pott
Cottrell	Lane
Sr. Thos. Carew	Ld. Cantaloupe
Manning	Mr. West
Talbot	Duke
Saunders	Saunders
Milward	Hawkins
Shipton	

O'Connor
Ld. Murray
Croft
Pott
Gunthorpe
Hamilton
Holdsworth
St. Leger
Agar
Hale
Grimston
Stratfield
Mr. Walpole
Hume

Unplaced.

Pack
Chafei
Woodhouse

2d Form Opps.

Rowles
St. Leger
Neville
Melson
Allen
Sparke
Ryan
Pratt

Coventry
Langston

Barrow
Townshend
Mr. Marsham

1st Form Opps.

Lane
Dennis
Daxton [Daxon]
Repkombe
Buckeridge
Mr. Villers
Mr. North
Mr. Monson
Mr. Bennet
Cooke
Prince
Bagnall
Trustler
Scott
Manby
Gordon
Wyatt
Roberts
Ashton
Blackwell
Brown
Gee   423 [424]

A BILL OF ETON COLLEGE,
AUGUST 1770.

Provost.

Dr. Barnard

Vice Provost.

Dr. Burton

Fellows.

Dr. Cooke
Dr. Apthorpe
Dr. Ashton
Mr. Hetherington
Mr. Southernwood
Dr. Dampier

Upper Master.

Dr. Foster

Lower Master.

Mr. Sleech

Upper Assistants.

Mr. Roberts
Mr. Edwards
Mr. Davis
Mr. Heath
Mr. Sumner

Lower Assistants.

Mr. Jepson
Mr. Norbury
Mr. Prior
Mr. Langford
Mr. Hawtrey

Collegers 6th Form

Holt
Baker
Gibbs
Emly *ma.*
Stanhope
Randolph
Plumptree *ma.*
Butler *ma.*
Foster
Barton
Froud
Reynell

5th Form Coll.

Cook *ma.*
Charters *ma.*
Cole
Reeves
Ellison
Hayter
Key
Charters *mi.*
Knapp
Beauchamp
Ward

Portall
Hinckley
Cutler
Scott *ma.*
Fleet

Remove Collrs.

Wigsell
Paddon
Wingfield
Wooley
Cole
Luxmore
Andrew

4th Form Coll.

Sampson
Haggitt
Goodall
Monk
Emly *mi.*
Lowndes
Butler *mi.*
Mitchell

3d Form Col.

Hanbury
Maule
Simpson
Naylor
Chafie
Duke
Sparke
Bury
Dominiceti

2d Form Coll.

Scott *mi.*
Leigh

1st Form Col.

Draper

Oppidans 6th Fo.

Hayes *ma.*
Boscawen
Eden
Calvert
Milles
Fitzherbert
Hawes
Kynaston *ma.*
Barrington
Ld. Roos
Danby

5th Form Op.

Ellis
Backwell
Leigh
Grenville [*ma.*]
Ld. Kilwarlin
Delabere
Ld. Lumley
Keene
Ripley
Garrick *ma.*
Mr. Stanley *ma.*
Ld. Middleton
Bramston
Rutherford
Bagnall
Ennis
Mr. Stanhope
Mr. Walpole *ma.*
Mr. Townshend *ma.*
Adamson
Garforth
Plumer
Mr. Stanley *mi.*
Mr. Grimston
South

Baker
Calley
Rice
Fanshaw
Mr. Broderick [ma.]
Hutchinson ma.
Walpole ma.
Sr. H. Moore
Edmonstone
Jenner
Welch
Pollard
Corbet
Mr. Hyde
Willis
Colthurst
Wilmot
Doughty
Cornwall
Hand
Woodroffe
Cecil
Jacob
Featherston
Tripe
Weller [ma.]
H. Lewis
Chessyre
Davison
Dutton
Mr. Monson ma.
Mr. Watson ma.
Mr. Watson mi.
Mr. Clive
Husbands
Gibson
Burrell
Luttrell
Manby
Egerton
Taylor
Mr. Waldegrave
Ld. Jo. Clinton
Fenton
Wilson
Rous
Booker
Clapp

H. Lewis
Mr. Fox
Warburton
Sumner
Manley
Richardson
Morant
Powell
Irish
Buckeridge ma.
Simeon ma.
Best
Peirse
Gibbons ma.
Monk
Hervey
Mitchell
Frere
Way
Davis
Dobbs
Coote
Walcot
Harding
Kynaston [mi.]
Mr. Legge
Dyson
Maynard [ma.]
Snow
Ld. Ludlow
Luxmore
Thoroton
Vansittart
Elton

Remove Opps.

Otley
Buxton
Coke
Delavaux
Pott ma.
Ld. Graham
Croft ma.
Cooke
Weller mi.
Baker

J. Cooke

Woodhouse *ma.*

Brice

Parker

Hayes *mi.*

Stewart

Battine

Shelley

Lemoine

4th Form Opps.

Brown

Donnellan

Mr. Vaughan

Twigg

Collier

Blagrove [? Blagrave]

Mr. Townshend *mi.*

Johnston

Bastard *ma.*

Johnes

Heywood

Gibbons *mi.*

Oxendon

Poole

Newport

Obrien

Harding *mi.*

St. Leger [*ma.*]

Lawrie

Swinnerton

Maynard *mi.*

Walpole *mi.*

John

Mitchell *ma.*

Burton

Præd

Jarvis

Smith *ma.*

Gregory

Dampier

Pott *mi.*

Shubrick

Trower

Bishop *ma.*

Norbury

Chauvet

Ld. Tullibardin

Hatch

Mr. Monson *mi.*

Ackland

Coke

Mr. Phipps *ma.*

Schutz

Smith *mi.*

Buck

Johnes

Oliver

Bosanquet

Dury

Rives *ma.*

Rives *mi.*

Robinson

Musgrave

Mr. Broderick *mi.*

Menzies

Fowkes

Mathews

Nourse

Rastall

Lutterell

Mr. Manners

Mr. Villers *ma.*

Mr. North *ma.*

Ld. Lindsay

Baker

Montgomery

Bishop *mi.*

Simeon *mi.*

Buckeridge *mi.*

Beeby

Cottrell

Sr. Tho. Carew

Manning

Talbot

Saunders

Millward

Shipton

Bernard

Amyat

Saunderson

Wells *ma.*

Raper
Townshend
Colthurst
Calvert
Mr. Lumley *ma.*
Hayes *min.*

_____

3rd Form Op.

Garrick *mi.*
Burton
Scudamore
Fuller
Langrish
Bastard *mi.*
Angelo
Mr. Monson *min.*
Brotherson
Wilmot
Gascoigne
Estwick
Pogson
Griffith
Newnham
Kynaston *min.*
Hodges
St. Leger *mi.*
Hutchinson *mi.*
Molesworth
Grenville *mi.*
Brown
Parris

_____

Dodd
Hurt
Beckwith
Fitter
Coote *mi.*
Greyhurst
Gunthorpe *ma.*
Simeon *min.*
Pott
Lane *ma.*
Ld. Cantaloupe
Mr. West
Brown
Hutchinson *min.*

Saunders
Hawkins
Edwards

_____

O'Connor
Croft *mi.*
Pott *min.*
Duke
Gunthorpe *mi.*
Hamilton
Holdsworth
St. Leger *mi.*
Agar
Hale
Grimston
Stratfield
Mr. Walpole *mi.*
Lee
Goodall
Hennington
Woodhouse *mi.*
Nourse
Mitchell

_____

Mr. Lumley *mi.*
Mr. Lumley *min.*
Hume
Rolles
St. Leger *min.*
Neville
Allen
Ryan
Langston
Birch
Pratt
Mitchell

_____

Thorp
Barrow
Mr. Marsham
Townshend
Pack
Tollfree

_____

2d Form Opp.

Mr. Villers [*mi.*]

Lane [*mi.*]
Prince
Wyatt
Buckeridge *min.*
Browne
Daxon

Roberts
Repkombe
Manby
Scott
Dennis
Bagnall
Mr. Bennet
Manning *mi.*
Tickell
Wells *mi.*
Ashton
Mr. North *mi.*

1st Form Opp.

Sr. John Ladd
Cook
Gee
St. Leger
Gordon
Mr. Monson
Wells *min.*
Blackwell
Manby
Hurd
Boddam

Unplaced.

Cooksey
Sauberg
Wright
Wheeley [? Whaley]
Shipphard   [391]

1771.

Provost.

Dr. Barnard

Vice Provost.

Dr. Apthorpe

Fellows.

Dr. Ashton
Dr. Cooke
Dr. Dampier
Mr. Southernwood
Mr. Roberts
Mr. Betham

Upper Master.

Dr. Forster

Lower Master.

Mr. Sleech

Upper Assistants.

Mr. Edwards
Mr. Davis
Mr. Heath
Mr. Sumner
Mr. Cooke

Lower Assistants.

Mr. Norbury
Mr. Prior
Mr. Hawtrey
Mr. Langford

Sixth form Collegers.

Randolph
Plumtree *ma.*
Butler *ma.*
Barton
Foster
Frowd
Rennell
Cooke *max.*
Charters
Cole *ma.*
Reeves
Ellison
Hayter

5th form Collegers.

Key
Knapp
Plumtree *mi.*
Hand
Woodroofe
Beaucham[p]
Jacob
Ward
Portall
Hinckley
Manby

Cutler
Simons
Scott *ma.*
Kynaston
Fleet
Wigsel
Padden
Wingfield
De la Veaux
Cole *mi.*
Luxmore
Andrew
Sampson
Haggit

Remove Collegers.

Emly
Goodall *ma.*
Butler *mi.*
Lowndes

4th form Collegers.

Mitchell
Hanbury
Kynaston
Sheppard
Smith
Maule
Simpson
Chaffie

Lower School,
Collegers 3d form.

Naylor
Duke
Berry
Sparke
Dominicetti
Tolfrie
Scot *mi.*
Wright

2d form Collegers.

Lee
Draper
Trusler

1st form Colleger.

Kirk

Sixth form Oppidans.

Ld. Granby
Greenville *ma.*
Garrick *ma.*
Ld. Midleton
Bramston
Rutherforth
Garforth
Plummer
South
Mr. Brodrick *ma.*
Hutchinson *ma.*
Walpole *ma.*
Jenner
Welch
Pollard

5th form Oppidans.

Corbet
Willis
Wilmot [*ma.*]
Doughty
Cornwall
Fetherston
Blount
Cheshire
Davison
Weller *ma.*
Mr. Watson *ma.*
Mr. Watson *mi.*
Gibson
Egerton
Taylor
Mr. Waldegrave

M

Booker
Warburton
Sumner
Manly
Richardson
Morant
Irish
Simeon
Best [ma.]
Gibbons ma.
Monk
Mitchell
Way
Davis
Coote ma.
Hardinge ma.
Mr. Legge
Dyson
Maynard ma.
Snow
Ld. Ludlow
Thoroton
Elton
Otley
Coke
Pott max.
Ld. Graham
Croft max.
Cooke ma.
Weller mi.
Woodhouse ma.
Baker
Parker
Hayes
Stewart
Batten
Mr. Vaughn
Collier
Blagrave
Mr. Townsend
Bastard
Johnes
Heywood
Pole
Newport
Hardinge mi.
St. Leger max.
Lawry

Swinnerton
Maynard mi.
Walpole mi.
Skeeles
Matthews
Nourse
Rastall
Lemoine

Remove.

Brown ma.
Gibbons mi.
Oxenden
Praed
Mitchell
Pott ma.
Dampier
Trower
Bishop ma.
Norbury
Hatch
Mr. Monson ma.
Acland
Cooke mi.
Mr. Phipps ma.
Schutz
Smith
Buck
Jones
Oliver
Bosanquet
Rives ma.
Rives mi.
Robinson ma.
Musgrave
Mr. Brodrick mi.
Menzies
Luttrell
Beevor ma.
Beevor mi.

4th form Oppidans.

Burton
Jervis

Dury
Mr. Manners
Mr. Villers *ma.*
Mr. North [*ma.*]
Ld. Lindsey
Baker
Montgomery
Bishop *mi.*
Buckerid[g]e
Beeby
Cottrell
Gregory
Sr. Th. Carew
Manning
Talbot
Saunders
Milward
Barnard
Amyatt
Saunderson
Wells [*ma.*]
Raper
Townsend
Colthurst
Calvert
Mr. Lumley *ma.*
Hayes
Longmore

———————

Garrick [*mi.*]
Brereton
Fuller
Bastard
Angelo
Mr. Monson *mi.*
Wilmot *mi.*
Gascoyne
Llewellyn
Griffith
Molesworth
Grenville *mi.*
Browne *mi.*
Patterson
Robinson [*mi.*]
Hutchinson [*mi.*]
Hodges
Paris
Smith
Whelpdale

Gouldburne
Beevor *min.*
Walton
Waite
Pemberton
Dupuis
Newnham
Scudamore
Pogson
Dauvert
Oldmeadow
Dodd
Beckwith
Coote *mi.*
Gunthorpe *ma.*
Simeon
Pott *mi.*
Lane
Ld. Cantilupe
Mr. West
Brown
Hutchinson [*min.*]
Saunders
Edwards
Hawkins
Mitchell
Fitzakerly [Fazakerley]
Baker
Oldnall
Mason
White

Lower School.
———————

3d form Oppidans.
———————

Croft
Pot [*min.*]
Gunthorpe [*mi.*]
Holdsworth
St. Leger [*ma.*]
Agar
Hale
Grimston
Streatfield
Mr. Walpole
Goodall
Hannington

M 2

Woodhouse [*mi.*]
Nurse
Duffield

Oconner
Coxe
Mr. Lumley *mi.*
Mr. Lumley *min.*
Hume
Roles
St. Leger [*mi.*]
Neville
Allen
Ryan
Prat
Mitchell
Basset
Metcalfe

Tharpe
Barrow
Mr. Marsham
Townsend
Pack
Brown
Cookesey

Mr. Villers [*mi.*]
Lane
Wyatt
Buckeridge
Brown
Daxon
Mr. Bennet
Porter
Radcliffe

Taylor
Roberts
Repkombe
Manby [*ma.*]
Scott
Dennis
Manning
Tickell
Wells
Whaley
Dawes
Mr. Phipps *mi.*

2d form Oppidans.

Ashton
Mr. North *mi.*
St. Leger *min.*
Best *mi.*

Cooke
Hirde
Saubergue
Wells *mi.*
Sr. John Lade
Blackwell
Boddam
Manby *mi.*
Mr. Monson *min.*

1st form Oppidans.

Gordon
Gunthorpe
Warner
Priest
Wood
Charters *mi.*
Tolfree

Unplaced.

Newnham
Ourry
Vand
Leighton
Harwood
Scot
Packington
Jefferson
Sumpter
Webb

Colleger[s].. 62
Oppidans ..285
347

A BILL OF ETON SCHOOL [1772].

Provost.

Dr. Barnard

Vice Provost.

Dr. Apthorpe

Fellows.

Dr. Ashton
Mr. Southernwood
Mr. Roberts
Mr. Betham
Mr. Bernard
Mr. Chamberlain

Upper Master.

Dr. Forster

Lower Master.

Mr. Sleech

Upper Assistants.

Mr. Edwards
Mr. Davies
Mr. Sumner
Mr. Langford
Mr. Cooke

Lower Assistants.

Mr. Norbery
Mr. Prior
Mr. Hawtrey

Collegers.
Randolph
Plumtree
Butler
Rennell
Cooke
Charters
Cole
Hayter
Ellison
Key
Knapp
Plumtree
Hand

Woodroofe
Beauchamp
Jacob
Ward
Portal
Sumner
Cutler
Simeon
Simons
Scott
Kynaston
Fleet
Paddon
Wingfeild
Cole
Luxmore

Andrew
Samson
Haggit
Skeels
Emly
Goodall
Hatch
Butler
Menzies
Lowndes
Michell
Hanbury
Kynaston
Shephard
Smith
Maule ·
Symson
Chafie
Purney
Berry
Sparke
Sumpter

Dominiceti
Tolfrey
Cropley
Griffies
Wrighte
Lodington
Jefferson
Lee
Draper

Trusler
Kirke
Wood

Tolfrey

Oppidants.

Rhutterforth [Rutherford]
Mr. Broderick
Hutchinson
Walpole
Willis
Blount

Cheshire
Mr. Watson
Gibson
Ejerton
Mr. Waldegrave
Booker
Manley
Richardson
Morant
Irish
Monk
Mitchell
Way
Davies
Harding
Mr. Legg
Dyson
Maynard
Ld. Ludlow
Otley
Pott
Ld. Graham
Croft
Weller
Hayes
Battine
Mr. Vaugn [Mr. Vaughan]
Colier
Mr. Townshend
Bastard
Johns
Heywood
Pole
Newport
St. Leger
Lawry
Swinnerton
Maynard
Rastall
Lemoine
Præd
Brown
Oxendon
Michell
Dampier
Pott
Gibbons
Bishop

Norbery

Chauvett

Mr. Monson

Ackland

Cooke

Shutz

Buck

Oliver

Bosanquet

Robinson

· Musgrave

Mr. Broderick

· Luttrel

Anstey

Anstey

Rives

Rives

Mr. Viliers

Mr. North

Montgomery

Beeby

Saunderson

Townshend

Longmore

Gregory

Cottrel

Barnard

Amyatt

Wells

Raper

Colethrust

Calvert

Mr. Lumley

Hayes

Manning

Dury

Talbot

Milward

—————

Baker

Burton

Jarvis

Brereton

Fuller

Bastard

Angelo

Mr. Monson

Brotherson

Wilmot

Grenville

Brown

Patterson

Robinson

Goulbourn

Walton

Dupuis

Michell

Fitzackeray [Fazakerley]

Oldnall

Lewellyn

Griffith

Molesworth

Hutchinson

Hodges

Paris

Sr. Thos. Carew

Smith

Welpdale

Bevor

Waite

Pemberton

————— — - - -

Gascoigne

Newnham

Scudamore

Dauvert

O[l]dmeadow

Dodd

Beckwith

Gunthorpe

Simeon

Pott

Ld. Cantilupe

Mr. West

Mr. Brown [? Brown]

Hutchinson

Saunders

Edwards

Hawkins

Baker

Mason

White

Graeme

Croft

Pott

Gunthorpe

Holdsworth
St. Leger
Agar
Hale
Streatfeild
Mr. Walpole
Goodall
Hannington
Woodhouse
Nourse
Sleech
Price
Kinlow [Kinloch]
Head
Yates
Riddle
Moore
Calvert
O'Connor
Cox
Mr. Lumleys 2
Hume
Rowls
St. Leger
Neville
Allen
Pratt
Mitchell
Basset
Metcalf
Aubrey
Crawford

Lower School.

Tharp
Barrow
Mr. Marsham
Townshend
Packe
Cooksey
Brown
Van
Harwood
Webb
Whitehorn
Riddle

Luxmore
Short

Mr. Viliers
Lane
Wyatt
Buckeridge
Brown
Daxon
Mr. Bennet
Porter
Radclive
Leighton
Oury
Samson
Harford
Newnham
Scott
Taylor
Roberts
Manby
Scott
Manning
Dennis
Pakington
Tickle
Wells
Whalley
Dawes
Roberts
Ld. Wellesley
Smart
Nelson
Cotes
Wright

Mr. Phipps
Mr. North
Bosanquet
St. Leger
Best
Pierce
Sr. Jas. Erskine

Cooke
Saubergue
Wells
Sr. Jn. Lade

Blackwell
Boddam
Willoughby
Streatfeild

Mr. Monson
Manby
Gordon
[*erasure*]
Buller
Gunthorpe
Roberts
Charters
Warner
Waring
Boyle
Hipworth
Cooke

Currie
Middlemore
Mr. Lumley
Couraud
Eldrigde
Jackson
Nelson
Cheslyn

New Boys.

Cross
Charlton

------

336 [328] Boys

[ELECTION] 1773.

Provost.	Lower Assistants.
Dr. Bernard	Mr. Norbury
	Mr. Hawtrey
Vice Provost.	Mr. Prior
Dr. Abthorpe	
	6 form Coll.
Fellows.	Knapp
	Hand
Dr. Ashton	Woodroofe
Mr. Southerwood	Beauchamp
Mr. Roberts	Jacob
Mr. Betham	Ward
Mr. Bernard	Sumner
Mr. Chamberlayne	Cutler
	Simeon
	Simons
Upper Master.	Scott
Mr. Davies	
	5 Form Coll.
Lower Master.	Fleet
Mr. Sleech	Paddon
	Wingfeild
	Cole
	Hays
Upper Assistants.	Luxmoore
	Sampson
Mr. Sumner	Haggitt
Mr. Langford	Sheels
Mr. Cooke	Emly
Mr. Forster	Goodall
	Hatch

Butler
Oliver
Menzies
Amyatt
Michell
Brown
Smith
Shephard
Smith

Remove Coll.

Chafie
Maule
Hanbury
Moore

4 form Coll.

Berry
Sparke
Sumpter
Haggit
Tolfrey
Cooksey
Griffies
Luxmoore
Cropley
Short
Cross
Sampson
Hinde

3 form Coll.

Wrighte
Lodington
Jefferson
Currie
Trusler
Kirke
Hipworth
Cooke
Jackson

6 form Oppis.

Plumtree
Portall
Blount
Cheshire
Gibson
Ejerton
Mr. Waldgrave
Monk
Way
Kynaston

5 form Oppis.

Mr. Legge
Dyson
Pott
Battine
Bastard
Johnes
Heywood
Newport
Maynard
Praid
Oxendon
Michell
Dampier
Gibbons
Norbury
Cheavett
Ackland
Cooke
Robinson
Musgrave
Mr. Brodericke
Anstey
Anstey
Rives
Mr. Villiers
Mr. North
Cottrell
Bernard
Wells
Raper
Calvert
Mr. Lumley

Hayes
Lens
Baker
Brereton
Bastard
Willmott
Grenville
Patterson
Robinson
Gouldbourn
Walton
Dupuis
Fazackerley
Mr. Monson
Molesworth
Hutchinson
Paris
Beevor
Waite
Pemberton
Soley
Askew
Simeon
Pott
Ld. Cantilupe
Mr. West
Hutchinson
Saunders
Edwards
Baker
Mason
White
Græme
Kinloch
Jarvis

Remove Oppi.

Scudamore
Dauvert
Beckwith
Parker
Croft
Pott
Mr. Walpoole
Goodall
St. Leger

Agar
Hale
Streatfeild
Hannington
Nourse
Sleech
Price
Hawkins
Head
Yates
Anguish

4 form Opps.

Holdsworth
Woodhouse
Calvert
Coxe
Cousmaker
Mr. Lumley
Hume
St. Leger
Allen
Pratt
Michell
Pratt
Basset
Aubrey
Crawford
Marsden
Atkins

Harwood
Mr. Marsham
Webb
Whitehorn
Neville
Townshend
Packe
Brown
Van
Riddle
Heywood
Barrow

Mr. Villiers
Radcliffe

Lane
Wyatt
Buckeridge
Brown
Daxon
Mr. Bennet .
Porter
Leighton
Oury
Sampson
Harford
Calvert
Morrison
White
Mason
Hill
Coffin

Lower School.

Newnham
Taylor
Roberts
Manby
Scott .
Manning
Dennis
Packington
Tickell
Wells
Whaley
Dawes
Roberts
Ld. Wellesley
Smart
Cotes
Wrighte
Hamilton
Pen
Atkins
Atkins
Smith

Lower Greek.

Mr. Phipps
Ashton

Mr. North
Bosanquet
St. Leger
Peirce
Best
Sr. Jas. Erskine
Hall
Charlton
Ingilby
Mr. Bathur[s]t
Penn
Fraser
Hughs

Blackwell
Boddam
Willoug[h]by
Streatfeild
Mr. Lumly
Cooke
Wells
Sr. Jno. Lade
Vezey
Gibbons

Mr. Monson
Buller
Manby
Gordon
Middlemore
Toulmin
Gunthorpe
Roberts
Charters
Waring
Warner
Boyle
Eldridge
Sr. Boughton
Gray

Unplaced.

Millner
Parks
Methold

---

2 Form Opp.

Bishop
Nelson
Couraud
White
Manby
Bearblock
Freeman

Hubbard
Chilcott
Scott
Tolfrey
White
Hardinge
Ward
Woodhouse [283]

'

A BILL OF ETON SCHOOL [1774].

[*Provost.*

Dr. Barnard

Vice Provost.

Dr. Apthorpe

Fellows.

Mr. Suthernwood
Dr. Ashton
Dr. Roberts
Mr. Beetham
Mr. Chamberlayne
Mr. Barnard

Upper Master.

Mr. Davies

Lower Master.

Mr. Sleech

Upper School Assistants.

Mr. Sumner
Mr. Langford
Mr. Cooke
Mr. Foster

Lower School Assistants.

Mr. Norbury
Mr. Prior
Mr. Hawtrey]

Hand C.
Woodroffe C.
Beauchamp C.
Jacob C.
Ward C.
Blount
Mr. Waldgrave
Sumner C.
Cutler C.
Simeon C.
Simons C.
Scott C.
Way
Mr. Legge
Kynaston
Pott
Fleet C.
Dyson
Battine
Bastard
Johnns
Newport

5 Form.

Paddon C.
Cole C.
Hayes C.
Luxmore C.

Maynard
Haggit C.
Skeeles C.
Praed
Emly C.
Mitchell
Dampier C.
Goodall C.
Norbury C.
Hatch C.
Butler C.
Oliver C.
Musgrave
Mr. Broderick
Menzies C.
Anstey
Anstey C.
Mr. Villiers
Mr. North
Barnard C.
Amyatt C.
Raper
Calvert
Hayes
Michell C.
Lens
Baker
Brereton
Bastard
Wilmot
Grenville
Browne C.
Patteson
Smith C.
Goulborne
Dupuis
Fitzakerley [Fazakerley]
Fuller
Molesworth
Shephard C.
Smyth C.
Askew C.
Simeon C.
Ld. Cantilupe
Mr. West
Hutchinson
Saunders
Edwards

Baker
Mason
White
Grame
Chafie C.
Maule C.
Mr. Walpole
Hanbury C.
Goodall
Deauvert
Parker
Pott
Agar
Streatfeild
Hannington
Sleech
Head
Moore [C.]
Anguish
Nourse
Yeate
Calvert
Mr. Lumley
Hume
Atkyns
Cousmaker
Holdsworth
Woodhouse
Emblyn C.
Coxe
Berry C.
Sparke C.
Mitchell
Basset
Marsden
Sumpter C.
Crawford
Haggit [C.]

Remove.

Allen
Prat
Harwood
Mr. Marsham
Tolfrey C.
Webb

Whitehorne
Barrow C.
Townshend
Packe
Cooksey C.
Brown
Van
Griffies C.
Luxmore C.
Cropley C.
Short C.
Heywood
Radcliffe
Porter

4th Form.

Neville
Mr. Villiers
Buckeridge
Browne
Whyatt
Daxon
Layton
Oury
Sampson C.
Harford
Cross C.
Hinde C.
Morrison
Mason
White
Hill
Biggin
Marsham C.
Strettle
Shipton
Beevor
Baldrow [Boldero]
Newnham
Taylor
Roberts
Scott
Manby
Manning
Dennis
Packington

Tickell
Whaley
Dawes
Wrighte C.
Roberts
Ld. Wellesley
Smart
Lodington C.
Nelson
Cotes
Wright
Hamilton
Penn
Atkyns
Atkyns
Smith
Coffin C.
Cobb C.
Stevenson C.
Farmer C.
Beecher
Ashton
Mr. North
Bosanquet
Best
Sr. Jas. Erskine
Jefferson C.
Hall
Charlton
Ingleby
Penn
Mr. Bathurst
Frazer
Hughes
Ld. Strathaven
Milne
Fonnerau

3d Form.

Blackwell
Boddam
Willoughby
Streatfeild
Sawyer
Mr. Lumley
Cooke

Wells
Sr. Jno. Lade
Vesey
Currie C.
Gibbons
Strettle
Mitchell
Tickle
Buller
Tolman [Toulmin]
Hewgill
Baker
Methold
Middlemore
Manby
Parkes
Gunthorpe
Kirke [C.]
Roberts
Charters
Waring
Warner
Boyle
Eldridge
Sr. T. Boughton
Grey
Strettle
Trusler C.
Bishop
Cooke C.
Hipworth C.
Nelson
Couraud
Farquason
Gordon
White

Manby
Freeman
Jackson C.
Harding
Tyndall

2d Form.

Warde C.
Hubbard
Scott
Tolfrey
Kent
Chillcot

1st Form.

Whinch
White
Mr. Westly
Clarke C.
Ware
Woodhouse
Sober
Roberts
Woods
Brown
French
Frazer
Sober
Harwood

---

[267]

[CHRISTMAS 1775.]

[1][Hayes C.
Luxmore C.
Emley C.
Dampier C.
Norbury C.]
Hatch [C.]
Butler C.
Oliver [C.]
Anstey ma. C.
Bernard C.
Amyatt C.
Mitchell C.
Calvert ma.
Hayes mi. C.
Baker ma.
Willmot
Grenville
Dupuis
Mason ma.
White ma.

Fifth Form.

[1][Smith C.
Smyth C.
Brow]ne C.
Askew C.
Simeon C.
Saunders C.
Chafie C.
Renouard
Mr. Walpole
Pott
Hannington

Goodall C.
Moore C.
Anguish
Calvert mi.
Mr. Lumley ma.
Atkins ma.
Cousmaker
Berry C.
Sparke C.
Sumpter ma. C.
Haggit
Anstey mi. C.
Mr. Marsham
Tolfrey ma. C.
Webb
Whitehorne
Packe
Cooksey C.
Griffies C.
Luxmore mi. C.
Short C.
Barrow C.
Cropley ma. C.
Ratcliffe
Heywood
Brown
King
Mr. Villiers
Browne
Cross C.
Porson C.
White mi.
Biggin
Buckeridge
Sampson C.

[1] Part of the roll is missing.

Hinde C.
Mason *mi.*
Marsham C.
Atkins *mi.*
Shipton
Harford
Dawes
Tinker
Roberts *ma.*
Scott *ma.*
Ld. Wellesley
Manning
Packington
Roberts *mi.*
Whalley
Lodington C.
Nelson *ma.*
Coates
Penn *ma.*
Tickell
Manby *ma.*
Coffin C.
Cobb C.
Stevenson C.
Farmer C.
Becher C.

Remove.

Ashton *ma.*
Mr. North *ma.*
Bosanquet
Sr. J. Erskine
Ld. Apsley
Ingilby
Penn *mi.*
Frazer *max. ma.*
Mr. Broderick *ma.*
Moss
Ld. Strathavon
Fonnerau C.
Fitz-Roy *max.*
Ld. Morton

Fourth Form.

Best

Jefferson C.
Gregory C.
Kinlock
Draper
Blackwell
Boddam
Willoughby
Streatfeild
Sawyer
Mr. Lumley *mi.*
Fitz-Roy *ma.*
Cooke C.
Wells
Sr. J. Lade
Vesey
Currie C.
Gibbons
Mitchell
Tickle
Reeves C.
Sr. Cs. Palmer
Lewis
Buller
Baker *mi.*
Edmonstone
Toulmin
Hewgill
Methold
Midd[l]eton
Middlemore
Manby *min.*
Parkes C.
Whitbread
Luxmore *min.* C.
Sumpter *mi.* C.
Nash
Hobhouse
Dickins
Tyrwhitt
French
Tollet
Grey
Gunthorpe
Grey
Roberts *min.*
Boyle
Waring
Warner

Sr. Theos. Boughton
Charters
Eldridge
Saunders *mi.*
Williams
Kirke [C.]
Mackarel [Mackrill C.]
Trusler [C.]

Chilcott *ma.* C.
Eaden
Mellish *ma.*
Ware C.
Clarke C.
Grover C.
Freeman *mi.*
Woods
Mellish *mi.*
Brown

Lower School.

Third Form.

Tyndall
Bishop
Hipworth C.
Cooke C.
Couraud
Hibbins
Nelson *mi.*
Farquaharson
Leycester *ma.*
Townshend
Baker
Syms *ma.* C.
Berkley C.
Mr. Broderick *mi.*
Matthias *ma.*
Freeman *ma.*
Manby *min.*
Bearblock
Harding
Hampson
Leycester *mi.*
Jackson C.
Ward C.
Hubbard
Scott *mi.*
Mr. Westley
Tolfrey *mi.* C.
Johnson
Fancourt C.
Fitz-Roy *mi.*
Hughes C.
Mr. North *mi.*
Kent
Sandys

Second Form.

Fraser *max. mi.*
Woodhouse
Treahearne C.
Leycester *min.*
Roberts
French C.
Chillcott *mi.*
Cropley *mi.* C.
Harwood
Sober *ma.*
Syms *mi.*
Hammersley
Cheap

First Form.

Ashton *mi.*
Elliot
Butcher
Fitz-Roy *min.*
Molesworth
Ld. Clifton
Novarre
Bell
Fraser *max.*
Fraser *ma.*
Fraser *mi.*
Mr. Stewart
Grant
Tighe
Fraser *min.*
Beadon
Raine

Matthias *mi.*
Sober *mi.*
Coote
Browne
Hird
Swinton

Unplaced.

Michaelstone

Nicbolls
Stichall

Boys.

246 Xmas
246 Xmas

1775

ELECTION 1776.

Dampier C.
Norbury C.
Butler C.
Anstey *ma.* C.
Barnard C.
Mitchell C.
Hayes C.
Wilmott
Grenville
Brown C.
Dupuis
Smith *ma.* C.
Smyth *mi.* C.
Askew C.
Simeon C.
Mason
White
Mr. Walpole
Pott
Hannington
Anguish
Saunders C.

Chafie C.
Goodall C.
Moore C.
Mr. Lumley
Berry C.
Sparke C.
Sumpter C.
Haggit
Anstey *mi.* C.
Mr. Marsham
Webb
Whitehorn
Ratcliffe
King
Mr. Villiers
Cooksey C.
Griffies C.
Luxmoore C.

Short C.
Barrow C.
Cropley C.
Brown
Cross C.
Porson C.
White
Biggin
Mason
Buckeridge
Sampson C
Hinde C.
Marsham C.
Atkins
Dawes
Tinker
Roberts
Scott
Manning
Packington
Whaley
Roberts
Ld. Wellesly
Lodington C.
Nelson
Cotes
Penn
Tickell
Coffin C.
Cobb C.
Stevenson C.
Farmer C.
Beecher C.
Ashton
Mr. North
Bosanquet
Sr. Js. Erskine
Ld. Apsley
Penn
Mr. Brodrick
Moss

Ld. Morton
Fonnereau C.
Fitzroy
Morris
___

Gregory C.
Kinloch
Draper
Blackwell
Boddam
Streatfield
Sawyer
Mr. Lumley
Fitzroy *mi.*
Cooke C.
Vesey
Ramsden
Currie C.
Tickell
Reeves C.
Sr. C. Palmer
Lewis
Dennis
. . . .
Sr. J. Lade
Gibbons
Buller
Baker
Edmonstone
Toulmin
Hewgill
Methold
Middleton
Middlemore
Manby
Parkes C.
Whitbread
Luxmoore C.
Sumpter C.
Dickins
Hobhouse
Tyrwhit
Nash
Tierney
Everett
___

French
Gray
Grey

Roberts
Boyle
Dyson
Anguish
Kirke C.
Waring
Warner
Sr. T. Boughton
Charters
Eldridge
Saunders
Williams
Edmonstone *mi.*
Colthurst
Ray
Wilkinson
Veel
Preston
Mackrill C.
Tyndall
Leycester
Cooke C.
Syms C.
Hibbins
Bishop
Hipworth C.
Nelson
Farquharson
Townshend
Baker
Berklly C.
Couraud
Gunthorpe
Tattnall
Earle
Bradshaw *ma.*
Bradshaw *mi.*
Wyndham
___

Lower School.
___

Mr. Brodrick
Hampson
Matthias *ma.*
Freeman
Bearblock
Harding

Manby
Jackson C.
Leister [Leycester]
Warde C.
Butt
Denis
Wilkinson
Scott
Heughs C.
Hubbard
Fitzroy
Johnson
Mr. Wesley
Fancourt C.
Chitter
Selwyn
Mr. North
Mayo
Sandys
Kent
Eden
Mellish
Roycroft
Ld. Glasgow
Pott
Crawfurd
Preston
Leycester
Mr. Dawnay
Chilcott C.
Ware C.
Clark [C.]
Brown
Grover [C.]
Freeman
Woods
Mellish
Green
Buller
Frazer
Trehearne C.
Cropley C.
Woodhouse
Leycester
French C.
Chilcott
Ld. Blanford
Roberts

Michaelson
Nicolls
Georges
Reid
Read
Marsh
Whitaker
Elliot
Harwood
Syms C.
Cheap
Hammersley
Roycroft
Sober
Frazer
Stichall
Western
Ashton
Ld. Clifton
Mr. Stuart
Beadon
Frazer
Frazer
Noverre
Bell
Tighe
Fitzroy
Roberts
Coote
Matthias
Raine
Grant
Sober
Pye
Browne
Hird
Ogilvie
Langford
Metcaffe
Swinton
Becket
Hankey
Broadhead
Cambell
Evans
Fosset
Maxwell

[266]

A BILL OF ETON SCHOOL, JULY 31ST, 1777.

VIth.

Michell C.
Hayes C.
Browne C.
Smyth C.
Askew C.
Simeon C.
Saunders C.
Chafie C.
Goodall C.
Hannington
Moore O.
Anguish
Mr. Lumley
Webb
King
Browne
Biggin
Mason
Dawes

Vth.

Anstey C.
Cooksey C.
Griffies C.
Luxmoore C.
Short C.
Barrow C.
Cropley C.
Porson C.
Sampson C.
Hinde C.
Marsham C.
Roberts
Scott
Packington

Whalley C.
Roberts
Ld. Wellesley
Lodington C.
Nelson
Cotes
Tickell
Stevenson C.
Becher C.
Ashton
Bosanquet
Sr. Jas. Erskine
Ld. Apsley
Penn
Fraser
Mr. Broderic
Moss
Ld. Morton
Fonnereau C.
Farmer C.
Gregory C.
Draper
Blackwell
Boddam
Sawyer
Mr. Lumley
Fitzroy
Cooke C.
Vesey
Ramsden C.
Currie C.
Reeves C.
Lewis C.
Dennis
Hutchinson
Baker
Edmonstone
Hewgill

Middleton

Whitbread

Hobhouse

Lloyd C.

Raine C.

Dickens

Gibbons

Methold

Manby

Luxmoore C.

Sumpter C.

Tyrrwhit

Nash

Tierney

Everett

Remove.

Grey

Roberts

Boyle

Dyson

Anguish

Kirke C.

Griffies C.

King C.

Waring

French

Sr. Theo. Boughton

Charters

Edmonstone

Coulthurst

Ray

· Wilkinson

Veel

Preston

Geraud C.

Lee

Williams

Mackrill C.

IVth.

Pawlett

Tyndall

Leycester

Cooke C.

Hampson

Hibbins

Bishop

Hipworth C.

Nelson

Farquharson

Townshend

Baker

Couraud

Berkeley C.

Earle

Bradshaw

Bradshaw

Wyndham

Tyrrwhit

Dyson

Squire

Crespigny

Mr. Broderic

Hampson

Mathias

Warde C.

Freeman

Bearblock

Jackson C.

Manby

Leycester

Butt

Dennis C.

Boggust C.

Stubbs

Macleod

Hume

Wilkinson

Scott

Selwin

Hughes [C]

Hill

Hubbard

Fitzroy

Fancourt C.

Chitter

Baley

Price

Blunt

IIIrd.

Grove C.
Mr. North
Mayo
Ld. Glasgow
Eden
Vesey
Mellish
Roycroft
Crawford
Sandys
Mr. Dawnay
Pott
Ld. Blandford
Reid C.
Evans C.
Preston
Leycester
O'brien
Chilcott C.

Browne
Ware
Freeman
Grover C.
Maxwell
Clarke C.
Mellish
Green
Reid
Elton
Blencowe
Gibbons
Gibbons
Lomax

Herne
Fraser
Leycester
Campbell
Woodhouse
Cropley C.
French C.
Buller
Michaelson
Chilcott

Roberts
Western
Elliot
Hammersley
Roycroft
Tonman
Fraser
Harwood C.
Syms C.
Fraser
Cheap
Stichall
Mr. Stuart
Beaden
Fraser
Lee

Whitaker
Ld. Clifton
Briggs C.
Tighe
Fraser
Ashton
Butcher
Novarre
Harding [C.]
Georges

IInd.

Marsh
Scott
Fitzroy
Fraser
Bell
Raine
Grant
Roberts
Pye
Worthington
Roberts
Griffiths

Mathias
Ogilvie
Herne
Hird

Browne	Snow
Fosset	Hankey
Campbell	Grey
Douglas	Boon
Broadhead	Arden
Langford	Adlard
Medcalf	

Ist.	Unplaced.
Novarre	Bartlam
Beckett	Oliver
Sykes	Morgan
Blake	Downes
Wallace	Lloyd
Mr. Flower	Copinger
Swinton	Wray
Sykes	Durelle

[271]

A BILL OF ETON SCHOOL
July 27th, 1778.

[Provost.

Dr. Barnard

Vice-Provost.

Dr. Apthorpe

Fellows.

Dr. Roberts
Mr. Betham
Mr. Barnard
Mr. Sleech
Mr. Chamberlayne
Dr. Young

Upper Master.

Dr. Davis

Lower Master.

Dr. Langford

Upper Assistants.

Mr. Sumner
Mr. Heath
Mr. Foster

Lower Assistants.

Mr. Norbury
Mr. Prior
Mr. Hawtrey
Mr. Cole]

6th Form.

Simeon C.
Goodall C.
Moore C.
Sumpter C.
Anstey C.
Cooksey C.
Griffies C.
Barrow C.
Cropley C.
Hinde C.
Browne
Biggin
Mason
Marsham C.
Dawes
Roberts C.
Scott
Packington
Ld. Wellesley
Nelson
Bosanquet
Ld. Apsley

5th Form.

Whalley C.
Roberts C.
Stevenson C.
Farmer C.
Becher C.
Fraser
Mr. Broderick
Moss
Fonnereau C.
Gregory C.
Draper
Boddam
Fitzroy
Cooke C.
Ramsden C.
Reeves C.
Lewis C.
Hutchinson C.
Baker
Edmonstone
Hewgill
Middleton
Whitbread
Lloyd C.
Raine C.
Dickins
Methold
Luxmoore C.
Manby
Sumpter C.
Tyrrwhitt
Nash
Everett
Grey
Roberts C.
Boyle
Dyson
Anguish
Griffiths C.
Kirke C.
King C.
Waring
French
Eldridge C.
Saunders
Edmonstone

Coulthurst
Ray
Wilkinson
Veel
Giraud C.
Mackrill C.
Tunstall
Tyndall
Powlett
Leycester
Bayley
Bayley
Hampson C.
Cooke C.
Chartres
Nelson
Farquharson
Townshend
Baker
Earle
Tyrrwhitt
Dyson
Squire
Bradshaw
Bradshaw
Wyndham
Crespigney

Remove.

Mr. Broderick
Crespigney
Hampson
Matthias
Warde C.
Freeman C.
Bearblock
Jackson C.
Manby
Leycester
Butt C.
Dennis C.
Boggust C.
Campion
Ilbert
Mr. Conway
. . . .

4th Form.

Upper Remove.

Macleod
Couraud
Hume
Wilkieson
Scott
Selwyn
Hughes C.
Hill
Hubbard
Fitzroy
Lambton
Bayley
Smith
Price C.
Blunt
Hunt C.
Chitter
Heartwell
Moore
Fancourt C.

Second Remove.

Mr. North
Grove C.
Mayo
Lord Glasgow
Eden
Vesey
Roycroft
Mellish
Sandys
Crawford
Mr. Dawnay
Pott
Ld. Blandford
Mr. Mountague
Waller
Reid C.
Preston
Evans C.
Leycester
Cooper

Pococke
Chilcott C.

Last Remove.

Langley
Browne
Maxwell
Mellish
Elton
Clarke C.
Freeman C.
Grover C.
Oliver C.
Reid
Greene
Jones
Alves

Lower School.

Upper Greek.

Lomax
Blencowe
Gibbons
Cropley C.
Herne
Woodhouse
Fraser
Leycester
Campbell
Philpott C.
Morse
Buller
Michaelson
Chillcott

Lower Greek.

Western
Hammersley
Roycroft
Cheap
Tonman

Stichall
Harwood C.
Syms C.
Ld. Clifton
Mr. Stuart
Beadon
Tighe
Lee
Ellison C.
Jenkinson
Roberts

Sense.

Briggs C.
Butcher
Georges
Harding C.
Whittaker
Blake
Wickes C.
Peach
Bridges
Orde
Calcraft

Nonsense.

Marsh
Scott
Raine
Fitzroy
Worthington C.
P. Fraser
Bell
Pye
G. Roberts
T. Roberts C.
Morgan C.
Griffiths
Grant
Woodbridge
Downes
Lloyd
Copinger
Durell

Lag Remove.

Hird
Matthias
Ogilvie
Herne
Browne
Douglass
Broadhead

2nd Form.

Upper Remove.

Spragge
Langford
Metcalfe
Wallace
Sykes
Noverre

Last Remove.

Beckett
Sykes
Mr. Flower
Trigg
Boone
Swinton
Hankey
Snow
Waller
Manning
Arden
Grey

1st Form.

Price
Bartlam [C.]
Bridges
Monk
Mr. Blighe
Grant
Campbell

Wombwell
Wright
Bridges
Prior
Prior
Boyce
Oliver
Leathes
Fitzroy
Blake
Roberts

Unplaced.

Jackson
Jackson
Calcraft
Craycraft
Oliver
North
Mr. Evans
Champness   [276]

A BILL OF ETON SCHOOL, JULY 29, 1779.

[*Provost.*

Dr. Barnard

Vice-Provost.

Dr. Apthorpe

Fellows.

Dr. Roberts
Mr. Betham
Mr. Barnard
Mr. Sleech
Mr. Chamberlayne
Dr. Young

Upper Master.

Dr. Davis

Lower Master.

Dr. Langford

Upper Assistants.

Mr. Sumner
Mr. Heath
Mr. Foster

Lower Assistants.

Mr. Norbury
Mr. Prior
Mr. Hawtrey
Mr. Cole]

Sumpter C.
Anstey C.
Griffies C.
Barrow C.
Cropley C.
Hinde C.
Marsham C.
Roberts C.
Scott
Whalley C.
Roberts C.
Stevenson C.
Farmer C.
Beecher C.
Gregory C.
Mr. Brodericke
Moss
Fitzroy
Baker
Edmonstone
Middleton
Whitbread
Dickins
Tyrrwhitt

24

Fifth Form.

Ramsden C.
Reeves C.
Lewis C.
Hutchinson C.
Loyd C.
Raine C.
Manby C.
Luxmoore C.
Nash
Grey
Roberts C.
Dyson
Anguish
Griffith C.
Kirke C.
King C.
Waring
Eldridge C.
Saunders C.
Edmonstone
Wilkinson
Giraud C.
Mackrill C
Tunstall
Tyndall
Powlett
Leycester
Bayley
Bayley
Hampson C.
Chartres
Townsend
Earle
Tyrrwhit
Dyson
Squire
Wyndham
Crespigny
Mr. Broderick
Hampson
Mr. Conway
Matthias
Ilbert
Warde C.
Freeman C.
Boggust C.

Butt C.
Bearblock
Leycester
Dennis C.
Manby
Jackson C.
Campion
Mcleod
Hume
Wilkinson
Scott
Selwyn
Fitzroy
Lambton
Davenport
Bayley
Smith
Price C.
Blount
Hunt C.
Moore C.
Hartwell C.
Lownds
Fancourt C.   70

Remove.

Mr. North
Grove C.
Mayo
Ld. Glasgow
Chitter
Eden
Vesey
Roycroft
Mellish
Crawford
Sandys
Mr. Dawnay
Pott
Ld. Blandford
Mr. Montague
Lockart
Leycester
Reid C.
Cooper
Waller

Preston
Pocock
Evans C.
Alves   24

_____

Fourth Form.
_____

Langley
Cotterell C.
Browne
Maxwell
Mellish
Lockart
Elton
Freeman C.
Oliver [? C.]
Grover [C.]
Reid
Green
Jones
Gregg
Durbin
. . . .
Turner
Ld. Stopford
Mr. Stopford
Clarke C.
Astley
Skinner
Harvey
Lomax
Blencowe
Cropley C.
Campbell
Herne
Woodhouse
Ellis
Fraser
Leycester
Morse
Phillpot C.
Michaelson
. . . .
Western
Hammersley
Anson
Tucker

Chilcott
Roycroft
Tonman
Stichall
Ld. Clifton
Harwood C.
Mr. Stewart
Beadon
Tighe
Lee
Mr. Windsor
Ibbot
Fennel
Syms C.
Smith
Page   55 [54]

_____

Third Form.
_____

Ellison C.
Briggs [C.]
Griffiths
Mr. Stopford
Roberts
Butcher
Bridges
Harding C.
Wickes C.
Blake
Peach
Calcraft
Orde
. . . .
Scott
Kirkpatrick *ma.*
Kirkpatrick *mi.*
Worthington C.
Marsh
Raine
Fitzroy
Morgan C.
West
Craddock C.
Walker C.
Cooper C.
Frazer
Bell

Pye
Roberts
Roberts C.
Griffith
Pittman
Woodbridge
Lloyd
Coppinger
Durell
Downs
Green
Whitaker
. . . .
Douglass
Hird
Matthias
Ogilvie
Herne
Broadhead
Martin C.
Browne
Mr. Evans
Wallace
Tillson
Beadle
Brooke
. . . .
Chambre
Langford
Metcalf
Jackson
Jackson
Mr. Bathurst
Sneyd
Noverre
Bridges
Sykes
Smith
Packington
. . . .
Cracraft
Smith
Sykes
Wombwell
Spragg
Calcraft
Becket C.
Browne

Snow
Littlehales
Trigg
. . . .
Beadle
Ld. Down
Leader
Brooke
Leith
Anson
Robinson
Palmer
Clarke
Rider
Scott
Roby
Mansell   88

2nd Form.

Mr. Flower
Champness
Price
Swinton
Hankey
Waller
Manning
Arden
Grey
Bartlam C.
Monk
Mr. Blighe
Bridges
. . . .
Hazlewood C.
Oliver
Oliver
North C.
Wright [C.]
Prior C.
Prior C.
Campbell
Grant
Clarke
Blake
Stocking
Langford   26

First Form.

Fisher
Concannen
Roberts
Fitzroy
Blake
Stewart
Moss
Dolphin
Kenrick
Kenrick
Careless
Mordaunt
Hill

Berry
Coppinger
Broadhead
Leigh
Mr. Dawnay
Prior   19

Sixth F.   24 ⎞
Fifth F.   70 ⎟
Remove   24 ⎬ 173 [172] ⎞
Fourth F. 55 [54] ⎠   ⎟ Total
                                    ⎬ 306 [305]
Third F.   88 ⎞   ⎟
Second F. 26 ⎬ 133 ⎠
First F.   19 ⎠

A BILL OF ETON SCHOOL, JULY 1780.

[*Provost.*

Dr. Barnard

Vice-Provost.

Dr. Apthorp

Fellows.

Dr. Roberts
Mr. Betham
Mr. Barnard
Mr. Sleech
Mr. Chamberlayne
Dr. Young

Upper Master.

Dr. Davies

Lower Master.

Dr. Langford

Upper Assistants.

Mr. Sumner
Mr. Heath
Mr. Foster

Lower Assistants.

Mr. Prior
Mr. Norbury
Mr. Hawtrey
Mr. Savage]

Sixth Form.

Roberts Colleger
Whaley C.
Roberts C.
Stevenson C.
Becher C.
Gregory C.
Ramsden C.
Reeves C.
Hutchinson C.
Loyd C.
Raine C.
Mr. Broderick
Edmonstone
Middleton
Whitbread
Dickins
Tyrrwhit
Grey
Anguish

5th Form.

Luxmore C.
Manby C.
Roberts C.
Dyson [C.]

Griffith C.

Kirke C.

Saunders C.

Edmonstone

Tunstall

Tyndall

Powlett

Leycester

Bailey

Bailey C.

Townshend

Earle

Dyson

Squire

Crespigny

Mr. Broderick

Crespigny

Hampson

Ilbert

Warde C.

Freeman C.

Boggust C.

Leycester

Bearblock

Butt C.

Dennis C.

Jackson C.

Manby C.

Campion

Hume

Wilkinson

Scott

Selwin

Fitz-Roy

Lambton

Bailey C.

Smith C.

Price C.

Blunt

Hunt C.

Moore C.

Lowndes

Fancourt C.

Mr. North

Grove C.

Mayo

Ld. Glasgow

Eden

Vesey

Roycroft

Mellish

Crawford

Mr. Dawnay

Pott

Ld. Blandford

Mr. Montague

Lockhart

Sandys

Cooper

Pocock

Evans C.

Waller

Preston

Heys

Mellish

Cotrell C.

Lockhart

Elton

Reid

Jones

Durbin

Turner

Remove.

Langley

Browne

Freeman C.

Grover C.

Ld. Stopford

Mr. Stopford

Astley

Skinner

Harvey

Lomax

Blencowe

Ellis

Fraser

Leycester

Phillpott C.

Westerne

Morse

Michaelson

Brogden

Burgh

4th Form.

Hammersly
Anson
Tucker
Roycroft
Tonman
Ld. Clifton
Stichall
Harwood C.
Beadon
Tighe
Pigott
Rolfe
Mr. Windsor
Hibbert C.
Fennel
Syms C.
Smith C. [O.]
Chilcot

Mackay
Plumbtree
Ellison C.
Briggs C.
Griffith
Bridges
Blake
Page
Roberts
Butcher
Harding C.
Wickes
Peach
Ord
Worgan
Parker
Blick
Jefferson

Scott
Worthington C.
Marsh
Morgan C.
West
Walker C.
Cooper C.
Scott C.

Bell
Pye
Smith
Roberts
Griffith
Woodbridge
Downes
Lloyd
Coppinger
Cradock C.
Roberts C.
Ashton
Whalley
Marshall

3 Form.

Pittman
Douglas
Hird
Herne
Bradhead *ma.*
Martin C.
Mr. Evans
Wallace
Tilsons 2
Bedell *ma.* C.
Browne *ma.*
Bullock

Chambre
Langford
Metcalf
Mr. Bathurst
Sneyd
Mr. Watson
Sawbridge
Smith *ma.*
Noverre
Pakington
Leith
Bedell *mi.* C.
Davis
Spencer
Abbott
Bligh

Sykes *ma.*
Rider C.

Wombwell
Smith *mi.*
Simmons
Cracraft
Sykes *mi.*
Spragge
Boone
Becket C.
Snow
Littlehales [C.]
Leader
Trigg

Clarke
Townshend
Price
Mr. Flower
Champness
Waller
Manning
Arden
Grey
Bartlam C.
Mr. Bligh
Monk
Bridges
Swinton
Hankey
Hart

Ld. Downe
Concannen
Palmer
Haslewood O.
Oliver *ma.*
Oliver *mi.*
Anson
Lacey
North C.
Wright C.
Priors 2 C.
Campbell
Careless

Hunter

Roby C.
Kitching
Walpole
Luke
Harvey
Crawfurd
Clinton
Griffinhoofe
Cropley
Poyntz
Dayrell

2nd Form.

Moss
Pigott
Roberts
Grant
Oxley
Langford *mi.*
Blake
Fitz-Roy
Stocking

Douglas
Mansell C.
Roberts
Steuart
Mordaunt
Kenerick *ma.*
Mr. Montague
Lord Huntly
Fisher
Dolphin
Robinson
Philpott
Way *ma.*
Lord Dalkeith

1st Form.

Parsons
Kenerick *mi.*
Hill [C.]
Berry
Yorke

Wragge
Way *mi.*
Leigh
Phillpott *mi.*
Broadhead *mi.*
Prior *mi.*
Mr. Dawnay

Broadley *ma.*
Broadley *mi.*
Pigott
Browne *mi.*
Fonnereau
Charteris
Parsons *mi.*　　[300]

A LIST OF ETON SCHOOL, AUG. 1st, 1781.

[*Provost.*

Dr. Barnard

Vice-Provost.

Dr. Apthorpe

Fellows.

Dr. Roberts
Mr. Betham
Mr. Barnard
Mr. Sleech
Mr. Chamberlayne
Dr. Young

Upper Master.

Dr. Davies

Lower Master.

Dr. Langford

Upper Assistants.

Mr. Sumner
Mr. Heath
Mr. Foster

Lower Assistants.

Mr. Prior
Mr. Hawtrey
Mr. Norbury
Mr. Savage]

6th Form.

Becher C.
Reeves C.
Loyd C.
Raine C.
Manby C.
Luxmoore C.
Roberts C.
Dyson C.
Saunders C.
Bayley C.
Dyson C.
Middleton
Grey
Anguish
Edmonstone
Powlet
Leycester
Bayley
Townshend
Squire
Crespigny

5th Form.

Freeman C.

Boggust C.
Leycester
Bearblock C.
Mr. Brodrick
Hampson
Hume
Selwyn
Butt C.
Dennis C.
Manby C.
Bayley C.
Smith C.
Price C.
Mr. Fitzroy
Lambton
Lowndes
Hunt C.
Moore C.
Fancourt C.
Mr. North
Grove C.
Eden
Mellish
Evans C.
Heys C.
Ld. Downe
Pott
Ld. Blandford
Mr. Mountague
Sandys
Cooper
Pocock
Waller
Lockart
Cotterell C.
Mellish
Elton
Reid
Jones C.
Ld. Stopford
Mr. Stopford
Freeman C.
Grover C.
Astley
Skinner
Leycester
Lomax
Blencowe

Ellis C.
Philpot C.
Brogden
Burg
Deverell
Hamersly
Anson
Ld. Clifton
Tighe
Beadon
Pigot
Plumbtree
Harvey
Morse
Michaelson
Tonman
Tucker C.
Roycroft C.
Stichall
Mr. Windsor
Fennell C.
Smith C.
Parker
Power

Remove.

Rolfe
Gulstone
Griffith
Blake
Ellison C.
Briggs C.
Page
Butcher
Harding C.
Wickes
Peach
Ord
Worgan
Blick C.
Jefferson
Worthington C.
Cooper C.
Smith

4th Form.

Marsh
West C.
Bell
Pye
Smith
Roberts
Scott C.
Roberts C.
Griffith
Loyd
Woodbridge C.
Coppinger
Ellis C.
Douglas
Broadhead
Wallace
Mr. Evans
Anguish
Tilson
Bedell C.
Hird
Herne
Marshall C.
Tilson
Browne
Bullock
Cooper
Harrison
Knott
Martin C.
Coppin
Chambre
Langford
Metcalf
Mr. Bathurst
Sneyd
Mr. Watson
Sawbridge
Davis
Smith
Spencer C.
Abbot
Naverre
Bedell C.
Packinton
Hunter

Sykes
Lewin
Woodcock
Lambton
Mr. Clive
Frere
Webb
Harvey
Reid

Upper Greek.

Bligh
Sr. Geo. Wombwell
Smith
Simmons
Mr. Lamb
Ryder C.
Littlehales C.
Spragg
Boone
Leader
Snow
Crawford
Sykes
Becket C.
Moore

Lower Greek.

Ld. Henry Spencer
Clarke
Townshend
Price
Ld. Ashbrook
Bartlam C.
Mr. Bligh
Waller
Manning
Arden
Chamness
Monk
Grey
Bridges
Hart
Luke C.

Palmer
Hankey
Cropley
Walpole
Adams
Plummer

Sense.

Trigg
Baker
Ld. Downe
Pogson *ma.*
Oliver *mi.*
Mr. Westly *ma.*
Mr. Westly *mi.*
Moore
Hazlewood C.
Concannon
Anson
Lacy
Pogson *mi.*
Careless
Sr. Grifs. Boynton
Langley
North C.
Prior *max.* C.
Prior *ma.* C.
Whitmore

Nonsense.

Moss
Pigot
Mr. Craven
Langford *mi.*
Ld. Huntley
Marsh
Stocking
Briggs
Roberts
Grant
Oxley
Blake
Clinton
Harvey

Sr. Cs. Cope
Dayrell
Anson *mi.*

Lower Remove.

Roby C.
Mansell C.
Mordaunt
Freeman C.
Douglas
Roberts
Kenrick
Dolphin
Robinson
Way
Bateman

Unplaced.

Lewin
Boldero
Elton
Parnther
Forester
Mr. King *ma.*
Langham
Churchill
Dalling
Cambwell

2nd Form.

Upper Remove.

Ld. Dalkeith
Poyntz
Berry C.
Hill C.
Way
Parsons *ma.*
Kenrick
Griffinhoofe C.
Hulse
Wragge

Lower Remove.
———————

Mr. Dawnay
Earle
York
Broadhead
Leigh
Pigot
Langford
Philpot
Prior *mi.* C.
Broadley
Broadley

———— ————

1st Form.
———————

Prior *min.* C.

Fonnereau
Charters
Browne
Parsons
Parry
King
Way *mi.*
Ld. Holland
Pigot *mi.*
Mr. King [*mi.*]
Batson
Tomkinson
Morant
Boone
Price
Mr. King *min.*   [300]

A BILL OF ETON SCHOOL, JULY 26TH, 1782.

[*Provost.*

Dr. Roberts

Vice-Provost.

Dr. Apthorpe

Fellows.

Mr. Betham
Mr. Barnard
Mr. Sleech
Mr. Chamberlayne
Dr. Young
Mr. Tew

Upper Master.

Dr. Davies

Lower Master.

Dr. Langford

Upper Assistants.

Mr. Sumner
Mr. Heath
Mr. Foster

Lower Assistants.

Mr. Prior
Mr. Hawtrey
Mr. Norbury
Mr. Savage]

Raine C.
Manby C.
Luxmoore C.
Roberts C.
Dyson C.
Saunders C.
Bayley C.
Dyson C.
Mr. Broaderick
Crespigny
Hampson
Freeman C.
Boggust C.
Hume
Selwyn
Mr. Fitzroy
Lambton
Lowndes
Mr. North

5th Form.

Bearblock C.
Butt C.
Smith C.
Dennis C.
Manby C.

Bayley C.
Hunt C.
Moore C.
Fancourt C.
Eden
Mellish
Ld. Blandford
Mr. Mountague
Cooper
Pocock
Evans C.
Heys C.
Cotterell C.
Lockart
Mellish
Freeman C.
Jones C.
Grover C.
Mr. Stopford
Astley
Skinner
Leycester
Western
Lomax
Blencowe C.
Ellis C.
Philpot C.
Burgh
Deverell
Hammersly
Anson
Tucker C.
Roycroft C.
Ld. Darnley
Tighe
Beadon
Pigott
Plumbtree
Michaelson
Tonman
Mr. Windsor
Fennell C.
Smith C.
Parker
Rolfe
Gulston
Harwood C.
Hibbert C.

Ellison C.
Briggs C.
Griffith
Blake
Page
Wickes
Peach
Ord
Worgan C.
Blick C.
Smyth
Jefferson
Worthington C.
Cooper C.
Ashton
Harding C.
West C.
Ingram
Pye
Marsh
St. George *ma.*
Smith
Belle
Roberts
Lloyd
Roberts C.
Street C.
Douglass
Jolliff

Remove.

Woodbridge C.
Scott C.
Marshall C.
Broadhead
Wallace
Anguish
Tilson
Hird
Herne
Tilson
Symes
Martin C.
Bullock
Cooper
Harrison C.

Knott
Chambre
St. George *mi.*
St. George *min.*
Secker

4th Form.

Ellis C.
Langford
Metcalfe
Mr. Bathurst
Mr. Lumley
Sneyd
Mr. Watson
Ld. Lesley
Jefferson
Smith
Beedell C.
Abbot C.
Noverre
Pakington
Hunter
Sykes
Lewin
Woodcock
Lambton
Mr. Clive

Webb
Frere
Reid C.
Harvey C.
Ferrier
Milnes
Clarke
Bligh
Sr. G. Wombwell
Smith
Mr. Lamb
Scott
Spragge
Littlehales C.
Rider C.
Snow
Crawford
Becket C.

Skinner
Winch
Morris
Bullock
Mr. Lumley

Moore
Ld. H. Spencer
Clarke
Ld. Ashbrook
Mr. Bligh
Price
Waller
Arden
Monk
Grey
Manning
Champneys C.
Bridges
Hart
Palmer
Luke C.
Cropley C.
Walpole
Carless
Hankey
Jebb
Gifford
Moore

3rd Form.

Upper Greek.

Ld. Downe
Pogson
Baker
Oliver
Plumer
Adams
Mr. Westley *ma.*
Mr. Westley *mi.*
Moore
Sr. G. Boynton
Pogson
Concanen
Anson

Lacy
Langley
Haslewood C.
Prior C.
Whitmore
Buller
Blencowe

Lower Greek.

Moss
Mr. Craven
Ld. Huntley
Langford
Marsh
Briggs C.
Blake
Clinton *ma.*
Anson *mi.*
Warington
Roberts
Grant
Robinson
Harvey
Dayrell
Ekins
Quarrel
Bethell
Lyford

Sense.

Mordaunt
Mr. Mountague
Stocking
Roby C.
Mansell C.
Freeman C.
Douglass
Way *ma.*
Dalling
Deare
H. Roberts
Kenrick
Dolphin
Forester

Churchill
Campbell
Boldero
Estwick
Ibbetson
Hucks
Hart

Nonsense.

Ld. Dalkeith
Poyntz
Way *mi.*
Griffinhoofe C.
Hulse
Mr. Herbert
Berry C.
Hill [C.]
Parsons *ma.*
Kenrick *mi.*

Lower Remove.

Yorke
Wragge
Mr. Dawnay
Earle
Broadhead
Leigh
Pigott
Mr. King
Langham
Clinton *mi.*
Mellish

Unplaced.

Burford
Bold
Watts
Smith
Shortt
Kerrison
Bullock
Rogers

Floyer
Nicholls
Bainbridge
Mr. Meade
Beauclerk
Michod

2nd Form.

Upper Remove.

North
Prime
Ld. Holland
Parry [C.]
Langford
Philpot
Broadley
Way
Broadley
Prior [C.]
Parnther
King
Baker
Tomkinson
Welton

Lower Remove.

Fonerau
Charteris

Boone
Payne
Harris
Mr. King *mi.*
Elton
Parsons *mi.*
Hulse *min.*
Wright
Ld. Broome
Roper
Leycester
Morant

1st Form.

Ekins *mi.*
Batson
Branscomb
Gambier
Buller
Mr. P. King
Blackman
Lawrence *ma.*
Lawrence *mi.*
Hulse *min.*
Hammersly
Bosanquet
Hunter
Mr. King *min.*

[Smith]   [326

A BILL OF ETON SCHOOL,
EASTER 1783.

6th Form.

Luxmoore C.
Roberts C.
Dyson C.
Saunders C.
Bayley C.
Dyson C.
Freeman C.
Boggust C.
Bearblock C.
Butt C.
Smith C.
Dennis C.
Selwyn
Mr. Fitzroy
Eden
Mellish
Ld. Blandford
Mr. Montagu
Pocock

5th Form.

Hunt C.
Moore C.
Manby C.
Fancourt C.
Evans C.
Heys C.
Cottrell C.
Lockart
Mellish
Freeman C.
Jones C.

Grover C.
Mr. Stopford
Astley
Skinner
Leycester C.
Western
Lomax
Blencowe C.
Ellis C.
Philpot C.
Burgh
Deverell
Hamersley
Anson
Roycroft C.
Ld. Darnley
Tighe
Beaden
Michaelson
Fennell C.
Smith C.
Parker
Rolfe
Gulston
Harwood C.
Hibbert C.
Ellison C.
Briggs C.
Griffith
Blake
Page
Wickes
Worgan C.
Blick C.
Jefferson
Cooper C.

West C.
Ingram
Marsh
Smith
Roberts
Loyd
Roberts C.
Street C.
Douglass
Jolliff
Scott C.
Marshall C.
Broadhead
Wallace
Anguish
Tilson
Hird
Tilson
Symes
Martin C.
Cooper
Harrison C.
Knott
Chambre
Secker

Remove.

Bullock
St. George
Canning
Langford
Metcalfe
Mr. Batthurst
Mr. Watson
Mr. Lumley
Ld. Leslie
Jefferson
Smith C.
Bedell C.
Abbott C.
Noverre
Sykes
Lewin
Woodcock
Lambton
Mr. Clive

Packington
Webb
Frere
Reid C.
Harvey C.
Ferrier
Clarke
Scott
Vause
Mellish
Herring

4th Form.

Milnes
Bligh
Sr. G. Wombwell
Smith
Wickam
Mr. Lamb
Spragge
Littlehales C.
Rider C.
Snow
Crawford
Beckett C.
Skinner
Wynch
Morris
Mr. Lumley
Ponsonby
Moore
Ld. H. Spencer
Clarke
Ld. Ashbrook
Mr. Bligh
Price
Waller
Jones
Monck
Grey
Champneys C.
Bridges
Hart
Palmer
Luke C.
Cropley C.

Walpole
Carless
Hankey
Jebb
Gifford
Moore C.
Groves
Cosens
Burgh
Bootle
Rosoman
Mr. Windsor
Keck
Kitson
Walwyn
Ld. Downe
Pogson
Baker
Oliver
Mr. Wesley
Mr. Wesley
Moore
Walwyn
Sr. G. Boynton
Plumer
Pogson
Concanen
Langley
Haslewood C.
Anson
Adams
Blencowe
Moss
Mr. Craven
Ld. Huntley
Langford
Marsh
Blake
Anson
Lyford
Briggs C.
Clinton
Warington
Quarrell
Roberts
Grant
Robinson
Harvey

Ekins
Bethell C.
Dayrell
Burford
Bold
Whitmore
Buller
Butler

3rd form.

Upper Greek.

Mordaunt
Mr. Montagu
Way *ma.*
Stocking
Forester
Mansell C.
Roby C.
Freeman C.
Dolphin
Deare
Douglass
Roberts
Kenrick
Churchill
Campbell
Boldero
Ibbetson
Hart
Bainbridge
Estwick
Coates
Hunt
Bethell

Lower Greek.

Ld. Dalkeith
Poyntz
Mr. Herbert
Way
Hulse
Griffinhoofe C.
Hill C.

Berry C.
Parsons
Leigh
Kenrick
Kerrison
Hunt
Williams

York
Burningham
Smith
Wragge
Mr. Dawnay
Earle
Pigott
King
Langham
Clinton
Mellish
Short
Smith C.
North
Ld. Holland

Prime
Hucks C.
Parry C.
Langford
Parnther
Baker
Way [mi.]
Philpot
Broadley C.
Broadley
King
Prior C.

Orde
Tomkinson
Welton
Weston
Charteris
Boone
Rogers
Harris
Mr. King
Elton
Wright

Fonereau
Payne

Unplaced.

Ladbrook
Waring
Nicholls
Mr. Meade
Beauclerk
Michod
Fletcher
Chilcot
Mr. Wesley
Hare
Cooke
Smith
Dashwood
Kenrick
Butler
Butler

2nd Form.

Watts C.
Lake
Floyer
Callander
Bullock
Hulse
Ld. Broome
Roper
Morant
Parsons
Leycester
Ekins

Mr. Stopford
Batson
Branscomb
Blackman
Bosanquet
Gambier
Buller
Lomax
Lawrence

Beauchamp	Skinner
Mr. P. King	Polehampton
Hulse	Trevanion
Lawrence	Grey
Draper	Mr. De Grey
Hamersley	Seymour
Hunter	St. Paul
Mr. E. King	Witts
Ponsonby	Lyddell
Brookland	Mr. Townshend
Smith	Langford [346]

A LIST OF THE SCHOOL, [? Easter] 1784.

6th Form.

Dyson *ma.* C.
Dyson *mi.* C.
Boggust C.
Bearblock C.
Butt C.
Smith C.
Selwyn
Mr. Montagu
Hunt C.
Moore C.
Fancourt C.
Evans C.
Heys C.
Cottrell C.
Mellish
Western
Hammersley
Anson
Ld. Darnly
Tighe

5th Form

Freeman C.
Jones C.
Grover C.
Leycester C.
Ellis C.
Philpot C.
Roycroft C.
Beaden
Smith C.
Gulston
Harwood C.
Hibbert C.

Ellison C.
Briggs C.
Griffith
Page
Wickes
Worgan C.
Blick C.
Ingram
Marsh
Smith
Street C.
Douglass
Jolliff
Scott C.
Marshall C.
Wallace
Anguish C.
Hird
Martin C.
Cooper
Harrison C.
Knott
Bullock
Chambre
Secker
Canning
Langford
Metcalfe
Mr. Bathurst
Mr. Lumley
Mr. Watson
Ld. Leslie
Jefferson
Smith C.
Bedell C.
Lambton
Mr. Clive
Frere

Reid C.
Ferrier
Webb
Woodcock
Abott C.
Harvey C.
Noverre
Pakington
Vause
Mellish
Herring
Bligh
Sr. G. Wombwell
Smith
Wickham
Mr. Lamb
Littlehales C.
Snow
Wynch
Crawfurd
Morris
Mr. Lumley
. Taylor

Remove.

Rider C.
Clayton
Ld. Barymore
Baker
Wyatt
Ponsonby
Ld. H. Spencer
Clarke
Mr. Bligh
Price
Grey
Bridges
Jebb
Roe
Carless
Palmer
Monck C.
Jones C.
Champneys C.
Keate C.
Hart C.

Groves
Luke C.
Cropley C.
Gifford C.
Kitson
Sr. G. Boynton
Foster
Courthope
Cooper

4th Form.

Cosens
Burgh
Bootle
Mr. Windsor
Keck
Walwyn *ma.*
Miller
Ld. Downe
Frere
Baker
Oliver
Mr. Wesley
Moore
Walwyn *mi.*
Plumer
Langley
Anson
Haslewood C.
Campion
Blencowe C.
Moss
Mr. Craven
Ld. Huntley
Langford
Marsh
Anson
Lyford C.
Driffield C.
Briggs C.
Clinton
Warrington
Quarrell
Grant
Harvey
Ekins

Bethell C.
Dayrell
Burford
Bold
Whitmore
Butler
Simpson
Lane
Humphreys C.
Thackeray C.
Hughes
Harvey
Cross
Adams
Mordaunt
Mr. Montagu
Way
Forester
Cartwright
Deare
Mansell C.
Roby C.
Dolphin
Freeman C.
Roberts
Churchill
Kenrick
Boldero
Estwick
Ibbetson
Hart
Bainbridge
Coates
Bethell C.
Ridout
Keate
Corbould
Donithorn
Cambell
Ld. Dalkeith
Poyntz
Mr. Herbert
Williams
Brown
Way
Hulse
Griffinhoofe C.
Hill C.

Leigh
Hunt
Parsons
Harrison C.
Kerrison
Fletcher C.
Astley C.

Lower School.
Upper Greek.

Kenrick
York
Burningham
Ladbrook
Smith
Mr. Dawnay
Earle
Pigott
Mr. King
Langham
Clinton
Short
Smith C.
North
Ld. Holland
Abbott
Hare
Smith
Christie

Lower Greek.

Mellish
Boone
Ladbrook
Wagner
Baker
Prime
Hucks C.
Parry C.
Langford
Panther
Way
Philpot
Broadley C.

Broadley C.
King
Fitzthomas
Williams
Wagner

Sense.

Mr. King
Tomkinson
Orde
Charteris
Western
Rogers
Harris
Elton
Wright
Fonereau
Albert
Mr. Meade
Payne
Filewood
Ladbrook
Butler
Foster
Anson

Nonsense.

Floyer
Bullock
Hulse
Watts C.
Ld. Broome
Roper
Lake
Parsons
Lawrence
Hexter
St. Leger

Lower Remove.

Mr. Wesley
Leycester

Michod
Dashwood
Nicholls
Mr. Stopford
Bosanquet
Ekins
Branscomb
Blackman
Gambier
Price
Batson
Brown
Buller
Draper
Lomax

Unplaced.

Smith
Grant
Weston
Hartley
Groves
Wynch
Jonstone

Second Form.

Smith
Beauclerk
Hulse
Beauchamp
Hunter
Kenrick
Lawrence
Chilcot

Lower Remove.

Mr. King
Mr. King
Butler
Way
Brookland

Hamersley
Newbery

First Form.

Newbery
Rogers
Ponsonby
Mr. Craven
Thackeray
Skinner
Polehampton
Langford

Barnard
Mr. Townshend
Trevanion
Grey
Liddle
Dolby
Mr. De Gray
Seymour
West
St. Paul
Hexter
Grant
Smith   [339]

A BILL OF THE SCHOOL, DEC. 10th, 1785.

Sixth Form.

Cottrell C.
Freeman C.
Jones C.
Grover C.
Leycester C.
Ellis C.
Smith C.
Hibbert C.
Ellison C.
Briggs C.
Worgan C.
Blick C.
Gulstone
Smith
Cooper
Bullock
Canning
Mr. Bathurst
Mr. Watson

Fifth Form.

Scott C.
Marshall C.
Anguish C.
Hird C.
Harrison C.
Langford C.
Metcalfe C.
Sergison
Smith C.
Mr. Clive
Frere
Reid C.
Abott C.

Woodcock
Harvey C.
Vause C.
Mellish
Herring
Sr. G. Wombwell
Wickham
Mr. Lamb
Littlehales C.
Snow
Crawford
Mr. Lumley
Rider C.
Baker C.
Wyatt
Ponsonby
Ld. H. Spencer
Ld. Barrymore
Mr. Bligh
Monck C.
Jones C.
Carless C.
Grey
Bridges
Hart C.
Palmer
Luke C.
Cropley C.
Sr. G. Boynton
Foster
Groves
Courthope
Cooper
Champneys C.
Seymour
Burgh
Miller
Bootle

Q

Mr. Windsor
Baker
Moore
Keck
Walwyn
Anderson
Oliver
Mr. Westley
Walwyn
Plummer
Langley
Anson
Campion
Williamson
Moss
Mr. Craven
Ld. Huntley
Langford
Marsh
Anson
Lyford C.
Haslewood C.
Driffield C.
Briggs C.
Clinton
Quarrell
Bold
Simpson
Dayrell
Warrington
Harvey
Ekins
Bethel C.
Adams C.
Burford
Whitmore
Lane
Hughes C.
Harvey C.
Wyatt C.
Hammilton
Butler
Humfrey C.
Mordaunt
Mr. Montague
Way
Thackeray C.
Forrester

Cartwright
Deare
Jollife
Young
Freeman C.
Bainbridge [C.]
Roberts
Churchill
Ibbetson
Hart
Estwick
Coates C.
Bethel C.
Roby C.
Keate C.
Corbould
Donithon
Boldero
Cross
Blashford

Remove.

Ld. Dalkeith
Cambell
Poyntz
Mr. Herbert
Williams
Brown
Way
Hulse
Griffinhoofe C.
Loyd C.
Hill C.
Leigh
Parsons
Harrison C.
Astley C.
Fletcher C.
Stackpoole

Fourth Form.

Yorke
Ladbrooke
Seymour

Burningham
Kenerick
Mr. Dawnay
Smith C.
Earle
Pigott
Mr. King
Langham
Clinton ·
Short
Smith
North
Ld. Holland
Smith C.
Christie
Hare
Ld. Morpeth
Mr. Wallop
Wright C.
Mellish
Boone
Ladbrooke
Baker
Prime
Hucks C.
Langford
Parnther
Lambart
Way
Deare
Williames
Broadley C.
King
Cookson
Mr. Bromley
Calvert
Davie
Haggerston
Manbey
Fitztomas
Mr. King
Harris
Tomkinson
Wagner C.
Wright
Charteris
Rogers
Weston

Elton
Orde
Albert
Mr. Meade
Keck
Ladbrooke
Pitt
Foster
Hanson
Parker
Wandesford
Hartley
Forbes
Ld. Le Poor
Mr. Beresford
Hexter

Lower School.
3rd Form.

Stacpoole
Clark
Hulse
Ld. Broome
King
Parsons
Lawrence
Dashwood
Roper
Lake
Whynch
Mr. Westley
Leycester
Payn

Lower Greek.

Nicholls
Mr. Stopford
Bosanquit
Batson
Branscomb
Brown
Draper
Tims
Ekins

Q 2

Michod
Buller
Brodrip
Smith C.
Anson
Delmé
Cook C. [? O.]
Kingston
Law
Wilson [C.]
Welpdale
Davie
Blake
Sims

Sense.

Blackman
Mr. Wallop
Beauclerk
Mr. Leslie
Hunter
Laurence
Beauchamp
Hulse
Chilcot
Weston
Carter
Tomkins
Douglas
Wright

Nonsense.

Mr. P. King
Mr. E. King
Hoare
Newbery
Way
Newbery
Hammersly
Mr. Bligh
Butler
Brookland
Hanbury
Liddell

Colhoun
Hartley

Lag Remove.

Langford
Polehampton
Ponsonby
Rogers
Mr. Craven
Mr. Townshend
Dolby
Smith
Barnard
Aylmer
Lewis
Thackeray
West
Galway
Groves
Harvey
Rawlins
Blake
Welpdale
Welpdale
Oliver
Askew
Ld. Gower
Bond
Harvey
Bagwell
Snow
Munday
Satherthwaite

Second Form.

Tighe
Gibbons
Mr. De Gray
Gray
Seymour
Trevanion
St. Paul
Smith

| Langham | Dick |
| Smith | Clarke |

Lag Remove.	1st Form.
Grant	Lushington
Hexter	Mr. Dawnay
Langford	Mr. King
Shephard	Heath
Mr. Irby	Marsh
Ld. H. Montague	Taubman
Langford	Stanley
Morgan	Christian
Beauchamp	Neucomen
Yorke	Elliott

[348]

ETON, JULY 29, 1786.

UPPER SCHOOL ONLY.

Sixth Form.	
Grover C.	Snow
Leycester C.	Mr. Lumley
Ellis C.	
Smith C.	Baker [C.]
Hibbert C.	Wyatt
Ellison C.	Ponsonby
Briggs C.	Ld. Spencer
Worgan C.	Ld. Barrymore
Blick C.	Mr. Bligh
Scot C.	Monck [C.]
Marshall C.	Jones [C.]
Smith	Carless [C.]
Cooper	Hart [C.]
Bullock	Palmer
Canning	Cropley [C.]
Mr. Clive	Sr. G. Boynton
Frere	Foster
Woodcock	Groves
Mellish	Courthope
Herring	Cooper
	Champneys [C.]
Anguish C.	
Hird C.	Seymour
Harrison C.	Burgh
Langford C.	Miller
Metcalfe C.	Bootle
Smith C.	Mr. Windsor
Reid C.	Baker
Abott C.	Moore
Hervey C.	Keck
Vause C.	Walwyn
Sr. G. Wombwell	Oliver
Wickham	Mr. Westley
Mr. Lamb	Walwyn
Littlehales C.	Langley
	Campion
	Williamson

Moss
Mr. Craven
Ld. Huntley
Langford
Marsh
Anson
Lyford [C.]
Haslewood [C.]
Driffield [C.]
Briggs [C.]
Quarrell
Bold
Simpson
Dayrell
Warrington
Harvey
Ekins
Bethell [C.]
Adams [C.]
Whitmore
Burford
Lane
Hughes [C.]
Harvey [C.]
Wyatt [C.]

Humfrey
Mordaunt
Mr. Montague
Way
Forrester
Carthwright
Younge
Freeman [C.]
Bainbridge [C.]
Churchill
Ibbetson
Hart
Elswick
Coates [C.]
Bethell [C.]
Roby [C.]
Keate [C.]
Donithorne
Boldero
Cross
Blatchford
Thackeray [C.]

Ld. Dalkeith
Cambell
Pointz
Mr. Herbert
Williams
Brown
Way
Hulse
Abney
Griffinhoofe [C.]
Loyd [C.]
Leigh
Parsons
Harrison [C.]
Astley [C.]
Fletcher [C.]
Stacpoole

Remove.

Mr. Bowes
Powell
Yorke
Ladbrooke
Seymour
Burningham
Mr. Dawnay
Smith C.
Earle
Mr. Bowes
Pigot
Mr. King
Ld. Morpeth
Langham
Short
Smith
North
Ld. Holland
Smith C.
Jones
Christie
Hare
Mr. Wallop

Fourth form.

Mellish

Wright C.
Boone
Ladbrooke
Baker
Prime
Hucks C.
Langford
Parnther
Lambart
Way
Deare
King
Cookson
Mr. Bromley
Broadly C.
Calvart
Davie
Haggarston
Manbey

Fitzthomas
Mr. King
Harris
Tompkinson
Charteris
Wagner C.
Rogers
Weston
Elton
2 Wright
Albert
1 Orde
Mr. Meade
Keck
Ladbrooke
Pitt
Foster
Hanson
Parker
Wandesford
Hartley
Forbes
Ld. Le Poer
Mr. Beresford
Worgan
Sr. J. Shelly
Puller
Stevens

Wyatt

Hulse
Clarke
Selwyn
Stacpole
Dashwood
King
Mr. Westley
Roper
Lake
Wynch
Leycester
Payne
Anson
Williams

A Bill of ye Lower School,
Election 1786.

Ld. Brome
Filewood
Nichols
Mr. Stopford
Bosanquet
Batson 2
Browne 1
Draper
Timms
Ekins
Brodrip
Buller
Smith C.
Delme *ma.*
Kingston C. [O.]
Wilson C.
Whelpdale *ma.*
Davie
Blake
Penrose
Sims
Law
Branscombe
Sturges

Harris *ma.*
Blackman

Mr. Wallop
Mr. Leslie
Hunter
Beauclerk
Lawrence
Beauchamp
Carter
Hulse
Chilcott
Weston
Douglas
Wright
Delme *mi.*
Tompkins
Cotton

Dunbar
Graham
Miller
Mr. P. King
Mr. E. King
Hoare
Newbery *ma.*
Newbery *mi.*
Hamersley
Way
Mr. Bligh
Hanbury
Liddell
Colhoun
Hartley
Mundy *ma.*
Butler
Brookland
Snow
Estridge *ma.*
Saterthwaite
Rawlins
Douglas

C. Langford
Polhampton
Ponsonby
Rogers
Dolby
Mr. Craven
Mr. Townshend
Smith

Aylmer
Lewis
Thackeray
West
Galway
Groves
Mundy *mi.*

Barnard
Hervey
Blake *mi.*
Tighe
Gibbons
Mr. de Grey
Seymour
Trevanion
Grey
St. Paul
S. Smith
Langham
T. Smith
Stewart

Unplaced.
Mundy *min.*
Dimsdale
Clifton
Byam
Preedy

2d Form.

Oliver
Ld. Gore
Askew
Grant
Hervey *mi.*
Hexter
H. Langford
Shepherd
Mr. Irby
Ld. H. Montagu
W. Langford 2
Morgan 1
Dick 3
Beauchamp 1
Yorke 2

Clarke
Whelpdale *mi.*
Bagwell
Bond

Heath
Mr. Dawnay
Mr. H. King
Lushington
Stanley
Xtian
Whelpdale *min.*
Newcomen
Taubman
Hoare
Marsh

1st Form.

Eliot
Braddyll
Coxe
Estridge *mi.*
North
Sewel
Brummell *ma.*
Russell
Brummell *mi.*
Mr. W. King   [357]

A BILL OF ETON SCHOOL, July 28th, 1787.

[Collegers.]
6th Form.

Worgan
Blick
Scott
Marshall
Hird
Langford
Metcalfe
Smith
Abbott
Vause
Baker

5th Form.

Monck
Jones
Carless
Hart
Cropley
Champneys
Driffield
Briggs
Ekins
Bethell
Adams
Burford
Hughes
Harvey
Wyatt
Humfrey
Thackeray
Bainbridge
Hart

Coates
Bethell
Keate
Griffinhoofe
Loyd
Astley
Smith
Jones
Wright
Hucks
Broadley

Remove.

Worgan
Wyatt

4th Form.

Williams
Ekins
Penrose
Wilson
Sturges
Cotton

Lower School.

Dinsdale
Clifton
Preedy
Byam
Russel

[Oppidans.]
6th Form.

Canning
Frere
Woodcock
Wyatt
Ld. Spencer
Mr. Bligh
Sr. G. Boynton
Foster
Groves

5th Form.

Cooper
Seymour
Burgh
Miller
Baker
Moore
Mr. Westley
Walwyn
Campion
Moss
Anson
Bold
Simpson
Dayrell
Mordaunt
Mr. Montague
Way
Cartwright
Mr. Stewart
Younge
Ibbetson
Estwick
Donithorne
Blashford
Ld. Dalkeith
Campbell
Mr. Herbert
Williams
Way
Hulse
Abney
Brown

Leigh
Mr. Bowes
Powell
Yorke
Seymour
Burningham
Mr. Dawnay
Earle
Pigott
Mr. Bowes
Mr. King
Ld. Morpeth
North
Ld. Holland
Christie
Hare
Mr. Wallop
Ld. Templetown
Atherly
Ladbrooke
Baker
Prime
Langford
Parnther
Lambart
Way
Williames
King
Cookson
Calvert
Davie
Manbey
Cornwall
Haggerston
Mr. Stewart

Remove.

Mr. Bromley
Atherly
Mr. King
Harris
Charteris
Rogers
Elton
Wright
Albert

Mr. Meade
Orde
Keck
Ladbrooke
Pitt
Foster
Parker
Wandesford
Hartley
Forbes　　　.
Ld. Le Poer
Mr. Beresford
Sr. J. Shelly
Puller
Stevens
Fortescue ·
Hulse
Clarke
Birch
Weston

4th Form.

Selwyn
Stackpoole
King
Dashwood
Roper
Mr. Westley
Leycester
Payne
Anson
Skipwith
Morgell
Lowry
Holbech
Winstone
Onslow
Ricketts

Ld. Broom
Nicholls
Mr. Stopford
Brown
Bosanquet
Filewood
Draper

Tims
Batson
Broderip
Kingston
Buller
Delmè
Whelpdale
Blake
Davie
Sims
Law
Mr. Stewart
Terry
Grimstone
Eyres

Mr. Wallop
Mr. Leslie
Hunter
Beauclerk
Lawrence
Delmè
Turner
Morphew
Froome
Digby
Beauchamp
Carter
Blackman
Harris
Weston
Wright
Chilcott
Fury
Blackman

Lower School.

Upper Greek.

Hunt
Douglass
Douglass
Dunbar
Graham
Mr. E. King
Tomkins

Miller
Mr. P. King
Hoare
Newbery
Newbery
Mr. Bligh
Hartley
Hammersly
Way
Hanbury
Liddell
Mundy
Saterthwaite
Estridge
Butler
Brookland
Snow
Rawlins
Whitfield

Lower Greek.

Mr. Stuart
C. Langford
Polehampton
Rogers
Dolby
Mr. Craven
Mr. Townshend
Smith
Aylmer
West
Galway
Groves
Lewis
Thackeray
Mundy
Tighe
Trevanion
Dalling
Croft
King.
Ponsonby

Cameron
Mr. De Grey
Barnard

Harvey
Blake
Gibbons
Seymour
P. Smith
Langham
Smith
Hatch
Grey
Newcomen
Garrick

Oliver
Mr. Irby
Grant
Hexter
Ld. H. Montague
Beauchamp
Yorke
Dering
Williams
Bagwell
Stewart
Harvey
H. Langford
Shepherd
W. Langford
Morgan
Dick
Clarke
Whelpdale
Heath
Atkinson
Mr. Dawnay
Mr. H. King
Lushington
Stanley
Christian
Whelpdale
Newbery
Russel

Unplaced.

Dedell
Cartwright
Baron

Cotton
Fry
Smith

2nd Form.

Ld. Gore
Beckford
Taubman
Marsh
Grimes
Mr. De Grey
Mundy
Elliot
Russell
North
Mr. Irby
Tynte
Mr. Dawnay

Boynton *ma.*
Adams

1st Form.

Braddyl
Estridge
Methuen
Boynton *mi.*
Brummell *ma.*
Brummell *mi.*
Sewell
Hoare
Mr. W. King
Netterville
Stewart
Granville
Trevanion
Mr. Townshend   [341]

A BILL OF ETON SCHOOL,
July 28th, 1788.

[*Provost.*	King's Scholars.
Dr. Roberts	**6th Form.**
	Langford
Vice Provost.	Metcalfe
	Smith
Mr. Chamberlayne	Abbott
	Vause
	Baker
Fellows.	Monck
	Jones
Dr. Apthorpe	Carless
Dr. Norbury	Hart
Mr. Tew	Driffield
Dr. Barford	
Dr. Heath	
Mr. W. Roberts	. 5th Form.
	Briggs
Upper School Masters.	Ekins
	Bethell
Dr. Davies, *headmaster*	Hughes
Dr. Sumner	Wyatt
Mr. Heath	Humfrey
Mr. Forster	Thackeray
Mr. Goodall	Bainbridge
	Hart
	Coates
Lower School Masters.	Bethell
	Keate
Dr. Langford, *headmaster*	Griffinhoofe
Mr. Prior	Loyd
Mr. Savage	Astley
Mr. Stevenson	Smith
Mr. Hinde]	Jones

Wright
Hucks
Broadley
Worgan
Wyatt
Williams

Remove.

Smith
Turner
Furey
Froome
Wilson
Penrose
Sturges

4th Form.

Cotton
Blackman
Morphew
Whitfield
Dinsdale

Lower School.

Hexter
Shepherd
Preedy
Cotton
Russell
Russell
Byam
Fry

Oppidans.

6th Form.

Foster
Cooper
Baker
Moore

Mr. Wesley
Moss
Anson
Bold
Simpson

5th Form.

Mordaunt
Mr. Mountagu
Way
Cartwright
Mr. Stuart
Young
Donnithorne
Blachford

Ld. Dalkeith
Campbell
Mr. Herbert
Way
Hulse
Abney
Brown
Leigh

Mr. Bowes
Powell
Yorke
Burningham
Mr. Dawnay
Earle
Mr. Bowes
Ld. Morpeth
North
Christie
Hare
Mr. Wallop
Ld. Templetown
Atherly

Baker
Prime
Parnther
Way
King
Cookson

R

Calvert
Davie
Mawbey
Cornwall
Mr. Stuart

Mr. Bromley
Atherly
Mr. King
Rogers
Harris
Wright
Orde
Keck
Foster
Puller
Parker
Wandesford
Hartly
Ld. Le Poer
Mr. Beresford
Sr. J. Shelly
Fortescue
Hulse
Clarke
Birch
Weston

Selwyn
King
Lawrance
Skipwith
Lowry
Morgell
Taddy
Dashwood
Roper
Mr. Wesley
Leycester
Anson
Holbeech
Winston
Onslow
Rickets
Eden
Peploe

Remove.

Ld. Broome
Nicholls
Mr. Stopford
Bosanquet
Brown
Payn
Filewood
Draper
Brogden
Timms
Batson
Broderip
Kingston
Saxton
Buller
Delme
Whelpdale
Latouche
Blake
Burgh
Davie
Law
Terry
Grimstone
Eyres
Gwyn
Mandreaux
Tilt

4th form.

Mr. Wallop
Mr. Leslie
Hunter
Beauclerk
Lawrance
Delme
Digby
Woodhouse
Mordaunt
Harley
Beauchamp
Carter
Blackman
Harris

Hulse
Weston
Wright
Taloe ?
Ld. Andover
Ld. Ossestone [Ld. Ossulstone]
Gandy
Southcote

Hunt
Douglas
Douglas
Mr. E. King
Miller
Mr. P. King
Hoare
Newbery
Newbery
Hartly
Hammersly
Way
Hanbury
Liddle
Mundy
Satterthwaite
Estridge
Brookland
Snow
Rawlins
Medlicote
Featherstone
Mr. Howard
Bennett

Mr. Stuart
Langford
Rogers
Dolby
Butler
Polehampton
Mr. Craven
Mr. Townshend
Aylmer
West
Galway
Groves
Lewis
Mundy

Tighe
Colton
Trevannion
Dalling
Croft
Ponsonby
Ld. Blantyre
Mr. Stuart
Pepys

Unplaced.

Swift
Lukin
Vaughan
Woodburn
Ogle
Smith
Remmett
Spry
Church

Lower School.

Upper Greek.

King
Mr. De Grey
Smith
Blake
Hervey
Seymour
Gibbons
Langham
Smith
Newcomen
Garrick
Hatch
Grey
Thackeray
Buller
Bagwell
Latouche

Lower Greek.

Oliver
Mr. Irby
Grant
Ld. H. Montagu
York
Dedell
Beauchamp
Dering
Williams
Graves
Grantham
Stewart
Hervey
Langford
Langford
Morgan
Dick
Whelpdale
Heath
Atkinson
Smith
Broderip

Sense.

Mr. Bennett
Halifax
Mr. Dawnay
Mr. King
Lushinton
Stanley
Christian
Whelpdale
Newbery
Trevillion
Armitage
Ker
Powys
James
Hyde
Cock
Morrice

Beckford
Taubman

Marsh
Grimes
Sewell
Stewart
Adams

Mr. De Grey
Mundy
Elliott
North
Mr. Irby
Tynte
Mr. Dawnay
Braddyl
Hyde

Unplaced.

Peers
Pemberton
Purefoy
Broderip
Stanley

2nd Form.

Ld. Gore
Boynton
Brummell
Estridge
Hoare
Canning
Methuen
Tarlton
Dedell
Gunthorp
Cowan
Mudd
Young
Colhoun
Ld. Tullibardine
Trevannion

Brummell
Boynton
Granville

Church
Baron
Mr. Cust
Netterville
Mr. Bennett

First Form.

Cooke
Mr. W. King
Mr. Townshend
Stapleton
Lawrance

Don
Mr. R. King
Mr. Cust
Mundy
Church
Mr. Fitzmorris
Mundy
Tancred
Tancred
Price
Young
Hulse
Langford   368

A BILL OF ETON SCHOOL, JULY 27TH, 1789.

Kings Scholars.
6th Form.

Jones
Hart
Driffield
Briggs
Ekins
Bethell *ma.*
Hughes
Wyatt
Thackeray

5th Form.

Hart
Bethell
Keate
Loyd
Smith
Jones
Wright
Hucks
Langford
Broadley
Harris
Worgan
Wyatt
Williams
Bosanquet
Smith
Furey
Froome
Lukin
Tilt
Wilson

Penrose
Sturges
Swift
Hunter
Carter
Blackman *ma.*
Blackman *mi.*
Morphew
Gandy
Vaughan
Woodburne
Church

Remove.

Cotton
Whitfield

4th Form.

Polehampton
Colton
Ogle
Spry
Smith
Remmett
Broderip

Lower School.

Shephard
Preedy
Stanley
Cotton

Russell
Purefoy
Byam
Fry ·

Oppidans.
6th Form.

Mr. Montagu
Younge
Donithorne
Ld. Dalkeith
Mr. Herbert
Way
Abney
Birmingham
Mr. Dawney
Earle

5th Form.

Mr. Bowes
Ld. Morpeth
North
Ld. Holland
Mr. Wallop
Atherley *ma.*

Prime
Parnther
Way
King *ma.*
Calvert
Davie
Mawbey
Cornwall

Atherley *mi.*
Mr. King
Rogers
Orde
Keck
Forster
Puller
Parker
Wandesford

Ld. Lepoer
Mr. Beresford
Sr. J. Shelley
Fortiscue
Hulse
Clarke
Birch

Selwyn
King *mi.*
Lawrence *ma.*
Shipwith
Lowry
Taddy
Mr. Westley
Roper
Leycester
Holbech
Winstone
Eden
Peploe
Rawlins
Onslow
Gervais

Ld. Brome
Mr. Stopford
Browne
Filewood
Draper
Brogden
Batson
Broderip
Kingston
Saxton
Buller
Delme *ma.*
Whelpdale *ma.*
Letouche
Blake
Burghe
Grimstone
Gwynne
Mandreaux
Terry
Eyres
Davie
Law

Pollen
Dixon
Senhouse
Mr. Wallop
Mr. Leslie
Ld. Stanley
Beauclerk
Lawrence
Digby
Wodehouse
Mordaunt
Delme *mi.*
Beauchamp *ma.*
Harris *mi.*
Rashleigh
Hulse *mi.*
Weston
Wright
Tayloe
Ld. Andover
Ld. Ossulstone
Southcote
Satterthwaite
Harley

Remove.

Hornby
Hunt
Douglas *ma.*
Douglas *mi.*
Mr. King
Loveden
Morris
Hoare
Gwynne
Miller
Newbery *ma.*
Newbery *mi.*
Mr. Bligh
Hartley
Hammersley
Neville
Way
Hanbury
Liddell

Mundy
Estridge *ma.*
Brookland
Rawlins
Medlicott
Fetherstone
Mr. Howard
Bennett
Scott
Trevanion

4th Form.

Mr. Stewart
Langford
Rogers *mi.*
Dolby
Butler
Norris
Mr. Craven
Mr. Townshend
Aylmer
Galwey
Groves
Lewis
Mundy
Tighe
Dalling
Mundy
Croft
Ld. Blantyre
Mr. Stewart
Pepys
Wilder
Clifton
Hallam
Drury
Mr. Degrey
Smith
King
Blake
Hervey
Seymour
Langham
Smith

Gibbons
Newcomen
Hatch
Garrick
Grey
Thackeray
Bagwell
Letouche
Terry
Dixon
Hammond
Payne
Mortlock
Purchiss
Bayley

Oliver
Mr. Irby
Grant
Ld. H. Montagu
Dedel
Marsham
Yorke
Beauchamp
Williams
Graves
Stewart
Dering
Langford
Hervey
Morgan
Whelpdale
Heath
Bayley
Atkinson
Smith
Piers
Joddrell
Cleaver
Eden
Swift
Lomax
Turner
Grantham
Langford
Dick

Lower School.
3rd Form.

Upper Greek.

Railton
Weatherstone
Denman
Mr. Bennett
Halifax
Mr. Dawney
Mr. H. King
Lushington
Christian
Whelpdale
Newbery
Trevylian
Powys
James
Ker
Cocke
Hyde
Morice
Moseley

Lower Greek.

Mudd
Beckford
Taubman
Marsh
Grimes
Sewel
Adams
Stewart
Greenough
Cowan
Mr. Percy *ma.*
Garland
Mr. De Grey
Eliott
North
Mr. Irby
Tynte
Mr. Dawney
Bradyll
Gunthorpe

Mr. Lamb
Trevanion
Mr. Stuart *ma.*
Mr. Stuart *mi.*
Musters

Brummell *ma.*
Sturt
Boynton *ma.*
Methuen
Tarleton
Dedel
Wodehouse
Vernon
Estridge *mi.*
Young *ma.*
Brummell
Ld. Tullibardin
Colhoun
W. Young

Cornwallis
Boynton [*mi.*]
Barron
Church *ma.*
Mr. Cust [*ma.*]
Mr. Percy *mi.*
Mr. Bennett *min.*

Unplaced.

Marsh *mi.*
Trant *ma.*
Snowden
Jarrett
Charsley
Morgan

2nd Form

Granville

Pemberton
Don
Ede *ma.*
Cooke
Mr. Townshend
Lawrence

Mr. W. King
Stapleton
Ede [*mi.*]
Mills
West
Morgan
Mr. R. King
Mr. W. Irby
Mundy *mi.*
Young *mi.*
Cole *ma.*
Cole *mi.*

1st Form

Mr. Cust *mi.*
G. Langford
Mundy
Church *mi.*
Sir T. Tancred
Tancred
Mr. Fitzmaurice
Price
Hulse
Mr. Beresford
Trant *mi.*
Layton
Butler
Mr. G. King
Wilmot *ma.*
Wilmot *mi.*
Conyers
Lushington *mi.*
Tregonwell   [377]

A BILL OF ETON SCHOOL, MAY 18th, 1790.

Kings Scholars.

Jones
Hart
Driffield
Briggs
Ekins
Bethell
Hughes
Wyatt
Thackeray
Bethell
Keate

5th Form.

Lloyd
Smith
Jones
Wright
Hucks
Langford
Broadley
Harris
Wyatt
Williams
Bosanquet
Broderip
Smith
Furey
Froome
Lukin
Tilt
Wilson
Penrose
Sturges

Terry
Swift
Hunter
Carter
Blackman
Blackman
Harris
Morphew
Gandy
Vaughan
Woodburn
Church
Cotton
Gwynne
Whitfield

Remove.

Polehampton
Colton
Spry
Smith

4th Form.

Remmett
Terry
Grantham
Broderip
Swift
Bayley
Fowler
Preedy
Stanley

Lower School.

Purefoy
Fry
Charsley
Layton
Morgan

Oppidans.

6th Form.

Mr. Montagu
Earle
Ld. Morpeth
Mr. Bowes
North
Ld. Holland
Mr. Wallop
Atherley

5th Form.

Prime
Parnther
Way
King *ma.*
Calvert
Mawbey
Cornwall
Atherley
Orde
Keck
Puller
Birch
Selwyn
King
Lawrence
Skipwith
Taddy
Holbech
Winstone
Onslow
Eden
Peploe

Gervais

Ld. Broome
Mr. Stopford
Draper
Brogden
Saxton
Latouche
Blake
Burgh
Gwynne
Mandreaux
Davie
Eyres
Dickson
Senhouse
Mr. Wallop
Mr. Leslie
Ld. Stanley
Lawrence
Digby
Woodhouse
Mordaunt
Delme
Beauchamp
Rashleigh
Weston
Ld. Andover
Ld. Ossulstone
Southcote
Satterthwaite
Harley
Shapland

Hornby
Hunt
Douglas
Douglas
Loveden
Morris
Hoare
Miller
Mr. King
Newbery
Newbery
Mr. Bligh
Hartley
Way

Hanbury
Liddell
Mundy
Brookland
Fetherstone
Mr. Howard
Bennett
Trevanion
Ingram
Wilson
Hobhouse
Dean

Remove.

Mr. Stuart
Langford·
Rogers
Dolby
Butler
Norris
Sperling
Hall
Mr. Craven
Mr. Townshend
Aylmer
Galwey
Groves
Lewes
Mundy
Tighe
Dalling
Croft
Ld. Blantyre
Mr. Stewart ·
Pepys
Wilder
Clifton
Hallam
Joddrell
Cooke
Hall
Pepper
Hughes
Gooch
Birch

4th Form.

Drury
Mr. De Grey
Smith
King
Blake
Hervey
Seymour
Langham
Smith
Gibbons
Newcomen
Garrick
Hatch
Grey
Thackeray
Latouche
Dixon
Dixon
Hammond
Payne
Mortlock
Mr. Herbert
Barnard
Gooche

Walmesly
Oliver
Mr. Irby
Ld. H. Montagu
Dedel
Marsham
Yorke
Beauchamp
Graves
Dering
Stewart
Hervey
Langford
Morgan
Whelpdale
Heath
Bayly
Atkinson
Smith
Peers
Cleaver

Eden
Lomax
Turner
Tresilian
Forster
Smith
Vansittart
Morris
Ravenshaw
Boswell
Mr. Moreton
Railton
Wetherstone
Denman
Mr. Bennett
Hallifax
Mr. Dawnay
Lushington
Christian
Whelpdale
Newbery
Trevellian
Powiss
James
Ker
Cock
Hyde
Morrice
Mosely
Delme
Heseltine
Bethell
Elton
Locker
Birch
Freke

———

Adams
Simpson
Mudd
Taubman
Marsh
Beckford
Grymes
Sewell
Cowan
Mr. Percy
Mr. Herbert

Garland
Sumner
Wolfe

———

Lower School.

———

Upper Greek.

———

Mr. Stuart
Hall
Alexander
Lindagreen
Mr. De Grey
North
Mr. Irby
Mr. Lamb
Mr. Dawnay
Tynte
Braddyl
Elliott
Gunthorpe
Trevanion
Mr. Stuart
Mr. Stuart
Musters
Stuart
Sparling
Rawlings
Brummell
Methuen
Tarlton
Dedel
Sturt
Vernon
Woodhouse
Young
Brummell
Ld. Tullibardin
Young
Colhoun
Forster
Leathes
Trant
Lawrence
Marsh
Bower
Mr. Bennett

———

Sense.

Cornwallis
Cornwallis
Boynton
Barron
Church
Mr. Cust
Mr. Percy
Abdy
Oliver
Thomas
Kilpatrick
Serjeant
Bouverie
Don
Pemberton
Granville
Ede
Cook
Mr. Townshend
West
Mundy
Mr. W. King
Stapleton
Ede
Mills
Ingles

Unplaced.

Abdy
Scarlett
Briggs
Clifton
Graves

2nd Form.

Child

Mr. Irby
Snowden
Young
Cole
Cole
Mundy
Sr. T. Tancred
Tancred
Langford
Church
Ld. G. Beresford
Price
Trant
Osborn
Morgan

1st Form.

Hulse
Butler
Mr. G. King
Mills
Greathead
Sr. C. Hawkins
Hawkins
Conyers
Wilmott
Wilmott
Tregonwell
Lushington
Birch
Polehampton
Hexter
Heath
Smith
Kennett
Thackeray
Hawkins   [384]

APPENDIX.

ETON COLLEGE.　A.D. 1698.

Provost.	Collegers—6th Form.
Dr. Godolphin	Willis
	Plucknett
	Philips
V. Provost.	Lamb
	Walpole
Mr. Horne	Malcher
	Loveday
	Cole
Fellows.	Feild
	Powell
Mr. Upman	Harwood [Horwood]
Mr. Hawtrey	Dearle
Mr. Richardson	Mann
Mr. Fleetwood	Lytton
Mr. Young	Simmond × [Symonds]
Mr. Richards	Rooper
	Wray
	Wilson
	Cox
Masters.	Lee
	Wright
Mr. Newborough	Ingelo
Mr. Weston	
Ushers.	6 Form Oppidents.
Mr. Johnson	Mr. Campbell
Mr. Parry	
Mr. Lawley	Cheynell
Mr. Willymott	Pickerings ×
Mr. Upton	Grosvenour
Mr. Sleech	Wilson
Mr. Chair	Tempest

Welyn
Serlock
Rawlinson
Pratt

———————

Collegers—5th Form.

———————

Clark [C.]
Goldwin [C.]
Curtis [C.]
Hartcliffe [C.]
Crompton [C.]
Baker [C.]
Traheren × [Traherne C.]
Bigg [C.]
Pile × [Pyle C.]
Moody [C.]
Tuttell [Tutte C.]
Yate × [Yates C.]
Hanson [C.]
Wood
Kingdom
Cotton
Plummer
Parker
Williams
Legh
Cradock
Dashwood
Medley
Betts
Oldfield
Foster [C.]
Barobie
Bramston
Hethrington
Windham
Goodall
Orchard
Player [C.]
Gay [C.]
Lemman × [C.]
Mannington [? Maningham C.]
Luttrell ×
Slab
Fazakerley
Strengthfield [C.]

Salisbury [C.]
Bragg [C.]
Campion [C.]
Robinson [C.]
Cleaveland [C.]
Seymour
Dashwood
Berkeley
Brodrick
Manning
Mawe [C.]
Harrison

———————

4th Form.
—·—
Mr. Paston
Mr. Darcey
———

Thompson [C.]
Pemberton
Herne
Burford [C.]
Townshend [C.]
Copps [C.]
Haslewood
Marwood
Bromfeild
Pettewood
Masters
Strong
Woodward
Claridge
Philip
Lenthall
Barrett
Thungeford [?]
Lugg
Torret [? Torrent C.]
Barthelman
Whistler
Windus
Lowefeild
Grice
Dowdeswell
Whiston [C.]
Duke
Honeywood [C.]

S

Coventry
Westcombe
Tolderby
Points 2 [one C.]
Fleet
Parcan
Gore [C.]
Lamb [C.]
Newborough
Bowles [C.]
Finch
Mingay
Jennings
Walpole
Hall 2 [one C.]
Bradshaw
Thompson [C.]
Small
Moyes
Hescombe
Seymour 2
Day
Batten
Estoft
Tireman
Reynolds
Jenn
Collington
St. John
Cayley
Knight
Upton
Hodgskins
Whistler
Bothwell [? Rothwell C.]
Seymore
Brigland
Bellam
Raike

———

4 Form Oppidents.

———

Ld. Crompton [Ld. Compton]
Ld. Churchill
Mr. Fane
Mr. Egerton
Mr. Townshend

Mr. Dawnay's 2
Mr. Sidney
Mr. Conning ×
                [? Mr. Coningsby]
Mr. Hanwell
Mr. Howard
Sr. Shirby × [Sr. Shirley]

———

Elliston
Bartlett [C.]
Lowe [C.]
Meridith ×
Cradock
Mountague
Crown
Whithers
Harcourt
Willimott
Shorditch
Daws
Yeamonds ×
Gillman [C.]
Cotterell [? C.]
Honeywood
Gosfright
Peisehouse
Child
Kent
Cranmer
Osbourne
Windham
Pulkington [Pilkington C.]
Ballard
Newell
March

———

Lower School.

Dove
Troude
Owen
Simpson
Hancock
Oglethorpe
Willers
Collington

Smith
Windus
Start
Powell
Dearing
Shepherd
Eyres
Bathus × [? Bathurst]
Calemur

Lower Greek.

Clark [C.]
Hancock
Glover
Tracy
Norton
Young
Cox
Masters
Lewing
Fielder
Lowther
Blackett
Mallett
Bow
Beaulieu
Oliver
Shaw
Bell
Meggot
Harris
Jenings
Hartwell
Carter
Dalyson
Strout
Johnson
Treggenna
Conyers
Sumner
Tillard

Nonsense.

Bowles

Scan and Prove.

Price
Harris
Fane
Brocklett
Sawtell
Floyer
Bonithon
Marshall
Burton
Upton
Kerby
Hawse
Rees
Jones
Bowyer
James
Edwards

Prosodia:

Perkins
Boscawen
Cowfield
Cutrill
Young
Dorell
Douchett
Isaac

Lag Remove.

Hoar
Frewen
Wakeling
Hammond
Sawtell
Sawyer
Jenings
Harris
Black
Tempest
Snow
Hawtry ×
Bernard

Betts 2
James
Price
Rushout
Beer
Bonham

___ _____

2 Form.

___ ____

Ld. Lumley
Ld. Ridgenay × [? Ld. Ridgeway]
Ld. Sauntry × [Ld. Santry]
Sr. Windham ×

___

Bigg
Whill
York
Nordage [? Pordage]
Weddall
Smith
Ward
Hawtry ×
Mountague
Wood
Hamersley
Cherridge
Cooper
Yarborough
Glover
Knapp
Grosvenour
Hatter
Lounge
Powell
Dearing

Philip
Parker
Grice
Carrington
Vaughan
Burton
Lord
Gore
Thoronton
Windham
Seymours 2
Allum
Wendigate [? Wingate C.]
Richardson
Alien
Barredell ×
Clark
Terry
Doyghton
Pasmore
Hamersley
Tornesiges ×
Woodson
Moses ×
Longuille ×
Miller
Shepherd
Hutt
Price
Bowyer

- _____

Upper School 196
Lower School 148 [149]
        _____
        344 [345]

INDEX.

The names are as a rule entered under the spelling most frequently found in the Lists.

The names of Provosts, Fellows and Masters are in italics.

Bouverie (Bouvirie, Boverie, Bovery) 23, 27, 29, 31, 255
Bouverie (Boverie), Mr. 48, 53, 55, 58, 60, 62, 65, 70, 75, 81, 88, 95, 101, 108, 114
Bow 8, 259
Bowden 31
Bowen 2
Bower 254
Bowes, Mr. 231 (*bis*), 236 (*bis*), 241 (*bis*), 247, 252
Bowles (Boles) 6, 10, 19, 34, 36, 53, 58, 62, 68, 73, 258, 259
Bowmont (Boumont, Beaumont), Ld. 49, 54, 58, *see* Roxburghe, Duke of
Bowpous [Burroughs] 4
Bowrous, *see* Burroughs
Bowry 12
Bowyer 27, 30, 32, 259, 260
Bowyer, Sr. 21
Boyce 194
Boyd (Boyde) 71, 76
Boyfield 99, 106, 108, 119
Boyle 169, 173, 178, 180, 184, 187, 191
Boynton 239 (*bis*), 244 (*bis*), 250 (*bis*), 255
Boynton, Sr. Grifs. (Sr. G.) 208, 212, 217, 221, 225, 230, 236
Brabazon 96, 102
Brabourne 1 (*bis*)
Brackley, Ld. 15
Bradbourn 24
Bradbury 5, 18, 26, 27, 30 (*bis*), 35
Braddyl (Braddyll, Bradyl, Bradyll, Braddyle) 35, 36, 40, 43, 234, 239, 244, 249, 254
Bradhead, *see* Broadhead
Bradshaw 184 (*bis*), 187 (*bis*), 191 (*bis*), 258
Bradwell 2
Bragg 257

Brall 16
Bramston (Bramstone) 131, 138, 155, 161, 257
Brand 28
Brandfoot (Branfoot) 46, 51
Bransby 48, 53, 57, 62
Branscomb (Branscombe) 214, 218, 223, 227, 232
Breedon (Bredon) 19, 49, 54, 58, 63, 69, 74, 80, 87
Brereton 31, 33, 38, 41, 45, 47, 133, 140, 147, 152, 163, 167, 172, 176
Bretton 9
Brewer 6
Brice 133, 139, 146, 151, 157
Brickendon (Brickenden) 70, 75, 81, 88, 94, 101
Bridall (Briddall) [Brydall] 39, 42
Bridges (Brydges) 85, 91, 98, 105, 111, 117, 124, 130, 137, 144, 193 (*bis*), 194, 197, 198 (*bis*), 202, 203, 207, 212, 216, 221, 225
Bridges, Sir 41, 44
Bridgewater 17
Bridgman 21
Brigland 258
Briggs 188, 193, 197, 202, 206, 208, 211, 213, 215, 217, 220, 221, 225, 226, 230, 231, 235, 240, 246, 251, 255
Brinkman 49
Britton (Briton, Britten) 4, 16, 21, 26
Briver (Bryver) 8, 12
Broaderick, Mr., *see* Brodrick, Mr.
Broadhead (Bradhead) 185, 189, 193, 198, 199, 202, 204, 207, 209, 211, 213, 216
Broadley (Broadly) 204 (*bis*), 209 (*bis*), 214 (*bis*), 218 (*bis*), 222, 223, 227, 232, 235, 241, 246, 251

Buckeridge (Buckerigde, Buckridge) 7, 11, 18, 19, 59, 64, 69, 75, 81, 83, 87, 90, 96, 103, 109, 115, 122, 129, 132, 133, 139, 140, 145, 147, 151, 152, 153, 156, 157, 159, 163, 164, 168, 173, 177, 179, 183

Buckle 49, 54, 59, 63, 74, 80

Buckler 3

Buckley (Buckly) 3, [Bulkley] 4, 133, 139, 146

Buckridge, *see* Buckeridge

Buckston, *see* Buxton

Buckworth 6, 10, 16, 18, 35, 40, 41

Bucleugh, Duke of, *see* Buccleugh, Duke of

Budgett 12

Budworth 98, 104, 116, 123, 129

Bull 34

Buller 3, 32, 169, 173, 178, 180, 184, 185, 188, 192, 213, 214, 217, 218, 223, 228, 232, 237, 242, 243, 247

Bullock 14, 27, 29, 34, 35 (*bis*), 36, 38, 40 (*bis*), 41, 42, 43, 44, 202, 207, 211, 212, 213, 216, 218, 220, 223, 225, 230

Burch 2, 50, 52, 57, 62, *see also* Birch

Burchet, Mr. 14, 24

Burchett (Burchitt) 7, 8, 11, 12, 34, 39, 42

Burder 32

Burford 213, 217, 222, 226, 231, 235, 257

Burford, Ld. 6, 11, 35, 40, 43

Burgh (Burg, Burghe) 16, 17, 49, 54. 58, 63, 112, 118, 124, 131, 137, 146, 201, 206, 211, 215, 217, 221, 225, 230, 236, 242, 247, 252

Burgoyne 47, 53, 57, 62, 68

Burgoyne, Sr. 20

Burnaby 15

Burningham (Birmingham) 218, 222, 227, 231, 236, 241, 247

Burrell (Burrel, Burwell, Burwill) 1, 22, 26, 97, 99, 104, 106, 110, 113, 116, 119, 125, 132, 139, 145, 150, 156

Burrough (Borough) 19, 26, 31, 33, 63 (*bis*), 68 (*bis*), 74 (*bis*), 79 (*bis*), 86, 93, 100

Burroughs (Burrows, Bowrous, Bowpous) 4, 5, 8, 9, 10, 12, 13

Burslem (Buslem) 32, 119, 125, 129, 136, 143

Burton 4, 5, 7 (*bis*), 9 (*bis*), 11 (*bis*), 23, 26, 32, 151, 157, 158, 162, 167. 259, 260

Burton, Mr., Dr., 36, 38, 42, 51, 56, 61, 67, 79, 86, 93, 100, 107, 114, 121, 128, 135, 142, 148, 154

Burwell, *see* Burrell

Bury, *see* Berry

Busby 21

Buslem, *see* Burslem

Butcher 96, 103, 109, 115, 139, 181, 188, 193, 197, 202, 206

Bute, Ld. 22, 26

Butler 15, 17, 70. 75, 81, 88, 94, 101, 108, 130, 133, 137, 140, 142, 143, 148, 149, 154, 155, 160, 161, 165, 166, 171, 176, 179, 183, 217, 218 (*bis*), 222, 223 (*bis*), 226, 228, 233, 238, 243, 248, 250, 253, 255

Butt 185, 187, 191, 196, 201, 206, 210, 215, 220

T

Gravener, *see* Grosvenor

Graves 103, 109, 115, 244, 249, 253, 255

Gray, *see* Grey

Greathead (Greatheed) 96, 103, 109, 115, 121, 124, 130, 137, 255

Green (Greene) 4, 9, 12, 18, 20, 22 (*bis*), 29, 31, 32, 33, 65, 71, 76, 82, 84, 89, 90, 95, 97, 102, 104, 108, 110, 116, 122, 185, 188, 192, 197, 198

Greenly 44

Greenough 249

Greenville, *see* Grenville

Greenway 16

Gregg (Greg) 5, 9, 197

Gregor 6, 10

Gregory 1, 49, 54, 59, 83 (*bis*), 90 (*bis*), 96 (*bis*), 103, 109, 115, 119, 126, 133, 140, 146, 152, 157, 163, 167, 180, 184, 186, 191, 195, 200

Grenville (Greenville) 20 (*bis*), 25, 27 (*bis*), 28, 30 (*bis*), 31, 58, 59, 63 (*bis*), 68, 69, 73, 74, 116, 118, 122, 124, 129, 131, 136, 137, 143, 144, 149, 155, 158, 161, 163, 167, 172, 176, 179, 183

Greive, *see* Grieve

Gresham 3

Gretton 30

Greville, Lord 55, 60

Grey (Gray) 18, 20, 22, 27, 30, 66, 77, 83, 89, 91, 95, 102, 109, 173, 178, 180 (*bis*), 184 (*bis*), 187, 189, 191, 193, 196, 198, 200, 203, 205, 207, 212, 216, 219, 221, 224, 228, 225, 233, 238, 243, 249, 253

Grey, Mr. 74, 80

Grey, Sr. 19

Greyhurst 141, 147, 152, 158

Grice 16, 35, 257, 260

Griesdale (Grisdale) 70, 75

Grieve (Greive) 49, 54, 58, 63, 69, [?] 72, 74, 77, 83, 90, 96, 103

Griffies, *see* Griffith

Griffin 7, 83, 90, 96, 103, 109, 115

Griffinhoofe 203, 208, 213, 217, 222, 226, 231, 235, 240

Griffith (Griffiths, Griffies) 58, 63, 69, 134, 140, 147, 152, 158, 163, 166, 167, 171, 177, 179, 183, 186, 187, 188, 190, 191, 193, 195, 196, 197, 198, 201, 202 (*bis*), 206, 207, 211, 215, 220

Grigg [? Trigg] 16

Grimes (Grime, Grymes, Grymmes) 70, 75, 81, 88, 94, 96, 97, 101, 103, 104, 108, 109, 111, 116, 123, 239, 244, 249, 254

Grimstone (Grimston) 83, 90, 96, 103, 109, 115, 153, 158, 163, 237, 242, 247

Grimstone (Grimston), Mr. 27 (*bis*), 104, 110, 116, 118, 122, 124, 125, 129, 130, 131, 137, 138, 144 (*bis*), 150, 155

Grisdale, *see* Griesdale

Grosmith 61, 67, 73

Grosvenor (Grosvenour, Grosvener, Gravener) 7, 11, 48, 52, 57, 256, 260

Grove 188, 192, 196, 201, 206

Grover 32, 64, 69, 74, 79, 86, 93, 100, 181, 185, 188, 192, 197, 201, 206, 211, 215, 220, 225, 230

Groves 217, 221, 223, 225, 228, 230, 233, 236, 238, 243, 248, 253

Hand 132, 138, 145, 150, 156, 160, 165, 170, 175

Handley 12

Hanger, Mr. 125, 131, 138, 144, 150

Hankey 185, 189, 193, 198, 203, 208, 212, 217

Hanmer (Hanner) 30, 65, 71, 76, 78, 80, 84, 87, 91, 94, 97, 101 (*bis*)

Hanniker, *see* Henniker

Hannington (Hennington) 158, 163, 168, 172, 176, 179, 183, 186

Hanson (Henson) 28, 32, 49, 52, 57, 61, 65, 70, 76, 82, 134, 136, 143, 149, 227, 232, 257

Hanwell, Mr. 258

Harbrow 5

Harcourt 258

Harden 45

Harding (Hardinge) 3, 14, 15, 35 (*bis*), 48, 54, 58, 63, 68, 73, 80, 87, 98, 105, 111, 113 (*bis*), 117, 119 (*ter*), 124, 126 (*bis*), 130, 132, 133, 139, 140, 145, 146, 151 (*bis*), 156, 157, 162 (*bis*), 166, 174, 178, 181, 184, 188, 193, 197, 202, 206, 211

Hare 12, 34, 39, 93, 100, 107, 114, 121, 131, 138, 144, 218, 222, 227, 231, 236, 241

Harford 168, 173, 177, 180

Harison, *see* Harrison

Harley 242, 248, 252

Harman 6, 11

Harris 4, 32, 33, 36, 38, 41, 42, 44, 46, 51, 63, 69, 72 (*bis*), 130, 214, 218, 223, 227, 232 (*bis*), 236, 237, 242 (*bis*), 246, 248, 251 (*bis*), 259 (*ter*)

Harris, Dr. 36, 38, 42

Harrison (Harison) 4, 9, 25, 48, 53, 58, 62 (*bis*), 67, 73, 79, 86, 93, 100, 113, 119, 126, 133, 140, 207, 211, 216, 220, 222, 225, 226, 230, 231, 257

Hart 3, 30, 203, 207, 212, 213, 216, 217, 221, 222, 225, 226, 230, 231, 235 (*bis*), 240 (*bis*), 246 (*bis*), 251

Hartcliffe 257

Hartley (Hartly) 223, 227, 228, 232, 233, 237, 238, 242, 243, 248, 252

Hartwell (Heartwell) 192, 196, 259

Harvest 27, [? Hawest 30], 47, 51, 56, 61, 67

Harvey (Hervey) 7, 11, 54, 59, 64, 69, 74, 133, 139, 145, 151, 156, 197, 201, 203, 206, 207, 208, 212, 213, 216, 217, 221 (*bis*), 222, 225, 226 (*bis*), 228 (*bis*), 230, 231 (*bis*), 233 (*bis*), 235, 238 (*bis*) 243, 244, 248, 249, 253 (*bis*)

Harvey, Mr. 27

Harwood 1, 2, 3, 20, 25, 35, 40, 164, 168, 172, 176, 178, 181, 185, 188, 193, 197, 202, 211, 215, 220, [Horwood] 256

Hascarot 15

Haskins (Haskyns) 80, 87, 94, 101, 108, 116

Haslam 35

Haslewood (Hazlewood) 198, 203, 208, 213, 217, 221, 226, 231, 257

Hassard (Hazard) 8, 12

Hasted 41, 44

Hatch 35, 48, 53, 54, 58, 59, 63, 64, 67, 70, 75, 84, 91, 97, 104, 105, 112, 118, 124, 126, 131, 133, 140, 146, 152, 157, 162, 166, 170,

Johnston (Jonstone), *see* Johnson

Johnstone, Lord George 31

Jolliff (Jollife) 211, 216, 220, 226

Jones 4, 5, 9, 10 (*bis*), 15, 17 (*bis*), 26, 39, 47, 48, 49, 52, 53, 54, 56, 59, 61, 62, 63, 67, 68, 69, 70, 72, 73 (*bis*), 74, 75, 76, 77 (*bis*), 79, 80 (*bis*), 83, 84, 86, 87 (*bis*), 90, 91, 93 (*ter*), 97 (*bis*), 98 (*bis*), 100 (*ter*), 103, 104, 105 (*bis*), 107, 111 (*ter*), 114, 117 (*quater*), 123 (*bis*), 126, 130 (*bis*), 132, 139, 146 (*bis*), 151, 152, 162, 192, 197, 201, 206, 211, 215, 216, 220, 221, 225 (*bis*), 230, 231, 235 (*bis*), 240 (*bis*), 246 (*bis*), 251 (*bis*), 259

Jonson, *see* Johnson

Jonstone, *see* Johnson

Jukes 7, 11

Keate (Keat) 21, 25, 51, 56, 61, 67, 73, 221, 222, 226, 231, 235, 240, 246, 251

Keating 6

Keck 53, 58, 62, 68, 73, 74, 81, 84, 87, 90, 94, 97, 104, 110, 116, 217, 221, 226, 227, 230, 232, 237, 242, 247, 252

Keeble 24

Keeling 27

Keen (Keene) 20, 24, 112, 118, 124, 131, 137, 144, 149, 155

Kelham (Kelhan) 25, 30

Kelly 40, 84 (*bis*), 91, 97, 98, 104 (*bis*), 110, 111, 116, 117, 123 (*bis*)

Kemble [? Hemble] 15

Kemith [Kemeys] (Keymish, Kemmish) 5, 9, 44

Kemp 48, 53, 58

Kendall (Kendal) 22, 23, 28 (*bis*), 39, 42, 69, 74

Kenerick, *see* Kenrick

Kennedy 14

Kennett (Kennet, Kennit) 54, 59, 63, 69, 74, 255

Kenrick (Kenerick) 199 (*bis*), 203 (*bis*), 208 (*bis*), 213 (*bis*), 217, 218 (*bis*), 222 (*bis*), 223, 227

Kent 19, 106, 113, 178, 181, 185, 258

Keppell 120, 127

Ker 244, 249, 254

Ker, Ld., *see* Kerr, Ld.

Kerby (Curby) 7, 259

Kerr (Ker), Ld. (Ld. Rt., Ld. Robt.) 65, 71, 77, 82, 89, 95, 103, 109

Kerrick 116, 122

Kerrison 213, 218, 222

Key 40, 92, 98, 105, 112, 118, 125, 131, 138, 144, 149, 154, 160, 165

Keymish, *see* Kemith

Kilderben [Kilderbee] (Kilderby) 20, 24

Kilpatrick 255

Kilwarlin, Ld. 137, 144, 149, 155

Kimber 41, 44

Kindsman, *see* Kinsman

King 3, 7, 10, 11, 45, 46, 48, 52, 54, 58, 179, 183, 186, 187, 191, 196, 209, 214, 218 (*bis*), 223, 227 (*bis*), 232 (*bis*), 236, 237, 238, 241, 242, 243, 247 (*bis*), 248, 252 (*bis*), 253

King, Mr. 139, 146, 208, 209 (*bis*), 213, 214 (*bis*), 218, 222, 223 (*ter*), 227 (*bis*), 229, 231, 232, 236 (*bis*), 242, 244, 247, 248, 252

King, Mr. E. 219, 228, 233, 237, 243

York (Yorke) 81, 88, 203,
209, 213, 218, 222, 226,
229, 231, 233, 236, 238,
241, 244, 249, 253, 260

Young (Yonge, Younge) 3,
12, 33 (*bis*), 35 (*bis*), 38,
40 (*bis*), 43, 60, 65, 71,
77, 78, 83, 84, 89, 91, 96,
97, 103, 104, 109, 110,
111, 116, 117, 122, 124,
129, 130, 136, 226, 231,

Young—cont.
236, 241, 244, 245, 247,
250 (*bis*), 254 (*bis*), 255,
259 (*bis*)

Young, Dr. 190, 195, 200,
205, 210

Young (Younge), Mr. 24,
51, 56, 61, 67, 79, 86, 93,
100, 256

Young, W. 250

Younger 2

CHRISTIAN NAMES ONLY.

Adams, Ld. [? sc. Gordon]
35

Charles, Ld. 17, 31, 34

George, Ld. [? sc. Bentinck]
27

James, Ld. 15

Sidney, Ld. 15

Spencer, Ld. (sc. Hamilton)
49, 69, 74

William, Ld. 18

NOTES ON THE LISTS.

1678 In the Bodleian Library, Oxford (Rawlinson MS. B. 266), in a volume labelled "Rawlinson's History of Eton College, vol. ii. fol. 146, 4to." The list is written (evidently by Rawlinson himself) on three sides of a quarto sheet of paper, and is generally, but not always, easy to decipher. It was printed by the Rev. W. L. Collins in his book "Etoniana," pp. 216–220, ed. 1865, but not, I think, always quite correctly : for instance, Mr. Collins prints " Baston," " Tath," " Fenmore," " Wetton," " Cleas," " Hawpey," " Cheasey," " Lutley," where I think the correct names are " Barton," " Tash," " Farmore," " Weston," " Cheas," " Hawtrey," " Cheaney " and " Luttey." A few other names I have marked with queries. The list contains no Provost, Fellows, or Masters, but only the names of the boys arranged in six classes (counting the Bibler's Seat as the First Form). The classes, except the sixth and the last, are divided into Collegers and " Oppidanes." There appear to be seventy Collegers, but as all the boys in the Sixth Form were subsequently elected to King's, and must therefore have been in College at Eton in order to be eligible, commentators on the list have been puzzled to account for the apparent presence of seventy-eight Collegers. It is possible however, by a careful examination of the Eton Register, which shews approximately at what date boys entered and left College, to find out more or less accurately what boys ought to have been in College in 1678. The conclusion I have come to is that in none of the divisions labelled Collegers were all the boys really in College.

To begin with the Sixth Form, which is labelled neither Colleger nor Oppidan, all the eight boys in it but " Ogdin " (more properly " Ogden ") were on the indentures of 1678 for King's, and there can therefore be no doubt these seven were at this date in College. " Ogden " was fourth on the Eton College indentures in 1678, and as Bury (the boy just above him) does not appear as a Colleger in this list, I imagine Ogden must still have been an Oppidan. Of the Fifth Form Collegers, I find no boy of the name of " Pagitt " in the Eton College Register at this time : on the other hand there ought to be, but is not, a

Colleger of the name of " Pate " in the list, so possibly
" Pagitt " may be a mistake for " Pate." I doubt also if
" Brabourne *mi.*" was a Colleger. Of the Fourth Form Collegers
all are correct with the exception of " Woodward " and " Preston,"
who must, I think, have been Oppidans. There should probably,
however, be two boys of the name of " Staples." Of the Third
Form Collegers, " Pain " and " Rendall " seem to have been
Oppidans. Of the Second Form Collegers, only " Poole " and
" Crouch " were really in College.

On the other hand there should be Collegers of the names of
" Hensman," " Thraile," " Allen," and " Waddon."¹ " Waddon "
was fifth on the King's indentures for 1678, but does not seem
ever to have gone to King's, and three crosses are put against
his name: possibly he died at Eton before this list was made out.

Leaving out " Ogden," " Brabourne *min.*," " Woodward,"
" Preston," " Pain," " Rendall," and the seven boys below " Crouch "·
in Second Form, we get sixty-five Collegers. " Hensman,"
" Thraile," " Allen," " Waddon," and a second " Staples " would
make up the number to seventy.

With regard to the number of boys in the list, including the
one boy in the Bibler's Seat, the numbers should be 198, or 207
if the nine boys at the end are included. The number given,
" about 202," splits the difference as near as may be. Why the
last nine boys are thus inserted, it is impossible to say. Perhaps
they were " unplaced," or absent, or omitted by the writer from
their proper place. It has also been suggested that they were
Choristers, of whom there were always *ten* who took their meals
in Hall before the Civil Wars. But as " Buckler " seems from
some notes in the same MS. volume to have been the son of Sir
Christopher Buckler, I think this last explanation is unlikely, as
the Choristers would probably be drawn from a lower class.

It will be seen that a few names have notes after them
viz. " Price (Sr. John)," " Dashwood (Sr. Rob.)," " Conway (Sir
John)," " Raymund (Sr. Jemmatt)," " Puliston (Sr. Rod.)."
Mr. Sterry¹ however shews that Raymund was not knighted till
1680, and Dashwood not till 1682. The notes however seem to
have been written at the same time as the list itself.

Taking all these facts into consideration, it seems most
probable that the list was written, perhaps partly from memory,
at least as late as 1682.

The School does not appear to have been particularly fashionable

¹ *Annals of Eton*, by Wasey Sterry, p.   .

at this period. There are very few boys of title, the only nobleman being Lord Alexander, the son of the Earl of Stirling. Alexander *mi.*, who presumably was his younger brother, is not distinguished by the prefix of " Mr."

The date of the list must be between Herbert's admission to King's on Aug. 24, 1678, and that of Adams on Feb. 8, 167⅞.

The Head Master in 1678 was John Rosewell, who is said to have greatly increased the reputation of the School.

A few notes on the names are to be found in the same MS. volume, but they are extremely brief.

1698 Appendix I., p. 256. From a transcript (of which the original has disappeared) in G. J. Dupuis's handwriting, now in possession of his son, Rev. G. R. Dupuis, of Sessay Rectory, Thirsk. The transcript is in the form of a foolscap octavo book of twelve pages, of which the list, written in double columns, occupies some nine pages. The heading is "Eton College. A.D. 1698." The Staff is given, and the list has this peculiarity that after the Fellows it gives the Upper and Lower Master under the heading of " Masters." Then follow the Assistants, but under the unusual heading of " Ushers." In the Sixth Form the Collegers are given before the " Oppidents." Then come " Collegers—5th Form," but without any break to show where the Oppidans begin ; the break should apparently be after " Hanson," the thirteenth name, but a good many Collegers are scattered about among the remainder of the Fifth Form. Next comes " 4th Form," headed by " Mr. Paston " and " Mr. Darcey," followed by seventy-one names not divided into Collegers and Oppidans. After these however comes a heading " 4 Form Oppidents," with twelve noblemen at the top followed by twenty-seven names, some of which are certainly those of Collegers. The arrangement of Fourth Form is not therefore very intelligible and the easiest explanation (if the transcriber followed the original correctly) is that it consisted of two removes, and that the word " Oppidents " at the head of the second is a mistake.

The next heading is " Lower School," under which general title come seventeen names, then " Lower Greek," " Nonsense " (with only one name), " Scan and Prove," " Prosodia " and " Lag Remove ": finally " 2 Form," with four noblemen preceding fifty-two names. Thus no First Form or Bible-seat is indicated.

The various sub-divisions of the Third Form (which is not mentioned by name) are interesting. They show that it was divided into six parts from very early times. "Upper Greek," though not mentioned, is presupposed by "Lower Greek," but the absence of "Sense" is odd, while "Scan and Prove" and "Prosodia" occur as names in no other extant list, but Thomas James in his MS. Account of Eton Discipline in 1766[1] mentions the lessons learnt by each of these divisions.

The date of the list must be between January 19, 169$\frac{7}{8}$, and April 30, 1698, the dates when Edlin and Plucknett were dismissed respectively to King's. Willis, who heads the list, should come below Plucknett, whom he follows on the indentures for King's for 1697. According to the dates in the Eton Register of Admissions only four of the boys on the Eton indentures for 1697 had been admitted to College when the list was made out, but as "Edlin," who created the fifth vacancy (filled by "Cotterell"), had already gone to King's (for he is not in the list) I imagine "Cotterell" must already have got into College.

We can discover from the same Register what Collegers ought to have been in the School at this date, with the result that supposing "Mannington," "Torret," "Bothwell" and "Wendigate" to be mistakes for "Maningham," "Torrent," "Rothwell" and "Wingate," sixty-eight Collegers can be accounted for. The two remaining ones, "Errington" and "Hayward," seem either to have been omitted or to have been away at the time (they did not leave till 1701–2). Some interest attaches to Errington owing to the following note that appears to his name in the Register for Election 1696. "Francis Errington (in the 12th place) brought no certificate of his age, there being no Register thereof by reason of his father being a Roman Catholick and [having] had him baptized by a Romish priest, but upon the solemn affirmation of Mrs. Errington, the child's mother, that he was but nine years old the 14th of February, 1695, he was admitted to stand and was nominated as abovesaid."

I have added "C." to the Collegers (except in the Sixth Form, "where they all come under one heading"): in cases where there is more than one boy of the same name, there must be some doubt which is the Colleger.

The numbers of the Lower School are wrongly given and should be 149 instead of 148: I suspect they were not given in the original list, but added by the transcriber. The transcriber has also placed crosses against some of the names, indicating, I imagine, that he was uncertain if he had copied them correctly.

[1] See the periodical *Etoniana*, No. 8.

He had placed " 2 " after " Hawse " in " Scan and Prove " but
subsequently erased it.   Notice that where two brothers come
together they are written thus : " Points 2," which we shall find
to be a very common practice in the MS. lists.

     In the British Museum (Harl. MS. 7025 f. 135).   This
1706 being the first of some half dozen lists, of which all the
    others belong to Westminster School, had long been
tacitly assumed to belong to Westminster, though it has no
indication upon it of belonging to any particular school.   But
happening to look out of curiosity at these lists in November
1904, I was much struck with the number of Eton names that
occurred in this list.   At first I thought it merely shewed that
the tide of fashion, which afterwards took these families to Eton,
at this period took them to Westminster, which was then at the
height of its fame, but a closer inspection made me almost certain
that the list actually was an Eton List, and a comparison of it
with the Orlebar list for 1707 proved this to be a fact.

  The list itself is written on two sides of a half-sheet of
foolscap, and is very badly spelt, which probably points to its being
the work of a boy.   Numerals denoting the names of the Forms
are given at the bottom of each, and include a Sixth, Fifth,
Fourth, Third, Second, and another not enumerated, which is no
doubt the First (probably subdivided into a Bible-Seat beginning
with " Mr. Howard ").   Collegers are not distinguished from
Oppidans in any way, but seem placed above them in their forms
throughout the Upper School.   The exception in the Fourth
Form probably points to the boys from " Mr. Compton " to
" Burton " being in Remove.   Oppidans with titles are placed
above other Oppidans.   The names are numbered throughout.
There is no heading of any sort, and the first name begins at
the very top of the paper.   At the end is the following note :
" A copey of a list sent to West by Mr. Henry Drax : 1706."
As a curious instance of an editorial mistake, it may be mentioned
that Mr. Holgate, under the belief that the list was of Westminster, quotes the note, " A copey of a list sent to *Westminster*
by Mr. Henry Drax."   It is of course possible that " West "
may be a contraction for " Westminster," but now that the list
is known to be an Eton one, there is no reason to suppose it.

  Sixty-nine Collegers are shewn in the list. " Snape," who
should follow " Bilbe," and who was in College from 1702–1709,
being omitted.

The date is between June 27 and August 31, 1706, when Norton and Hemming respectively got King's.

Belongs to Mr. R. Orlebar, of Hinwick House, Beds.
1707 In the 3rd Report of the Historical Manuscripts Commission (c. 673), p. 276 Col. A, issued in 1872, upon Mr. Orlebar's MSS., is the following entry:

"1707—Narrow paper roll, 8 or 10 ft. long. Names of persons in Winchester School."

Mr. Holgate came across this entry, and on applying for the loan of the list, learnt it was a Roll of Eton, wrongly described. He further learnt that it had been given to Mr. Richard Longuet Orlebar about the years 1835-6 by Colonel Charles Hervey Smith, of Apsley House, Beds.

The Roll is 9 ft. 4 in. long by $2\frac{7}{8}$ in. wide, and only contains the names of the boys, without those of the Provost, Fellows or Masters. The names of the Forms come at the end of each, and consist of the Sixth, Fourth, Third, Second, and a final one, not named, but no doubt the First. It is evident that the scribe forgot to write "5 form" in its proper place, i.e. after "Tracey," for the fact that a block of Collegers follows "Tracey" shews that a new Form begins here. For the same reason a new Form should begin with "Humphris," and one may fairly conclude that the boys from "Lockett" to "Herne" belonged to Remove.

Each Form down to and including the Third Form is divided into Collegers and "Oppidents," the Collegers coming first. There were no Collegers below the Third Form. At the top of the Oppidans in each case come the boys with titles, the only exception being that in the Third Form the noblemen came above the Collegers. There was no such title as "Lord Buckcleare," who is at the top of the First Form, and Mr. G. E. Cokayne has suggested that "Buckcleare" is for "Beauclerk," meaning "Lord William Beauclerk," whose elder brother, "Lord Burford," appears at the top of Third Form.

The date of this list must be between November 6, 1707, when Sturges got into College, and January 20, 170$\frac{7}{8}$, when Lee got in.

The full complement of seventy Collegers is shewn.

In the Eton College Library. A Roll 9 ft. long by
1718 3 in. wide. It was presented to the Library by Dr. Okes, Provost of King's College, Cambridge, on August 2, 1862.

It is entitled, "A Bill of Eton Schole, 1718." It is the first extant list in which we get a definite mention of "Remove" as a form.

The list does not look as if it had been written by a boy, and from the curious mistakes made was evidently compiled from some written original. Thus the scribe was unable to decipher correctly the seventh name on the list, and has written "Loshu" instead of "Lofting." It is not difficult to detect the mistakes in the case of Collegers, but unfortunately there is no certainty in the case of Oppidans. Another hand moreover has been over the list and made certain corrections and insertions, e.g. "Corbet," the thirty-sixth name in Fifth Form, has been inserted. The "tor" in "Procktor," nine names below, has been added. The sixth name in Remove, "Archer," has also been inserted in a later hand. The twentieth name in Lower Greek was originally "Mackman," but has been altered to "Blackman." After "Barcroft," the twenty-ninth name in the last remove of Third Form, the original scribe had written "Besher," which has been erased and "Bertie" written at the side, with a further insertion of "Wise" at the side. The second name in the Lower Remove of Second Form is written "Holstone," but the *H* has been underlined and an *R* put at the side. The sixteenth name in the Bible Seat was originally written "Libthong," which has been erased and "Sibthorp" put at the side.

The numbers at the end of the Forms are in a later hand: the final number 353 is wrong and should be 350.

The Collegers though not distinctively marked are at the head of their Forms in Sixth, Fifth and Remove, and probably of the various removes of the Fourth: in the Lower School they are mixed up with the Oppidans. Noblemen are above other Oppidans in Sixth, Fifth, Fourth, Second and First Forms, but not in Remove or Third Form.

Red ink is used for the lines dividing off the forms. Notice in Remove "Ld. Sidney," in Fourth Form "Ld. James," in Third "Ld. Charles" and in First "Ld. William," without the addition of any surnames.

There are sixty-six Collegers for certain. Going by the Admission Book it would seem that Raby, Burroughs, Love and another (whose name I cannot discover) are missing, but on the whole it seems more likely that the Admission Register is not very exact with regard to who made the vacancies, and that Dongworth, Winder, Pearce and Wilkinson had got in *vice* the four above.

But if so, it is odd that Dongworth is not with the other Collegers at the top of Remove.

1725   This list was first brought to light in 1890. Its appearance was the outcome of a letter about Eton Lists from Mr. Sterry to the *Eton College Chronicle* on July 3 of that year. In consequence Major Godsal wrote to Mr. Sterry sending him a transcript of a list in the possession of his uncle Mr. T. C. Garth (the well-known M.F.H.), which had been discovered during a recent visit of Major Godsal's to Haines Hill. Major Godsal says that the boys for whose parents' edification the list was evidently made out were the "Colletons," and that one of the Colletons docketed it in 1787, "List of Eaton School 1725."

The list is written on three sides of a sheet of foolscap, each page containing four columns of names. It is endorsed "List of Eaton School 1725," and bears in another place at the back the date July 1725. At the top of page 1, too, is written in a later hand "July 1725." There are the remains of a red seal on the fourth page. The handwriting is fairly good.

The Collegers are not distinguished from the Oppidans; the names of the divisions are given at the end instead of the beginning of each. Fourth Form contains four blocks, shewn by dotted lines, Third Form has three blocks, similarly shewn, First Form two. Boys with titles are grouped together at the top of their forms or blocks in the Upper School, but not in the Lower School, except in the second block of the First Form. The number of boys in each form is added up at the end of it, but has been wrongly added in the case of the Fourth Form, which should read 97, not 98. The totals given at the end for Upper and Lower School are however correct, but they are in a later hand. It may be noted that the names of brothers, where occurring together, are written out in full. Number of boys 378.

1728   This list belongs to Mr. J. E. Eastwood, of Enton, Witley, Surrey, and I first heard of its existence on January 28, 1905. On March 7 Mr. Eastwood kindly lent me the list, informing me that he had it from his uncle J. J. Bumpsted, who left Eton in 1838, and was afterwards Bursar of King's College, Cambridge. The list was originally a Roll, 9 ft. 3⅛ in. long by 3 in. wide, but has since been cut up into five strips, pasted on a large sheet of paper, and placed in a glass frame. It is entitled "A Bill of Eton School, Nov. 2d,

1728," and is headed by the names of the Provost, Fellows and Masters : after these come the Collegers, of whom there are 71, and then the Oppidans. Boys with titles are put at the top of their forms in the Upper School, but not in the Lower, except in the Bible Seat. At the end of the list the names are added up thus : " Upper School 173, Lower School 205, Total 378." This however is not quite correct, for the numbers should be " Upper School 171, Lower School 205, Total 376." The handwriting is good and easy to read, but the spelling is occasionally at fault : the list is written in black ink, except that red ink is used to mark the divisions between the forms. It is curious that there should be 71 Collegers ; probably the scribe inserted some one who in reality had left. In 5th Form " Milford " should probably be " Midford " or " Mitford."

1732 This list is to be found printed on pp. 78-81 of Vol. I. of the " Memoirs of Horace Walpole," by Eliot Warburton (London, 1851). In a footnote to p. 78 the editor acknowledges his thanks to Dr. Hawtrey for granting and to Viscount Castlereagh for requesting the loan of the document. No list of Provost and Fellows is given, nor are the names of the forms, but certain spaces in the printing evidently denote the beginning of the forms, of which there would appear to have been six. Boys with titles appear in groups in the early part of the list, thus no doubt conforming to the general rule that they were placed at the top of their forms in the Upper but not in the Lower School. Notes are added to certain names, and are presumably by Eliot Warburton : these I have eliminated in printing the list. Unfortunately the original of the list has quite disappeared. I suspect that the thirty-ninth name should be " Harvest " and not " Hawest."

1742 In the Bodleian Library (Gough, Bucks 6). This list was discovered by Mr. Sterry, in 1888, bound up in a copy of Harwood's *Alumni Etonenses*, which had belonged to Thomas Okes, a physician. It is written in a clear, boyish handwriting, across the front and back sides of a sheet of foolscap. The first page contains thirteen columns of boys' names, the second two, followed by one giving the names of the Provost, Fellows, Masters, Assistants, and a table of the numbers in each form. To the right of the third column is written " John North, December 21, MDCCXLII," whom we may assume to have been the

writer of the list.   His name will be found in the first remove of
Fourth Form, followed by "Coll.," the only occasion in the list
where the more ordinary abbreviation of "C." is not used.   The
list is headed "The Names of the Boys in Eton School, December
21st, 1742."   Collegers are not given separately, but are distinguished by the letter "C." after their names.   The forms given
are Sixth, Fifth, Remove, Fourth, Third, Second, First and Bible
Seat : of these Fifth Form contains three removes, Fourth Form
three, and Third Form five.   The names of the forms are given
at the end of each in the Upper School, and at the beginning in
the Lower.   Noblemen are placed at the head of their form in
the Upper, but not in the Lower (there are none in the First
Form or Bible Seat).   Notice " Ld. Charles " at the top of Fourth
Form without any surname.   The list has in addition certain
peculiarities of its own that I will now indicate.   The top boy
both of the Upper School and Lower School is designated
" Captain."   Certain boys throughout the School have crosses put
against their names, viz. Frank, Harris *ma.* in Fifth Form,
Cardale in Remove, Williams *mi.* and Plumbe in Third Form,
and Hill in Second Form—but for what reason I am unable to
say.   Lastly Taylor, the Captain of the School, has "C. Prae." after
his name, and the third, fourth, fifth, sixth, seventh and eighth
Collegers have " C. P." after theirs.   Similarly Champion, the
twelfth name in the list, has " C. Op. P." after his name, where the
" C." must have been written in error, as Champion was not a
Colleger : similarly, omitting Mr. Cholmondly, the first name in
the Fifth Form, the six highest Oppidans have either " Op. Prae.,"
" Op. P." or " O. P." written after their names.   These abbrevia-
tions no doubt denote the several " Praepositors " (as they were
then styled) among the Collegers and Oppidans, and throw an interesting side-light on that institution.   Why Anstey, the second
Colleger, was not a Praepostor, cannot be said, but the case of
Mr. Cholmondly, the first Oppidan in Fifth Form, admits of an
easy explanation, viz. that this was not his proper place in Fifth
Form, but that he merely occupied it by courtesy, as being the
son of a peer.

  For early mention of praepostors we must turn to Richard Cox's
account of Eton in 1530 (*Archaeologia* xxxiv. p. 38), to Malim's account in 1561, and to Thomas James' account in 1766 (*Etoniana*
magazine, No. 7), but they do not come prominently into notice
until the Rebellion in 1768.   One of the duties of the
Praepostors was to keep the other boys in bounds, and they

claimed in consequence that they themselves were free to go out of bounds, though they recognised the obligation either to shirk or "cap" the Assistant Masters when they met them. Difficulties arose in 1768, when the Assistants claimed the right to send back Praepostors found out of bounds. Dr. Foster, the Head Master, supported his Assistants. Matters became worse when one of the Assistants complained of a Praepostor for making a noise in Church. It was one of the duties of the Praepostors to sit at the end of each seat and keep silence among the Lower Boys during Divine Service. The boy, who appears to have been merely performing his duty, was flogged; whereupon the Praepostors (it would appear that only the Oppidans were implicated) resigned their office *en masse*. Further they said that "as they were no longer praepositors, they would not speak (i.e. declaim) in school." The Head Master however said they were to speak not as Praepostors but as Sixth Form boys. The ex-praepostors disputed this, "imagining declaiming was the office of a praepositor," and giving as a reason "that the collegers of the sixth form, altho' as many, and senior to the oppidans, did not declaim till they enjoy'd the privileges of praepositorship, which only the seven seniors enjoy'd. That whoever declaimed missed three regular school exercises in consequence of it." But Dr. Foster said they must either declaim or quit the School. The result was the famous march to Maidenhead. Much of the above is to be found in a pamphlet in the Bodleian (Gough, Add. Bucks 8. 14. 4) which (from a note on it) was written by Jeremiah Milles, eldest son of the Dean of Exeter.

The above passage points to seven being the invariable number of College Praepostors, and to this day only the first seven Collegers in Sixth Form take part in the Speeches delivered in the Michaelmas and Easter Halves. But the School List of 1742 points to seven being also the regular number of Oppidan Praepostors, of whom only one is in Sixth Form. Was this rule altered later to one that all Oppidans in Sixth Form were Praepostors? A collection of old Speech Lists might help to decide this point. *Ten* did not become the fixed number of Oppidans in Sixth Form till much later.

1745 A list printed by Williams of Eton for Dr. Hawtrey (who edited it) in 1843. In the copy in the British Museum (G. 15126) is a letter dated Feb. 7, 1843, from Dr. Hawtrey—probably to Hon. Thomas Grenville, whose stamp

z

the book bears—in which he says, "A very early List of Eton School lately fell into my hands, which I have had printed by the Eton bookseller. As it is rather curious in itself and a very respectable specimen of our Typography, I venture to request your acceptance of it." The original has unfortunately disappeared, and as the list shews considerable signs of having been edited, it is difficult to be quite certain as to how much was in the original. Assuming however all except the notes to have been in the original list we may observe the following features. The list was entitled "Bill of Eton College & School 1745." It is headed by the Visitor, Dr. Thomas, Bishop of Lincoln, and is the only occasion on which the Visitor's name occurs in any known school list until Lent 1905, when the practice was revived at the writer's suggestion. Following the Visitor's name come those of the Provost, Vice-Provost, Fellows, Upper and Lower Masters, Upper and Lower Assistants and the Conducts. This again is the only list in which the Conducts' names appear until 1856. Then follow the Collegers, of whom there are 70, divided among the Sixth, Fifth, Remove, Fourth, Third and Second Forms. Then come the Oppidans, divided among the Fifth, Remove, Fourth, Third, Second, First Forms and the Bible Seat. It will be noted that there are no Oppidans in the Sixth Form. Boys with titles come at the head of their forms in the Upper School, but not in the Lower (there are none in the Bible Seat).

1747 Belonging to Mr. R. Orlebar of Hinwick House, Wellingborough, Beds. It is written on three sides of a sheet of foolscap, in a fair upright handwriting. The title of the list is as printed on p. 42 (without the date): the date must be between Dec. 17, 1747, and June 23, 1748. There are four columns to the page, and the forms are marked off by lines, but without any names given to them. Three names have been erased, viz. "Gibson," "Richards," and "Holles." Without counting these there are 68 Collegers and 182 Oppidans. The names of Ld. Herbert, Mr. St. John and Mr. Calvert are written at the top of the second page, between columns 1 and 2, and there is no indication of the exact place they should occupy in the list.

1753 There are three, if not four, lists extant for this year. I have printed two, one for January, the other for December, as they practically cover two different years. Both of these belong to Mr. R. Orlebar of Hinwick House.

(1) Written on three sides of a sheet of foolscap, each side containing four columns of names. Across the top of the first page is written "A Bill of Eton School, Jany 30th, 1753." The list does not give the Staff; the Collegers in each Form and in each Remove are placed first, and next to them any peers, or boys with titles. A peculiarity is the mention by name of three Removes in Fourth Form, six in Third Form and two in Second Form. In the First Remove of Fourth Form, after "Ld. Charles," a later hand has written "Spencer." The handwriting is probably that of a boy.

(2) Written on four sides of a sheet of foolscap, with three columns to the page. The handwriting is good. On the top of the first page is written "1753, December," and if this date is correct, it seems that "Tew" has been omitted at the head of the Collegers, for he did not go to King's till May, 1754. The names of the Staff are given and the Collegers all come together before the Oppidans. At the end of each Form of the Collegers a different hand has added the numbers, and this hand is the same that wrote the next list that will be described. Peers are placed above commoners in the Upper but not in the Lower School. It may be noticed that "Mr. Cornwallis," who was in the Fifth Form in the preceding list, has now become "Lord Brome," his father having been made an earl on June 30, 1753.

Besides these two lists, two others may be noted, viz.:

(3) A list now in the College Library. It was discovered in 1903 by a Reading bookseller among the leaves of a copy of Harwood's *Alumni Etonenses*, and bought by Mr. R. S. de Havilland, who presented it to the Library. It is written in a large ungainly hand, on three sides of a sheet of foolscap, with four columns to the page, and is headed "A List of Eton School in the year 1753." As far as the names of the boys go the list is identical, except for slight variations in spelling, with the Orlebar list for December 1753, except that in the First Form "Sumner" comes *after* instead of *before* "Lord Greville." In giving the names of the Assistants, this list is almost unique in prefixing the Christian names in four instances, viz. "Mr. Jn. Norbury, Batholomey (*sic*) Young, John Graham and Robert Sumner."

(4) Among Mr. Stapylton's transcripts is one which he describes as a copy by Lord Abingdon of a roll belonging to Lord Romney for the year 1752. But on closer examination this list proves to be later than the Orlebar list for January 30, 1753, so that it should be labelled as belonging to the latter year.

The late Lord Romney was unable to discover this roll when he lent me others in his possession, so that I have never seen the original. The transcript shews that the roll gave first the Staff, then the Collegers, and finally the Oppidans. Peers came at the head of their forms in the Upper School (except in Sixth Form) but not in Lower School. The lowest form of Oppidans is entitled "First form & B. S." (i.e. Bible Seat).

There are three lists for this year:

1754 (1) That which is printed belongs to Mr. Orlebar, and resembles those in his possession for 1753. The date of the list must roughly be between September 1, when "Harris" was admitted to King's, and October 20, when "Richards" was admitted. No list of the Staff is given, and that which is printed on p. 56 is taken from the third list described for this year. It will be seen that peers are placed at the top of their forms in the Upper School, except in Fifth Form, but not in Lower School, except in First Form. The exception in Fifth Form, where "Orlebar" precedes four boys with titles, may be due to the fact that this Orlebar was perhaps the writer of the list. The numerals at the end of each form of Collegers are in the same hand as the de Havilland lists for 1753 and 1754.

(2) A list now in the College Library, with the same history and in the same handwriting as No. 3 for 1753. It does not give the Staff, and as regards names is identical with the Orlebar list for this year, except that the spelling and order differ somewhat. Thus "Orlebar" comes after the peers in Fifth Form. A peculiarity about this list is that it is the only one that distinguishes brothers by the abbreviation (so common at Winchester) of *senr.* and *junr.*

(3) A list now in my possession. When Mr. Stapylton saw this list it was in the possession of a former assistant of Mr. E. P. Williams. It must have passed from him to Mr. Ingalton Drake, from whom I purchased it in March 1905. It is written on three sides of a sheet of foolscap with three columns to the page, and headed "A List of Eton College, Aug. 26, 1754," but the date seems in another hand: it is no doubt correct though "Harris" is not in the list, and as he was admitted to King's on September 1, his dismissal would probably have been about ten days earlier. The list gives in succession the Staff, Collegers, and Oppidans. Barnard had just succeeded Sumner as head master, and two more assistants have been added

since 1753. Peers head their forms in the Upper School, except in Sixth Form, but not in Lower School, except in First Form. The handwriting seems that of a boy. The list contains 336 names, six fewer than the Orlebar list, but " Mr. Collier " in First Form seems to be the only name that does not occur in any of the lists here printed. According to Barnard's Entrance Book, he entered the School on August 16, 1754.

Of a list for this year which Mr. Stapylton was lent in January 1884 by Mr. R. N. Cust, I have been unable to find any trace.

From 1756 onwards the lists begin to assume a more stereotyped character and with a few exceptions do not require much in the form of notes.

1756- **1761** I have used a series of lists belonging to Sir Lawrence E. Jones, Bt., of Cranmer Hall, Fakenham, Norfolk. The College Register gives us the information that Matthew Jones got on the indentures in 1755 and Daniel Jones in 1758, both coming from Fakenham, and no doubt these boys sent the lists home to their parents.

There are eight lists altogether, dated respectively (though the date has been in some cases added subsequently) August 1756, August 1757, Christmas 1757, August 1758, Christmas 1759, (August) 1760, August 1761 and Christmas 1761. The first four seem to be written by the same hand, probably by a boy ; the fifth also by a boy, and the last three in a formal, clerkly hand. They are written on four sides of a foolscap sheet : the list for August 1756 has only two columns on each page and consequently overflows on to a second sheet. The lists for 1757 and 1759 have three columns to a page, and those for 1758, 1760 and 1761 have four. Throughout the lists certain names have crosses affixed to them and others are underlined, perhaps denoting friends of the writers ; these crosses I have not reproduced.

I will now give a few details about each list, as well as about lists that survive.

1756 This list has the rare heading of " A Bill of Eton College and School " (cf. list for 1745). The distinction between the College and School is still noted in the Trials List of to-day, of which the title is " A List of Eton College," but the eleventh page of which has for heading " Eton School." The forms are as usual, Third Form showing six removes and Second Form two. Peers head their forms in the Upper School, except in Sixth Form, but not in the Lower School, except in First Form.

(1) (August.) This list does not give the Provost, **1757** Fellows and Masters, and I have added them from the Jones list for Christmas 1757 as no changes seem to have occurred between Election and Christmas. No removes are indicated in the various forms. Peers are placed at the head of their forms. At the end of the list in a sort of overflow column are six additional names, not included in the scribe's enumeration (which, it may be remarked, is faulty as usual). Possibly these had not yet been "placed" as four of them seem to have arrived on July 22, 1757, according to Barnard's Entrance Book.

"Grave," the second of these, seems to have been originally written "Grey" and altered to "Grave." Possibly the name should be "Grieve," who entered September 14, 1757.

(2) I have also a list dated October 1757, which I bought from Mr. Drake in 1905. It is the same as that mentioned by Mr. Stapylton, as "lent by Mr. Williams' assistant." It is written in an excellent hand on a sheet of foolscap, with four columns to the page; it bears no heading of any kind, and has one peculiarity, viz. that the Collegers are all placed *after* the Oppidans. The names of the forms are not given, but both forms and removes are indicated by lines. Peers are all grouped together at the head of their forms in the Upper but not in the Lower School. At the end the numbers are given as follows: "Upper School 146, Low. School 169, Coll. 69, In all 384." The date is given at the end.

(3) Christmas. Another list belonging to Sir L. E. Jones, Bt.: the order of this list is Provost and Staff, Collegers (69), and Oppidans (usually spelt *Oppidants*), showing a total of 401 altered to 403 (but should be 404). Peers are at the head of their forms in the Upper but not in the Lower School.

(1) August. Belonging to Sir L. E. Jones. It does **1758** not give the Staff, and does not separate the Collegers from the Oppidans: but certain groups of Collegers have been indicated by brackets, which seem in a later hand. Red ink has been employed for the lines dividing off the forms. Peers head their forms in Fifth, Remove, Fourth, Third and

First Forms (with the exception of " Sr. Jno. Nelthorpe," Lord Kerr and Lord Morpeth, who perhaps are at the top of removes). A feature of this list is that the Fifth, Fourth and Third Forms are each headed by a Duke, a fact denoting the repute which the School was gaining.

(2) There is also a fragment of a list for this year among Lord Brownlow's papers. I have not seen the original, but from a transcript of it kindly sent me by Mr. Lionel Cust, it seems to be a list of the Fourth Form, divided into four removes. It is headed " List of Eton 1758 " and contains 113 names, and was probably written by Brownlow Cust, eldest son of Sir John Cust, Bt., afterwards 1st Baron Brownlow. In Third Form " Thorpe " should probably read " Tharp."

1759   Christmas. Belonging to Sir L. E. Jones. Peers are placed at the head of their forms except in the Sixth Form. No removes are indicated, but at the end of Third Form two boys are shewn as " Not placed."

1760   Belonging to Sir L. E. Jones. Dated 1760 only, but endorsed "Augt. 1760." This is the earliest list belonging to a type that now becomes fairly frequent and which I shall call the " F. G." type (see the list for 1761). Each page is neatly divided into four columns by lines ruled in red ink : all lines dividing forms, or beneath the various headings, and all names of peers are also in red ink. The handwriting is very clear and of a clerkly character, with occasional flourishes and twirligigs. My own theory is that these lists were written by the writing-master, who perhaps added to his stipend by selling copies. Old-fashioned " e's " and " g's " and " r's " are occasionally used in this type of list. In this particular list the scribe seems to have forgotten the eleven names from " Mr. Montague " to " Cotes " inclusive near the end of the Second Form, and they have been inserted afterwards. In the same form " Lander " originally was written after " Skelton " but has been erased in red ink, and the same name appears as an insertion in the eighth place in First Form. The name " Pess " near the end of Third Form does not occur elsewhere in the lists or in Barnard's Entrance Book and may perhaps be a mistake. Three removes are indicated in Fourth Form. Peers are placed first in the Fifth, Remove, and in the first and third removes of the Fourth Form ; and perhaps the one commoner at the head of the second remove is a mistake.

(1) August. Belonging to Sir L. E. Jones. The month
1761 is written in a later hand. The type of this list is the same
as that of the last, but the names of the peers are written
in black ink. In the top left-hand corner of p. 1, written very
small, are the initials " F. G.," no doubt those of the scribe. Three
errors, viz. " Rime" for " Prime" and " Toote" for " Foote" in
Fourth Form and " Reylor " for " Paylor " in Third Form, indicate
that the scribe was copying, and not writing from memory. No
removes are indicated, except two in Third Form, and peers are
placed first only in Remove and Fourth Form (with the exception
of " Sr. Jas. Ibbetson," who perhaps heads a remove).

(2) Christmas. Belonging to Sir L. E. Jones. " Christmas "
is in a later hand. This is another list of the " F. G." type.
Red ink is used for marking off the columns and divisions, and
not for the names of peers. Three removes are shown in Fourth
Form, and the peers are placed first in them and in Remove.
There are 505 names in the list.

(3) and (4). I have seen two other lists of this date, lent me
by Miss Ellison of Kingsbury Lodge, St. Albans. One of these
is of the " F. G." type, being identical in almost every way with
the Jones list for Christmas 1761, with the exception that it contains at the bottom of the Fourth Form Collegers " Newland," who
is absent from the Jones list. As a result the list shows 506 names.

The second Ellison list is of the same date, but a much
rougher performance, and in black ink throughout, without any
list of Provost, etc., being evidently the work of a boy. There
are 503 names, and there is a new variant of the spelling of
Oppidans, viz. " Opidents."

For these four years I have used lists belonging to
1762-5 Mr. G. E. Lloyd Baker, of Hardwicke Court, Gloucester-
shire. This collection consists of sixteen lists, 1762-
1769, viz. one for 1762 (? July), four for 1763 (viz. March 28, and
three others bearing no date beyond that of the year), three for
1764 (viz. for April 16, August 1, and December), two for
1765 (viz. March 30 and August), two for 1766 (the first undated
and the second for August), two for 1767 (viz. April 12 and
December), one for 1768 (December 9), and one for 1769 (no date).
Nearly all of these seem to be written by the same hand, except
those for April 12, 1767, and for 1768; the handwriting of the
majority is fair, probably that of a boy: that of April 12,
1767, and of 1768 is less good. All the lists are written on similar

paper, viz. on four sides of a quarto sheet, with four columns on each page. They are now sewn together in a paper cover. They have undergone a good deal of editing, e.g. *ma.* and *mi.* have been freely added: where they are obviously additions I have omitted them. Further, at the end of each list, certain names are usually added in red ink, as "omitted." These are often inserted in red ink in the places they should occupy, and what is curious is that in the list of August 1, 1764, it appears as if in writing the list the scribe had left blank spaces for inserting these names; if this is so, the list cannot well be the original draft. The complete list of Provost, Fellows, Masters, etc., is only given in the lists for 1763 (No. 2), 1765 (August) at the end, 1766 (No. 1) and 1769. In 1762 the names of the Provost, Upper and Lower Masters alone are given. The peers, etc., are never given in red ink. Collegers are given by themselves at the beginning in the lists for 1762, 1763 (four lists), and 1769; in the others they are mixed with the Oppidans.

One or two points may be noted about some of the lists, viz.: the second list for 1763 gives a complete list of the forms and removes, viz.: Sixth, Fifth (Upper, Second, Third, Fourth and Lag Removes), Remove, Fourth (Upper, Second, Third and Fourth Removes), Third (Upper Greek, Lower Greek, Sense, Nonsense, Lag Remove and Unplaced), Second (Upper and Lag Removes) and First. The fourth list for 1763, the first for 1764, and the list for 1768 give the last form as "I. and Bible-seat."

The following are the chief peculiarities of the lists I have printed for the years 1762–5:

1762   (? July.) This list gives at the end in red ink "Omitted —Mr. Irby *ma.*, Baker."

1763   This list bears no date, but must be later than July 8, 1763, when "Manners," the last boy, was admitted. It gives at the end in red ink as "Omitted—Budworth, Dutton *min.*, Mr. Fox, Jones, Thomas, Morant, probably Mr. Townshend, and Jesse."

1764   Aug. 1. It gives at the end "Omitted—Eden, Hanbury, Johnson, Cole, and Vincent." In the text it inserts in red ink "Vincent" (aft. "Farrer" No. 93), "Hanbury" (aft. "Vanderpool" No. 272), "Eden" (aft. "Stanley" No. 296), "Curtis *mi.*" (aft. "Thomas" No. 315).

1765   Aug. It gives at the end " Omitted—Piggot."

1762–5   Other lists existing for these years are:

(1) A list, belonging to the Duke of Rutland among the
1762 Belvoir Castle Papers, entitled "Letters and Papers,
Supplementary, 1471–1799." It is a list of the "F. G."
type, but the right hand quarter of the first page is missing. Red
ink is used only for the dividing lines, not for the peers. The
list is slightly later in date than the Baker list that is printed
and no doubt is for Election, as Capstack, who came on July 26,
is in the list. It contains 520 names. A playful note at the end
says " Pray whip the bearer, Wm." The spelling of the names
is occasionally peculiar, e.g. " Cæmer " for " Seymour." Peers
are placed at the top in Remove, and probably in the removes of
Fourth Form.

(2) A list, written on eight pages of foolscap octavo, and
bound up at the beginning of a volume of printed School-
lists 1791–1810, in the possession of Messrs. Spottiswoode & Co.
The volume seems once to have belonged to G. Davis, who was
Mr. Williams' assistant. The writing is small and neat, but
whether the list is an original or merely a transcript is uncertain.
The list is headed " A Bill of Eton School, Election 1762." The
list of the Staff is not given, nor are the Collegers in any way
distinguished from the Oppidans. There are 511 names. Peers
seem placed first only in the Remove.

(3) A list belonging to Sir J. W. Buchanan Riddell, Bt., of
Hepple, Whitefield, Rothbury. This was originally a roll, but
has been cut into strips and pasted into a book. The strips put
together would measure about $13\frac{1}{2}$ ft. $\times$ $2\frac{1}{10}$ in. The list as it
survives begins with " Harrison," but a later hand has written
" Sumner " above his name, and probably he was originally in the
list, as the top seems wanting. The boys number 489. The
handwriting and spelling are both very inferior: thus " Lord
Ophaley " is written " Lord Ophelia," and Lord Roos " appears as
" Lord Ruse." Peers come first only in Remove. Besides the
names of the forms, five boys are described as " Unplaced " at
the end of Third Form. At the end of the strips composing
the list a piece of paper is pasted which formed without doubt
the wrapper of the roll. On it is written " The following note is
in my Father's hand—' G. J. Cholmondely, b. 1752, d. 1830, and
an Etonian,' F. S. B. Riddell. ' A Bill of Eton School made

probably about the year 1762, shewing there to be in the Upper School, Collegers 45, Oppidans 219=264, Lower School, Collegers 11, Oppidans 207=218 [Total] 482 Total Collegers only 56 i.e. 14 below Complement. Given to me by Mr. Parry of Warfield.' " But the numbers should read: Upper School, Collegers 45, Oppidans 222=267; Lower School, Collegers 10, Oppidans 212=222, Total 489.

(1) A list in the Eton College Library, presented by
1764 Mr. R. M. Harvey, in July, 1889. It is written on four sides of a quarto sheet, in a moderate handwriting, and badly spelt. The list gives in order the Staff, Collegers, and Oppidans. There is nothing remarkable about the list except that after writing page 1 the scribe turned his paper upside down and so continued, and in setting out the forms, he has made one heading of Remove and Fourth Form. The list contains 57 Collegers and 445 Oppidans and is perhaps slightly later than Baker's list for August 1, 1764, as it omits " Bouverie " in the Oppidan Sixth Form. There are various other differences among the names, the only important one being the insertion of " Arden " in the First Form. "Arden" came to Eton on March 16, 1764, according to Barnard's Entrance Book, but for some reason does not appear in any of the Baker lists.

(2) A transcript now in possession of Mr. A. Clark-Kennedy, of 17 Langham Street, W. On it is written this note, " Mem. The List from which this was taken was lent to me by Rev^d. Th^os. Hatch of Walton. It was badly written and in many instances the Names were wrongly spelt." This note was probably written by the Rev. R. B. Byam, once Rector of Petersham, who seems originally to have owned the transcript, and from whom Mr. Stapylton appears to have borrowed it. The date of the list must be about Election 1764; there are 491 names given, and the order is Staff, Collegers, Oppidans. I have no idea where the original is.

(3) A transcript in the possession of Miss B. Chetwynd Stapylton, bound up at the beginning of an interleaved and annotated copy of " Montem " lists. This transcript seems to have been made by Mr. Stapylton from a list lent him by Mr. Jesse.

A list in possession of Mr. S. H. le Fleming, of Rydal
1765 Hall, Ambleside. The existence of this list is noted in the twelfth Report, App. Pt. VII. of the Historical MSS.

Commission, p. 357, 5684 e " 1765. Bill of Eton School." The list bears no actual date but was probably made out at Election 1765. It is written on four sides of a sheet of foolscap in a fairly good hand, no doubt that of a boy. It gives the Staff, but does not separate the Collegers from the Oppidans. There are 512 names.

1766   A list belonging to the Duke of Rutland and to be found among the "Letters and Papers supplementary 1471–1799 —Belvoir Castle," f. 190. This is one of the "F. G." lists, being written on four sides of a sheet of foolscap, with four columns to the page, in an excellent clerkly handwriting, with the usual flourishes. Red ink is used for the lines between the columns, for the dividing lines between the divisions, and for the names of peers, etc. It is headed "A List of Eton School" with "Election 1766" written in the top right-hand corner. The order is Provost, Fellows, etc., Collegers and Oppidans. The forms are as usual, but three removes are shewn in the Fifth Form, three in the Fourth, six in the Third (the last alone having a heading, viz. "Unplaced"). Peers are not put above others, except in the three removes of Fourth Form. The total number of boys is 498. At the end of the list is a drawing in red ink representing a quill pen, and a note in another hand below it saying, " N.B. This was a fellow, named Pen, if it is intended for a joke."

N.B. In Second Form " Croftes " should apparently be "Croft" and " Blagrove " " Blagrave."

Other lists for the year 1766 are :

(1) Sir R. Payne-Gallwey, of Thirkleby Park, Thirsk, has another list for this year, made out by Sir Thomas Frankland : he says that it gives the names of peers, etc. in red ink. I have not seen the list.

(2) A list on two sides of a single large sheet, sent me loose among the Baker lists. It is headed " A Bill of Eton School for July 1766 " and is made out in five columns, red ink being used for peers, names of forms, dividing lines, etc. An explanatory note says : " N.B. Those boys who have *C.* after their names are Collegers or on the foundation. Those boys whose names are wrote in red ink are noblemen. Those whose names are followed by *ma.* or *maj.* are the eldest brothers, by *mi.* or *minor* or *min.* the second, by *mini.* or *minimus* the third." There are 486 names. The handwriting is that of a boy, but does not seem the same as that of the Baker lists.

(3) A roll belonging to V. F. Tufnell, Esq., Norwood House, Leamington. This roll is 15 ft. 7 in. long by 3⅓ in. wide, and is written in fairly good handwriting on stoutish paper. It bears no date but must have been made out about Election 1766. The top portion of the roll is gone, and the first name now to be seen on it is a fragment of Mr. Southernwood's, one of the Fellows. After the Fellows come the Collegers, and lastly the "Oppidents." The spelling of the names is very poor. On the reverse side of the roll, at the top, has been written in a later hand, " Provost Dr. Barnard." The names number 469. Some notes in a later hand have been added to many of the names. The usual forms are given in Upper School; three removes are shewn in Fourth Form. In Lower School we have Upper Greek, Lower Greek, Sense, Nonsense, Second and First. Only in Fourth Form do peers come at the head of their removes.

(4) A roll belonging to the Right Honble. L. V. Harcourt, 14 Berkeley Square, W. This is one of the three rolls that were originally in the possession of either the Bramston or Beach families. The late Lady Portal (daughter of Mr. William Hicks-Beach), into whose possession they passed, gave one to Mrs. Chute, another to Sir Michael Hicks-Beach (now Lord St. Aldwyn), and retained the third herself. Sir Michael, possessing no other Eton curiosities, gave his to Mr. Harcourt, who, as is well known, has long collected everything relating to Eton. This roll is unfortunately only a fragment, ending at name No. 281 (Smith). The remainder has evidently been torn off and lost. It is written in a large boyish hand, and the spelling is bad. It is headed " A Bill of Eton Colledge 1766," and gives the Provost, Fellows, Collegers and Oppidans. It was probably made out at Election. Asterisks have been placed against the names of Bramston, No. 241, and Lord Midleton, 250. The first asterisk probably denotes the writer of the list. The reason of the second is not apparent.

(5) Belonging to Mr. A. Wyatt Edgell, of Cowley Place, Exeter. It is written on four sides of a sheet of quarto paper. The handwriting is good, and Mr. Wyatt Edgell says that it looks to him like the handwriting of his great-grand-father, Richard Wyatt, of Milton Park, Egham.

The list has no heading, but at the top of the first column occurs the date 1766. There is no list of Provost, Fellows, etc., the Collegers are not separated from the Oppidans, nor are peers put at the heads of their forms. Fourth Form contains an Upper, Second and Third Remove; Third Form has Upper Greek,

Lower Greek, Sense, Nonsense, Lag Remove and Unplaced; Second Form, Upper Remove and Second Remove. The boys number 474, viz. Upper School 231, and Lower School 243. The list is endorsed " Eton Boys."

(6) A roll belonging to Eton College Library, $9\frac{1}{2}$ ft. long by $2\frac{7}{10}$ in. wide. It belonged formerly to Sir W. S. Trelawny, Bt., of Trelawne, Duloe, who gave it in 1873 to the late Mr. Chetwynd-Stapylton, whose son, Mr. H. G. Chetwynd-Stapylton, gave it to the College on November 7, 1904. The roll is written in a small, neat handwriting, on stout white paper, which bears a watermark of 1810. If as seems almost certain these figures give the date of the make of paper, this roll must be a transcript of an older one. The heading is " Eton List 1766," beneath which comes " Upper School—Doctor Foster, Head," followed by the names of four assistants, and similarly " Lower School—Doctor Dampier, Head," followed by five assistants. Thus the Provost and Fellows are not given. The Collegers are not given apart from the Oppidans, nor are peers at the head of their forms. Fourth Form shows an Upper, Second and Third Remove; Third Form has Upper Greek, Lower Greek, Sense, Nonsense, Lag Remove, and Unplaced; Second Form has Upper and Second Remove. The list contains 484 names.

1767–1770 For these years I have used a set of lists written by Sir Thomas Frankland. These lists are written in a copy-book bearing on the inside of the cover the name of " Thomas Frankland," apparently in the same handwriting as the lists themselves. They cover the years 1766–1770. The list for 1766 is dated " June," the others " August." They are written in a very neat hand, the columns—three to a page —being ruled off with red ink, which is also used for separating the forms and for the names of peers, etc. The different lists succeed each other without any interval, and look almost as if they had been all written at the same time: if so, they must of course be copies from older originals.

The writer of these lists was Sir Thomas Frankland of Thirkleby Park, afterwards President of the Royal Society, etc., a careful chronicler of all that went on around him during all his life. One of the only two extant MSS. of *Nugae Etonenses* (c. 1765) is in his handwriting. His descendant, Sir Ralph Payne-Gallwey, tells me that he has in his possession another list for 1766 written by Frankland, framed and hung in his billiard room. The following account of Sir Thomas Frankland is quoted from the *Herald* of 1786 : " Sir Thos. Frankland was sent by his father Adm. Sir Thomas to Domine Evans because the house looked quiet from having some greens nailed all over it. He was the head boy of that house. As a scholar he was diligent more than distinguished, and he had a talent for every mechanic art that distinguished him from every boy of his time."

These lists were bought at a London sale by Mr. Ingalton Drake about 1886, and passed into my hands in 1904.

Other lists for the years 1767—1770 are the following :

1767 A transcript in possession of Mr. A. Clark-Kennedy, of 17 Langham Street, W., having at the end this note : " Copied from a list lent by Mr. Angelo, author of Reminiscences, Aug. 16, '34." This therefore must be the transcript seen by Mr. Stapylton and described by him as the " Copy of a list in possession of the late Rev. R. B. Byam, taken from a list lent by Mr. Angelo, author of Reminiscences, etc., 16th August 1834." The list is headed " Eton School 1767," and gives the Provost, Fellows, etc., Collegers and Oppidans. The transcript is on a sheet of foolscap with three columns to the page ; a good many pencil notes have been added by some commentator. Peers are not at the heads of their forms. Note that the Lewis's are written thus : J. Lewis, H. Lewis, David Lewis and W. Lewis. An interesting feature is that about half way down the Fifth Form comes the heading " Lower Division." The list contains 417 names.

1768 In my possession, lately belonging to Mr. Drake. Mr. Stapylton mentions it as " belonging to Mr. Williams' assistant." It is written on four sides of a sheet of quarto in an excellent but rather formal handwriting. The writer had not quite sufficient space for all the names, and the last ten names are written across the last page. The list is headed " A List of Eton School, July 20, 1768," and gives the Staff, Collegers and Oppidents (*sic*). Peers, etc. are not put at the heads of their forms, but are written in red ink. The names number 465.

1768 A list belonging to the Earl of Romney ; it is one of the " F. G." type, being written on a sheet of foolscap with four columns to the page ; the dividing lines which separate the columns and the forms, as well as all boys with titles being in red ink. The writing contains the usual flourishes and twirligigs. The list is practically the same as the Portal roll, and contains 462 names, wrongly counted on the list as 463. The removes are shewn in Fifth Form. The order is Staff, Collegers, Oppidans.

1768 A roll belonging to Sir W. W. Portal, Bart., Malshanger, Basingstoke. This roll, which is 12 ft. 2 in. long by $2\frac{5}{16}$ in. wide, is preserved in a parchment bag, drawn together with strings at the top. For its history see the notes on the Harcourt roll of 1766. Its heading runs "A Bill of the | School," and over this has been written by a later hand "1767," but the date should probably be 1768. It is in the same handwriting as the Chute roll for 1771. The roll gives the Provost, Fellows, etc., and the "Colledgers" (*sic*) precede the "Oppedants" (*sic*). Some care has been taken to differentiate the several boys of the name "Lewis." Thus we find "John Lewis," "Windham Lewis" and "H. Lewis." There are 462 names.

1769 A roll in the School Library. This roll was purchased from Mr. W. G. Griffith of Croughton, Brackley, and presented to the School Library in January 1903 by Mr. A. B. Ramsay and others. It has been mounted on a long strip of parchment, with wooden rollers at the top and bottom, so as to make it easy for purposes of reference. The roll bears no date in itself, and as Pote, the first Colleger, was admitted to King's on January 24, 1769, it is not unlikely that the date is 1768, subsequent to July 7, when Poynter was admitted to King's. The list is headed "A Bill of Eton School," and gives the Staff, Collegers and Oppidans. Red ink is used for the names of peers and for the dividing lines.

1766
1767
1768
1769 These four lists were presented to the Eton College Library by the Rev. John Ayre, curate of St. John's, Hampstead, on July 20, 1855. They are all written in the same handwriting, of a poor character with spelling to match—and are no doubt the work of a boy. They are each written on the first three sides of a sheet of foolscap, with four columns to the page, in black ink throughout. In each case the Provost and Fellows, etc., are given, and the Collegers come before the Oppidans; peers are not at the head of their

forms. In the first three lists the Lower Master is described as "Head Master of the Lower School," but in the fourth as "Lower Master." The dates of the lists are June 1766 with 481 names, July 1767 with 478 names, July 1768 with 461 names, and November 1769 with 400 names. There is an interesting note at the end of the 1769 list, where no names are given under First Form, viz. "N.B. The Bill of the 1st Form was lost: from the July Bill are these few following," and then follow twelve names under the heading "1st Form."

1771 A roll, 7 ft. 7¼ in. long by 2¼ in. wide, belonging to Mrs. Chute, The Vyne, Hampshire [see list for 1766 (4)]. The handwriting is fair and is the same as that of the Portal roll. Black ink is used throughout. It is headed "1771" and gives in order Provost, etc., Collegers and Oppidans. Two removes are shown in Fourth Form, five in Third, and two in Second, and then ten boys under the heading "Unplaced" in First Form. Peers are not at the head of their forms, and the names number 347 (Collegers 62).

1772 A roll, 2 1/10 in. wide, belonging to the Earl of Romney : it is written in a poor hand, and the spelling is inferior. The heading is "A Bill of Eton School," and the list bears no date. Mr. Stapylton thought it belonged to the year 1771, but it must be between April 14, 1772, when Mr. Chamberlayne became a Fellow, and August 15, 1772, when Randolph was admitted to King's. Red ink is used for the lines dividing the forms, for the names of boys with titles, for the heading "Collegers," for the first and last letters of "New Boys," which heading appears over the last two boys in the School, and for the numerals at the end, viz. 336. The list gives the Staff, Collegers and Oppidans. The names are wrongly counted and should number 328.

In the last remove of the Upper School "Mr. Brown" seems an error for "Brown."

1773 (1) In the Eton College Library. The list is written on two sides of a half sheet of foolscap in a poor hand. It has no heading, but some one has added a date which appears to be "1772" converted into "1773." The date is probably about Election 1773, for Dr. Foster, who is said to have resigned the headmastership in July of that year, does not appear in the list, nor does Key, who was admitted to King's on Aug. 14. There are 283 names including fifty-eight Collegers, and the list gives in order the Staff, Collegers and Oppidans.

N.B. In Fifth Form (Coll.) "Sheels" should be "Skeels."

(2) A roll belonging to the Rev. J. H. Snowden, S. Vedast, 25 Carlton Road, Putney Hill, S.W. This is a very interesting roll, much time and labour having evidently been spent upon it. The roll is $2\frac{3}{5}$ in. wide, and is preserved in a small particoloured silk bag, green below and black above. This bag was evidently made to fit it, and is tied together at the top by means of black strings. The bag is enclosed in another bag much larger and made of green silk. Mr. Snowden says that the list, enclosed in these bags, came into his possession some fifty years ago, on his father's death. At the top of the roll on the reverse side is written "I | Thos. Hughes July 14th 1773 | Aetas 14," but this does not seem in the same writing as any part of the roll itself. Nor does it seem possible that this date is correct, as thirteen boys who were placed on the indentures of 1773 appear as being already in College, and the Election did not take place until July 26. The date would seem to be between July 26, 1773, and February 15, 1774, when Knapp, who is the first Colleger, was admitted to King's. The roll is headed "A List of Eton School" without any date. The Provost, Fellows, etc., are given, after which comes the heading BOYS. Collegers are not separated from Oppidans, nor are peers at the head of their forms. Six removes are shewn in Fifth Form; Fourth Form contains Upper, Middle and Lower Removes; Third Form (the title of which is omitted) has Upper Greek, Lower Greek, The Sense, The Nonsense, and Lower Remove; Second Form Upper and Lower Removes. There are 291 names. The peculiarity about the roll is the liberal use of red ink, and the large amount of ornamentation between the various forms. Thus red ink is used for the headings to all forms, for abbreviations such as *Coll.* (which is so written throughout, except after the head boy's name when *Colleger* is written in full), for names of all boys with titles, for numerals at the side, and for many dividing lines. The ornamentation is of a childish nature, and consists mainly of flourishes (partly in red and partly in black ink). In one instance hearts and diamonds have been drawn in red ink, and spades and clubs in black. Hidden among the ornamentation is in most cases the name of the youthful artist. Thus down to and including Upper Greek we find " I. Goodall

fecit" constantly, but from Lower Greek onwards Hughes is the artist. The handwriting changes similarly, so that there seems no doubt that Joseph Goodall—the future head master—No. 101, wrote the greater portion of the list, and that Hughes, No. 224, wrote the remainder. It would seem that Hughes was dissatisfied with his first attempt at ornamentation, viz. at Lower Greek, for a new bit of work has evidently been executed over a former one. At the bottom of the list on the reverse side is written " 276 Names," which is certainly incorrect.

When advertising for Eton lists, two transcripts of this list were sent me—one by the Rev. N. T. Garry of the Rectory, Taplow; it had been made by Mr. Snowden, who had written in several places "·sic J. H. S." Mr. Garry informed me that it contained the name of his mother's father, "Vesey," in Lower Greek.

The second came from Mr. C. W. Campbell of Ivy House, Hampton Court, and was a transcript of the last. Mr. Campbell said it had been in his possession since the death of his cousin Arthur Vesey.

1774 In the Eton College Library. It is written on three sides of a sheet of foolscap in a poor hand. The heading is " A Bill of Eton School, Election 1773," but the date is in a later hand and is certainly wrong, for it must be at least as late as February 1774, Knapp, who does not appear in the list, having been admitted to King's on February 15 of that year. It is somewhat earlier in all probability than Election-time as there are five more Collegers who were on the indentures of 1773 who had still to get into College. The list does not give the Staff, but I have added it from the Snowden list, which may belong to this year. The Collegers and Oppidans are mixed together and the names number 267, including seventy Collegers.

1775 A roll belonging to Miss M. A. J. Mason of Aldenham Cottage, Yateley. It is in an incomplete state, a portion of the top having been lost, as well as a piece at the beginning of Fifth Form and a third portion having become detached at the bottom. Its present length is 4 ft. 2¾ in. + 4⅝ in. (the detached piece) by 1¾ in. On a wrapper is written

"Bill Eton College, 1760," which date is plainly wrong, and the real date is to be found at the end of the list, viz. Christmas 1775. Owing to the top portion of the roll being missing the names of the first five boys have been lost. This is rendered certain by the fact that " Bernard," the fifth name as the list stands at present, is numbered " 10." The missing Collegers are easily supplied from the King's indentures for 1775. Whether the roll ever contained the names of the Staff cannot be said. There is an incomplete list, finishing in the middle of Third Form, for Christmas 1775 in the bound volume of MS. lists in the College Library. According to that list " Hatch " and " Oliver " had already left College, while " Kirke," " Mackarel " and " Trusler " had got in. If this were so the Mason list would contain exactly seventy Collegers. As a matter of fact it does not mark " Hatch " or " Oliver " with a " C." so that it is just conceivable that they had left College and become Oppidans for a Half. The roll contains 246 names, allowing for the five lost, and represents the lowest ebb to which the School sank after its glorious career under Barnard.

A peculiarity of this list is the way the six Frasers are distinguished from one another, viz. Fraser *max. ma.*, Fraser *max. mi.*, Fraser *max.*, Fraser *ma.*, Fraser *mi.* and Fraser *min.*

1776–ퟏퟕퟗퟎ The remaining lists are taken from a MS. collection in the College Library. There are a great many of these, the majority being bound together in two volumes, entitled " Eton School Lists. MS. 1775–1799 " and " 1799–1834." The origin of these lists is not apparent ; but most of them are probably the official lists which it became the custom at some period for the Head and Lower Masters to deliver each Half to the Provost. Practically all the Bills are written on four sides of a quarto sheet of paper, with three columns to the page. The handwriting varies much, in some cases being that of a boy, in other cases being a formal hand, while many of the separate lists of the Lower School are, I believe, written by the Lower Master (Dr. Langford) himself. The dates of the lists have frequently been added by a later hand. In the case of the list printed for Election 1784, the original date seems to have been erased, and " Decr 1783 " to have been written over it. But the proper date seems to be about Election 1784. In many cases there are duplicate lists, as well as lists for the Easter and Michaelmas Halves. This series of lists does not present any very striking features, the form having apparently become more or less stereotyped. The list of Provost, Fellows, and Masters is never given; but I have occasionally been able to add it from other extant lists. The Collegers are rarely given separately from the Oppidans, but an important change occurs in the lists for 1788, 1789, and 1790, when all the Collegers are put at the head of the list under the title of King's Scholars. The same thing happens in the MS. lists for 1791. At Easter 1793 (there is no MS. list between December 1791 and Easter 1793) Collegers are once more mingled with the Oppidans, but are distinguished by the initials K.S. instead of C. The first time, however, that the expression "King's Scholar" occurs is in a list dated December 8, 1786, in which crosses are put to various names, and are said by a note in a later hand to denote "King's Scholars."

The following peculiarities in the whole series of lists may be noted. In the corner of one of the lists dated August 1, 1781, is written "Dr. B.," the initials evidently denoting that it was a list intended for Dr. Barnard, the Provost, and it must have been his last list, for he died December 2. 1781.

There is a note added to the list for December 6, 1791—which is just beyond the series printed in this volume—" My last bill— on yᵉ 16th I became Provost," evidently by Dr. Davies.

Similarly a note, probably in Dr. Davies' hand, to the list for Christmas 1801, says it was taken "when Dr. Heath vacated the Mastership being elected Fellow, and Dr. Goodall was elected Master."

At the end of the list for Easter 1802 is written "Easter 1802 Dr. Goodall."

Most of the lists in Dr. Goodall's headmastership and all in Dr. Keate's are evidently written by the Head Master himself. At the end of the last bill in the second volume of the MS. book, viz. for Election 1834, is written "Dr. Keate's last Bill." Four sides of a quarto sheet sufficed, with a certain amount of management, to contain the School till the end of Dr. Keate's rule, except for the halves from Easter 1830 to Easter 1833 inclusive, when the School does not conclude at the fourth page, but must have overflowed on to another sheet. But whoever had these lists bound up, did not notice this (or else the second sheets were missing), so that the MS. lists for these particular Halves are incomplete. But as the lists were printed annually at Election from 1791, this is not of course a matter of any importance.

I will add a few further remarks about each of the lists printed in this book.

1776 Election. The date has been added by a later hand. The list is in a boy's handwriting, and contains 266 names, including sixty-three Collegers.

1777 July 31. The date is in a later hand, and so are the "C.'s "denoting the Collegers. The list itself is written in a very good, formal hand. From the lists for 1776 and 1778 it seems that "Sumpter C." has been omitted from either the Sixth or Fifth Form; also "Eldridge C." and "Saunders" from Remove. (Eldridge was on the Indentures of 1776.) "Hughes" in Fourth Form should have "C." after his name. The list contains 271 names, of which sixty-one (including "Hughes") are Collegers.

1778 July 27. The date is again added in a later hand. I have added the Staff from a list in my possession (see p. 361). The list, which is poorly written, contains 276 names, including sixty-seven Collegers (including Bartlam, which is not marked with a "C.").

1779 July 29. The Staff is again taken from a list in my possession (see p. 361). The list, which is in a moderate hand, contains 305 names (wrongly added up as 306), of which sixty-eight are marked as Collegers. But it seems that "Oliver" and "Grover" in Fourth Form, "Briggs" in Third, and "Wright" in Second should also be marked as Collegers, which would bring the number to seventy-two. "Oliver" seems to have left this year, and may have become an Oppidan, but this would still leave one too many, and I do not know how to explain the fact.

N.B. "Ibbot" in Fourth Form must be a mistake for "Hibbert."

1780 July. The date is in a later hand. The Staff is added from the printed Tighe list (see *infra* pp. 361-2). There are 300 names, of which sixty-four are marked as Collegers, but "Smith" in Fourth Form ought not to be marked as a Colleger, while "Dyson" in Fifth, "Littlehales" in Third, and "Hill" in First Form should also be marked C., bringing up the number of Collegers to sixty-six. Of the boys on the indentures for 1779 only eleven out of the twenty-one who eventually got in appear as Collegers, which is odd as College does not seem to have been full at the moment.

Note that "Hampson" in Fifth Form and "Wickes" in Fourth Form seem to have left College and become Oppidans. A good many boys in the Upper part of the School have dashes placed after their names, and there is a note at the end of the list, written by the same hand that added the date "The boys mark'd C. are on the Foundation, those mark'd — were confirmed Jul. 8. 1780."

Aug. 1. The date is in a later hand. The Staff is from **1781** a list in my possession (see *infra* p. 361). There are 300 names of which sixty-nine are marked as Collegers, but "Harwood C." and "Hibbert C.," who were in Fourth Form in the last list and who reappear in Fifth Form in the next list, seem to be temporarily absent. Notice that the list contains two "Lord Downes," one in Fifth Form, who appears in the previous list as "Mr. Dawnay," and the second in Sense, who should probably be written "Ld. Doune."

July 26. The date is in a later hand, and some one has **1782** drawn a pencil through "July 26th" and written "Election" over it, but as the date of Election that year was July 29, the difference is not great. Similarly pencil marks have been drawn through the names of the various forms, and "Smith" has been added in pencil at the end of the list. The Staff has been added from a list of 1781 in my possession (see *infra* p. 361) which has evidently been corrected for use in 1782. Dr. Roberts became Provost on December 12, 1781, and Mr. Tew Fellow on December 24, 1781. Including "Smith," there are 326 names, of which sixty-eight are marked Collegers; but the C. added to "Reid," "Harvey," and "Champneys," all in Fourth Form, is only in pencil. They were the last three on the indentures for 1781, and if they had got in, "Hill" in Nonsense, and "Parry," "Prior," and one "Broadley," in Second Form, Upper Remove, must also have got in. This, however, would give seventy-one Collegers, one too many.

Easter. There are 346 names, including seventy **1783** marked as Collegers.

1784 The date of this list, which is in a later hand, was originally " Election 1784," but this has been erased and " Election 1783" written over it; the list, however, is certainly for 1784, though it may be Easter rather than Election. The list contains 339 names, of which seventy are marked as Collegers, and as twelve of these on the indentures for 1783 were already in, the list must at any rate be later than Election 1783.

1785 December 10. There are 348 names, of which sixty-four are marked as Collegers. But " Bainbridge " in Fifth Form and " Wilson " in Lower Greek should be marked with a C., while " Cook " in Lower Greek is apparently thus marked by mistake, as there does not seem to have been a Colleger of that name at this time.

1786 This is compiled from two lists, (1) in the volume of MS. lists marked " Upper School only " with " Eton, July 29, 1786," written above in another hand; (2) from a packet of loose lists in the College Library marked " A Bill of yᵉ Lower School, Election 1786," which seems to be in the hand-writing of the Lower Master (Langford). There are altogether 357 names, but only thirty-one are marked as Collegers, and of these " Kingston " in Third Form seems marked by mistake. There should be probably 58 Collegers. In the Upper School list the names of the Forms are added in pencil, and several names, i.e. " Ellis C." in Sixth Form, " Thackeray " in Fifth Form, both " Smith C." in Remove, " Wright C., Hucks C., Broadley C., and Wagner C." in Fourth Form, are added in another hand.

N.B. In Fifth Form, for " Elswick " read " Estwick."

1787 July 28. There are 341 names. The Collegers are placed first, and number fifty-four.

1788 July 28. The Staff are given from a list in my possession (see *infra* p. 362). There are 368 names. The Collegers are given first, under the heading of King's Scholars, and number fifty-four. " F. Langford," who was second on the indentures of 1787, seems missing from among them. " Lord Templetown " has been erased with a stroke of the pen in Fifth Form, while " Stanley " has been inserted in another hand in Unplaced, but both are counted in according to the enumeration given in the MS.

1789 July 27, 1789. There are 377 names, including fifty-nine King's Scholars, who came before the Oppidans.

1790 May 18. There are 384 names, including sixty-four King's Scholars, who come first. Half-way down " Upper Greek," " Lower Greek " has been faintly written in pencil opposite Methuen's name, and similarly " Lower Remove " opposite Pemberton's name in Sense. In the first remove of Fourth Form the name of " Parkiss " has been erased between " Mortlock " and " Mr. Herbert."

In addition to the above-mentioned lists for the period 1776–1790 the following are also known of, viz. :

1778,
1779,
1781 Three lists in my possession, which I bought from Mr. Drake. They are mentioned by Mr. Stapylton as being " in the possession of Mr. Williams' assistant." They are all three in the shape of small 12mo books, two columns to the page, in marbled covers. They do not all appear to be by the same hand however.

The list of 1778 is styled " A List of Eton College, at Easter 1778," and gives the Provost, Fellows, etc. Collegers are not given apart from the Oppidans. Red ink has been used for the names of the Provost, Vice-Provost, Fellows and Upper and Lower Master, and for peers, etc. Fourth Form contains Upper, Middle and Lag Removes ; Third Form Upper Greek, Lower Greek, Sense, Nonsense, Lag Remove and Unplac'd ; Second Form Upper and Lag Remove.

The list of 1779 is styled " A List of Eton College, Feb. 79." The arrangement is similar to that of the last list, but no red ink is used. The names are numbered in fives, and shew 292. A good many names in the Upper School have crosses set against them.

The list for 1781 is styled " Eton College 1781 " and is more or less similar to the last. Black ink is used throughout. Several names have had lines drawn through them, notably the Provost, Dr. Barnard : it looks as if the list had been edited for use in the following year.

1780 Among Mr. Stapylton's collection of transcripts is a list printed on a broadside, and dated " Election 1780."

There is a pencil note in the corner, in Mr. Stapylton's hand-writing, saying that the list was sent him in July 1877 by Colonel Tighe of Rossana. The list gives the Staff across the top of the sheet, and then the boys, numbering 301, in eight columns, the Upper School being on the left-hand half of the sheet, the Lower School on the right. Mr. Stapylton seems to have made a transcript of the same list and in the corner of his MS. transcript is this note: "Copied from a List printed by Col. Tighe of Rossana, lent me by C. C. James of Eton: Jan. 1884."

1781 (1) A list printed in the *Gentleman's Magazine*, January 1832. The list is prefaced as follows: "December 30 [1831 ?]. Mr. Urban. I have transcribed, from the original, a List of the boys at Eton in the years 1779–1780, upwards of half a century ago," and is signed "Zo." The list seems really to be for Election 1781 and contains 296 names. It gives the Staff and is peculiar in giving "The Provost of King's" after the Provost of Eton. After the Assistants come the "Private Tutors to Noblemen and others, not assisting in the school." The Collegers are not distinguished in any way from the Oppidans. Most of the names have short biographica notes appended, and those boys still thought to be living have asterisks placed against them.

(2) A list belonging to Lord Darnley at Cobham Hall: the original (which I have not seen) is said to be enclosed in a letter from Lord Clifton to his father, John Bligh, third Earl of Darnley, from Eton, dated June 17, 1781. The writer says: "I send you a list of the school, which I believe is accurate." The Collegers are not put first, but are differentiated by a cross placed after their names. There are 302 names altogether.

1782 Mr. Stapylton was lent a list (or a transcript of a list) in the possession of Rev. J. W. Hawtrey, in the hand-writing of one of Dr. Hawtrey's sisters. I have been unable to see the original, but Mr. Stapylton's transcript shews that it gave the Staff and the names of 322 boys: the Collegers are mixed with the Oppidans and distinguished by the initials "K.S.," but I feel doubtful if "K.S." would be found in the original.

1788 A list in my possession, bought from Mr. Drake in 1905. This is a very rough list, but of great interest. It is written in a very poor hand on several sheets of foolscap quarto. It

is headed "A List of Eton Colledge, Anno Domino (*sic*) 1788," and
begins with the Provost, Vice-Provost, and Fellows. Then came
"Busers (i.e. Bursars) Dr. Norbury and Mr. Tew," whose
names have already appeared among the Fellows. Then follow
the "Upper School Masters" and "Lower School Masters," with
Dr. Davies "head" of the former and Dr. Langford "head" of
the latter. Then follows a list of thirteen Private Tutors with
the names of their pupils. Then thirteen Dames, then the Extra
Masters, and finally the boys with the names of their Dames and
Tutors, much as in the present School List. The list stops after
"Nonsense." The heading of the next remove has been written,
viz. "Lag Remove," but no boys are given.

1789 Mr. Stapylton was lent a list, dated December 1789, by
Archdeacon Holbech of Farnborough, Warwickshire: I
have not seen the original, but Mr. Stapylton's transcript
shews that it contains 372 names, including sixty-six Collegers
who are placed before the Oppidans. The first seven Collegers
have "P." affixed to their names, to indicate, no doubt, that they
were Praepostors.

1789, Lists belonging to the Earl of Romney. These three
1790(2) lists, dated respectively November 12, 1789, June 10, 1790,
and December 1, 1790, present no special features of
interest. They are each written on the first three sides
of a sheet of foolscap, in black ink throughout, and all in the
same handwriting, which is fairly good. None of them contain
the Provost or Fellows, etc., nor place the Collegers first. The
names of the forms are not given, but the forms are indicated
by lines. The numbers given in the three lists are respectively
369, 395 (wrongly given as 392), and 386.

APPENDIX II.*

ETON SCHOOL.

Anno Dom.	Informator	Num.	Ostiarius	Num.	Tot.	
1693	Newboro'	240	Weston	89	338	
1697		230	..	170	400	
1698	Newboro'	..	Weston	..	402	
1705	do.	..	do.	..	367	
1707	Newboro'	..	Weston & Carter	..	349	
1708	do.	149	Carter	201	350	
1713	Dr. Snape	146	Carter	187	333	
1714	do.	155	do.	169	324	
1715	do.	149	do.	170	319	
1716	do.	148	do.	174	322	
1717	do.	170	Mr. Goode	183	353	
1718	do.	161	do.	194	355	
1719	do.	186	do.	221	407	
1720	Dr. Bland	171	do.	245	416	
1721	do.	165	do.	222	387	
1722	do.	170	do.	227	397	
1723	do.	159	do.	219	378	
1724	do.	157	do.	226	383	
1725	do.	176	do.	202	378	
1726	do.	176	do.	240	416	
1727	do.	170	do.	238	408	
1728	Dr. George	173	..	205	378	
1729	..	..	..	..	..	
1730	..	..	..	..	..	
1732	..	..	..	..	212	
1734	..	..	Mr. Sumner	..	..	
1735	..	120	do.	111	231	
1737	..	..	..	..	239	
1739	..	120	..	145	265	
1741	..	..	..	..	238	
1743	Mr. Cooke	137	..	145	282	
1744	..	134	..	118	252	

* From a paper probably in Dr. Goodall's handwriting: the few entries in the last column seem to be in a later hand.

Anno Dom.	Informator	Num.	Ostiarius	Num.	Tot.	
1745	Dr. Sumner	135	{ Sumner Dampier	113	248	
1746	..	129	Mr. Dampier	121	250	
1747	..	126	..	134	260	
1748	..	128	..	133	261	
1749	Dr. Sumner	122	Dampier	138	260	
1750	..	134	..	140	274	
1752	..	132	..	167	299	
1753	..	133	..	179	312	
1754	Dr. Barnard	148	..	174	322	
	..	153	..	184	338	
1755	..	173	..	194	367	
1756	..	188	..	212	400	
1757	..	205	..	194	390	
1758	..	225	.	206	431	
1759	..	245	..	215	460	
1760	..	257	..	224	481	
1761	..	262	..	243	505	
1762	..	267	..	246	515	
1764	..	262	..	252	505	500
1765	..	272	..	250	522	
1765	Dr. Foster	..	..	.	527	
1766	..	244	..	240	484	
1767	..	273	Mr. Sleech	211	484	
1768	..	276	..	168	444	
1769	..	272	..	140	412	437
1770	..	264	..	127	391	
1772	..	266	..	89	355	
1773	Dr. Davies	207	..	83	290	
1774	..	171	..	66	237	
1775	..	163	Mr. Langford	83	246	
1776	..	163	..	105	268	
1777	..	159	..	119	278	
1778	..	166	..	110	276	295
1779	..	173	..	111	284	
1780	..	174	..	134	308	
1781	..	..	..	..	..	
1782	..	..	..	..	..	
1783	..	..	..	..	..	
1784	..	..	..	..	..	
1785	..	..	..	..	..	
1786	Davies	199	Langford	142	341	
1787	..	..	..	..	..	

Anno Dom.	Informator	Num.	Ostiarius	Num.	Tot.	
1788	..	..	..	..	..	.
1789	..	..	.	..	..	
1790	..	..	..	..	..	
1791	..	299	..	132	431	446
1792	Dr. G. Heath	..	..	..	..	
1793	..	345	..	144	489	
1794	..	344	..	106	450	
1795	..	348	..	88	436	
1796	..	334	..	88	422	
1797	..	..	..	..	..	
1798	..	355	..	50	405	.
1799	..	..	..	..	..	
1800	..	311	..	46	357	
1801	..	..	..	..	337	
1802	Goodall	..	..	..	..	

APPENDIX III.

TABLE OF NUMBERS AT ETON,* WINCHESTER, WESTMINSTER, HARROW AND RUGBY.

	Eton	Winchester	West-minster	Harrow	Rugby
1653	..	96	..	..	..
1655/6	..	..	241	..	..
1678	207	127	..	..	..
1698	345	111	..	..	..
1706	353	117	..	..	..
1707	357	118	..	..	..
1718	350	..	..	..	..
1719	..	91	..	..	..
1725	378	108	..	..	..
1728	376	127	434	..	..
1732	205	181	348	..	(100)
1739	[265]	128	..	..	..
1742	283	98	..	..	..
1745	244	103	363	..	..
1747	250	92	322	..	..
1753	284 (Jan.)	75	..	..	..
	326 (Dec.)				..
1754	342	83	327	..	..
1755	[367]	78	..	..	..
1756	403	84	..	..	..
1757	413	94	..	..	..
1758	443	96	..	..	..
1759	472	108	..	..	..
1760	486	123	..	..	..
1761	505	123	..	..	..
1762	503	158	..	..	..
1763	513	119	..	..	..
1764	513	110	244	..	..
1765	522	109	..	..	..
1766	487	114	..	..	..
1767	474	129	..	..	..
1768	453	138	..	..	..
1769	424	155	..	..	..

* The numbers for Eton for the years 1678–1790 are taken from the lists in this volume, with the exception of those within square brackets which are taken from the *Eton Calendar*: for the years 1791–1800 from the printed lists.

	Eton	Winchester	West-minster	Harrow	Rugby
1770	391	159	..	235	..
1771	347	162	248	..	..
1772	328	160	260	..	..
1773	283	163	283	..	..
1774	267	165	306	..	..
1775	246	172	302	225	..
1776	266	179	299	243	..
1777	271	179	..	..	80
1778	276	186	282	..	52
1779	305	175	..	..	..
1780	300	147	272	173	..
1781	300	142	..	..	..
1782	326	123	..	..	..
1783	346	113	..	..	..
1784	339	120	..	..	..
1785	348	124	291	150	..
1786	357	117	..	..	..
1787	341	110	..	..	..
1788	368	108	..	..	..
1789	377	109	..	..	..
1790	384	111	..	..	240
1791	434	119	..	119	..
1792	467	116	..	..	..
1793	477	111	..	123	..
1794	450	122	..	124	(200)
1795	436	123	243	..	..
1796	422	145	..	131	..
1797	427	152	267	141	..
1798	404	159	..	166	.
1799	378	153	..	200	144
1800	364	159	..	..	149

APPENDIX IV.

DATES OF ELECTION 1683—1800.

(Taken from the Register of Scholars.)

1683.	August 9	1716.	July 16
1684.	July 28	1717.	July 29
1685.	(not given)	1718.	August 4
1686.	August 2	1719.	July 20
1687.	July 25	1720.	July 25
1688.	August 6	1721.	August 7
1689.	August 5	1722.	July 23
1690.	August 11	1723.	August 5
1691.	August 3	1724.	July 27
1692.	August 8	1725.	July 26
1693.	August 7	1726.	July 25
1694.	August 6	1727.	July 24
1695.	August 5	1728.	July 29
1696.	August 3	1729.	August 4
1697.	August 2	1730.	August 3
1698.	August 8	1731.	August 2
1699.	August 7	1732.	July 31
1700.	August 5	1733.	July 23
1701.	August 4	1734.	August 5
1702.	August 3	1735.	August 4
1703.	August 2	1736.	August 2
1704.	August 7	1737.	August 1
1705.	July 30	1738.	August 7
1706.	August 5	1739.	August 6
1707.	July 28	1740.	August 4
1708.	July 26	1741.	August 3
1709.	August 1	1742.	August 2
1710.	July 24	1743.	August 1
1711.	July 23	1744.	July 30
1712.	July 28	1745.	July 29
1713.	August 3	1746.	August 4
1714.	August 2	1747.	August 3
1715.	July 25	1748.	August 1

1749.	August 7		1775.	July 24
1750.	July 30		1776.	July 29
1751.	July 29		1777.	July 28
1752.	July 27		1778.	July 27
1753.	July 30		1779.	July 26
1754.	August 5		1780.	July 24
1755.	July 28		1781.	July 30
1756.	August 2		1782.	July 29
1757.	July 25		1783.	July 28
1758.	July 31		1784.	July 26
1759.	July 23		1785.	July 25
1760.	July 28		1786.	July 31
1761.	July 27		1787.	July 30
1762.	July 26		1788.	July 28
1763.	August 1		1789.	July 27
1764.	July 30		1790.	July 26
1765.	July 29		1791.	July 25
1766.	July 28		1792.	July 30
1767.	July 27		1793.	July 29
1768.	July 25		1794.	July 28
1769.	July 31		1795.	July 27
1770.	July 30		1796.	August 1
1771.	July 15		1797.	July 31
1772.	July 27		1798.	July 30
1773.	July 26		1799.	July 29
1774.	July 25		1800.	July 28

APPENDIX V.

NUMBER OF BOYS PLACED ON INDENTURES FOR COLLEGE, 1661—1800.

*1661. 1+24	1723. 11
*1662. 1+24	1724. 16
1663. 24	1725. 13
*1664. 1+24	1726. 23
1665-70. 24	1727. 17
*1671. 25	1728. 16
1672-5. 24	1729. 14
*1676. 25	1730. 18
1677-95. 24	1731. 24
1696. 22	1732-5. 24
1697. 23	1736. 22
1698-1704. 24	1737. 18
1705. 21	1738. 20
1706. 17	1739. 24
1707. 22	1740. 21
1708. 21	1741. 18
1709. 19	1742. 16
1710-11. 24	1743. 14
1712. 17	1744. 16
1713. 24	1745. 18
1714. 21	1746. 16
1715. 20	1747. 19
1716. 17	1748. 13
1717. 13	1749. 15
1718. 14	1750. 21
1719. 21	1751. 15
1720. 19	1752. 14
1721. 14	1753. 15
1722. 20	1754. 13

* In 1661, 1662 and 1664 the first boy has no number against his name, the second name being numbered "one." These boys, *extra numerum*, were no doubt royal nominees. Probably the extra boys in 1671 and 1676 were likewise royal nominees, though enumerated with the rest.

APPENDIX V.

1755.	15	1778.	17
1756.	24	1779.	24
1757.	18	1780.	23
1758.	15	1781.	12
1759.	12	1782.	14
1760.	13	1783.	21
1761.	11	1784.	13
1762.	18	1785.	5
1763.	18	1786.	16
1764.	16	1787.	12
1765.	12	1788.	21
1766.	11	1789.	12
1767.	17	1790.	15
1768.	13	1791.	26
1769.	17	1792.	20
1770.	14	1793.	16
1771.	14	1794.	15
1772.	17	1795.	7
1773.	21	1796.	12
1774.	8	1797.	13
1775.	15	1798.	7
1776.	19	1799.	12
1777.	21	1800.	19

ETON COLLEGE:
PRINTED BY SPOTTISWOODE AND CO., LTD.
AT THE SAVILE PRESS